Seeing It on Television

Seeing It on Television

Televisuality in the Contemporary US 'High-End' Series

Max Sexton and Dominic Lees

BLOOMSBURY ACADEMIC
NEW YORK • LONDON • OXFORD • NEW DELHI • SYDNEY

BLOOMSBURY ACADEMIC
Bloomsbury Publishing Inc
1385 Broadway, New York, NY 10018, USA
50 Bedford Square, London, WC1B 3DP, UK
29 Earlsfort Terrace, Dublin 2, Ireland

BLOOMSBURY, BLOOMSBURY ACADEMIC and the Diana logo are trademarks
of Bloomsbury Publishing Plc

First published in the United States of America 2021
This paperback edition published 2022

Volume Editor's Part of the Work © Max Sexton and Dominic Lees

Each chapter © of Contributors

For legal purposes the Acknowledgements on p. vi constitute an extension
of this copyright page.

Cover design: Namkwan Cho
Cover image © 2014 Home Box Office/Collection Christophel/ArenaPAL

All rights reserved. No part of this publication may be reproduced or transmitted
in any form or by any means, electronic or mechanical, including photocopying,
recording, or any information storage or retrieval system, without prior
permission in writing from the publishers.

Bloomsbury Publishing Inc does not have any control over, or responsibility for, any
third-party websites referred to or in this book. All internet addresses given in this
book were correct at the time of going to press. The author and publisher regret
any inconvenience caused if addresses have changed or sites have ceased to
exist, but can accept no responsibility for any such changes.

Library of Congress Cataloging-in-Publication Data
Names: Sexton, Max, 1966- author. | Lees, Dominic, 1964- author.
Title: Seeing It on Television: Televisuality in the Contemporary US 'High End' Series /
co-authored by Max Sexton and Dominic Lees.
Description: New York, NY: Bloomsbury Academic, [2021] |
Includes bibliographical references and index.
Identifiers: LCCN 2020036400 | ISBN 9781501359422 (hardback) |
ISBN 9781501359415 (epub) | ISBN 9781501359408 (pdf)
Subjects: LCSH: Television mini-series–United States–History–21st century. |
Television–Aesthetics.
Classification: LCC PN1992.8.F5 S44 2021 | DDC 791.45/75–dc23
LC record available at https://lccn.loc.gov/2020036400

ISBN: HB: 978-1-5013-5942-2
PB: 978-1-5013-7596-5
ePDF: 978-1-5013-5940-8
eBook: 978-1-5013-5941-5

Typeset by Deanta Global Publishing Services, Chennai, India

To find out more about our authors and books visit www.bloomsbury.com and
sign up for our newsletters.

Contents

Acknowledgements	vi
Introduction	1
1 Reconfiguring Televisuality in high-end television	9
2 Passionate realism: Paolo Sorrentino's *The Young Pope*	33
3 Independent style: Stephen Soderbergh's *The Knick*	57
4 *Fargo*: Adaptation of a cinematic text	81
5 A wealth of allusiveness: *Stranger Things*, *Boardwalk Empire* and *Vinyl*	105
6 Performance modes in collision: *The Leftovers*	131
7 Televisual spectacle: *Mars*	153
Conclusion	175
Index	179

Acknowledgements

We would like to thank Alison Smith, Holly Neko, Annelies Lovell and Theodore Lees for their support; the 'Sewing Circle' at the University of Reading, led by Doug Pye and John Gibbs, for rigorous analysis; University Centre, Farnborough; and Bernhard Gross at the University of the West of England for their help in completing this book.

Introduction

Seeing It on Television: Televisuality in the Contemporary US 'High-End' Series is about the theorizing of aesthetics in contemporary US television drama. It examines a range of cultural, technological and formal practices that continue to maintain a distinctive dramatic mode in the high-end series, which acknowledges both television's history and a high degree of variability in its use of recent televisual conventions.

Television specificity

A discussion of style in television drama presents certain initial problems. How style has been defined historically suggests television's aesthetics have been mandated by its specificity. For example, in an earlier era, theorists acknowledged the impact on television's aesthetics of the medium's technological foundations and modes of distribution, including its smaller screen size.[1] It was argued that formalist definitions of television's small screen relied on close-up and medium shots, which, with its ability to be live, hoped to achieve an intimate view of the world.[2] However, since the 1980s, the US television industry has been greatly altered by technological and economic shifts. If theory about the medium had tried to prove that television was *essentially* different from other media in its methods of production and consumption, as well as formal aspects, a countervailing tendency has developed. The recent growth of streaming and video on demand has led to a rethinking of television specificity amid the growth of cable and computer technologies. An increased media convergence suggests the erosion of specificities. But the aim of this book is to demonstrate that newer distribution channels have also led US networks to produce a form

---

[1] For examples of an earlier era of television theory, see William Lafferty, 'Film and Television', in Gary Edgerton (ed.), *Film and the Arts in Symbiosis* (New York: Greenwood Press, 1988), 273–310, and John Ellis, *Visible Fictions: Cinema, Television, Video*, 2nd revised edn (London: Routledge, 1992).

[2] Glen Creeber, *Small Screen Aesthetics: From TV to the Internet* (Basingstoke: Palgrave Macmillan, 2013), 15–17.

that continues to be distinctively televisual. The chapters of this book serve to explain the continuing appeal of specificity in high-end television drama for the producer and audience, as well as remaining an important method of analysis. If technological convergence has been shown by theorists such as Henry Jenkins to undermine distinctions between different media, it is important to examine how aesthetics in high-end drama continue to afford specific televisual pleasures.[3] This book argues that distinct cultural systems in television continue to promote the study of Televisuality by referring to various discourses around technology and formal practices, as well as types of engagement with style in high-end television.

Television's dramatic stylistics have always been part of a wider cultural process of shaping aesthetic form. From the 1970s, the cable era of television not only altered the consensus about American political and social values but also supported a number of stylistic innovations, maturing by the 1980s and 1990s into an era of talented producers such as Steven Bochco, Chris Carter, Mark Frost and David Lynch. Now, as shows like *Hill Street Blues*, *X-Files* and *Twin Peaks* recede into the past, television theory acknowledges that a discussion about contemporary shows further demonstrates the need to move beyond fixed categories of style. Instead, the blurring of generic boundaries and the use of intertextuality create a complex understanding of style and cultural worth. John T. Caldwell and Greg M. Smith discuss how aesthetics in television drama have constructed discourses in older shows like *Miami Vice* (1984–90) or *Ally McBeal* (1997–2002) to achieve a 'special event' status,[4] including in the case of the latter, a quirky aesthetic tone.[5] Increasingly, US television drama has permitted greater stylistic development with complex visual and aural strategies than those which governed it in the past. Meanwhile, to meet the challenge of distinguishing one era of television production from another, a methodology of historical poetics has appeared in Jeremy Butler's *Television Style* (2010), Jason Mittell's *Complex TV: The Poetics of Contemporary Television Storytelling* (2015) and Trisha Dunleavy's *Complex Serial Drama and Multiplatform Television* (2018). Each of these books deals with debates on television specificity amid distinct historic production contexts.

[3] Henry Jenkins, *Convergence Culture: Where Old and New Media Collide*, revised edn (New York University Press, 2008).
[4] John T. Caldwell, *Televisuality: Style, Crisis and Authority in American Television* (New Brunswick: Rutgers University Press, 1995).
[5] Greg M. Smith, *Beautiful TV: The Art and Argument of Ally McBeal* (Austin: University of Texas, 2007).

Seeing It on Television is, therefore, an account of the changing use of style in US drama during the second decade of the twenty-first century. If media convergence threatens older paradigms about the specificity of television drama, it should be recalled that producers have always exploited the tensions between different aesthetic systems, while allowing television to be distinguished from other mediums like film. This book addresses the need to take a broader view of the possibilities of style in recent US drama without ignoring the continued challenges to television specificity, including the claim of the high-end series becoming 'cinematic'.

High-end television serial drama

During the second decade of the twenty-first century, the continuing development of a 'high-end' aesthetic in US television depended on a complex set of industrial and cultural circumstances. To examine this, *Seeing It on Television* utilizes eight case studies in order to develop a sense of what can be defined as high-end television drama. Since the 1990s, high-end television has been applied to a type of serial drama whose structure of narrative deferral has been increasingly sought by media conglomerates.[6] Using these antecedents, high-end television drama has become well suited to the digital age because of the market conditions of delivering to a desirable demographic, leading to customer loyalty for a particular series. Within methods of pay-per-view distribution, high-end drama capitalizes on the fact that audiences are no longer loyal to a network or channel but remain loyal to particular television shows.[7]

Prior to digitalization, television drama could be characterized by what have been termed by Marie-Laure Ryan as 'semiotic affordances' of the medium.[8] These affordances distinguished film from television because of the varying use of image, sound and language. *Seeing It on Television* focuses on evolving practices that determine techniques of style – such as approaches to mise en scène – which contribute to distinct affordances in contemporary television storytelling. Ryan further argues that a medium should be defined by its

---

[6] Robert Nelson, *State of Play: Contemporary High-End TV Drama* (Manchester: Manchester University Press, 2007).
[7] Michael Curtin and Jane Shattuc, *The American Television Industry* (Basingstoke: Palgrave Macmillan, 2009).
[8] Marie-Laure Ryan, *Avatars of Story* (Minneapolis: University of Minnesota, 2006), 18–23.

'cultural use', determining how a distinct media culture mandates a programme's specific affordances.[9] High-end drama invites comparisons with cinema due to its recent technological changes and the desire for certain types of prestigious drama to rival film in its quality and complexity.[10] In many ways, the 'film look' on television has been a moniker about rising high production values and investment in feature cinematography.[11] Nevertheless, the value, scope and meaning of formalist definitions of high-end drama must be considered in a cultural context, as much as an economic or technical one.

Television's distinct forms suggest notions of worth about types of high-quality drama that are predicated less on technical quality – the choice of camera and so on – than its cultural significance as a *creative* medium. In this way, 'high-end drama' is a term that is flexible enough to include a plurality of styles, albeit remaining distinct from mainstream practices. This book deals with some of the problems of how high-end television has maintained its distinctiveness in recent years. Often boundaries between high-end television and mainstream practices depend on concepts to do with 'original content'. Ultimately, this defines high-end drama as an aspirational idea of television. Chapters in this book examine how style in high-end television, as both a concept and a practice, reveal how it can be understood in terms of cultural, as well as economic, value.

The central claim in *Seeing It on Television* is that selected programmes possess distinctiveness within a discourse of 'original content' allied to authorship. However, this book is careful not to devise a hierarchy or set of aestheticist ideas that operates as a dramatic mode. Rather than argue that a high-end series comes from one person's vision, there is, for example, a dialectic between the role of the showrunner or director as the guarantor of quality and a production aligned with the cultural shift to the audience. In fact, what is usually striking within the shows discussed in this book is a pluralization of televisual style across a serial narrative as its ongoing story world demands engagement by its audience. One consequence has been that a distinctive style is more robust than ever in high-end drama. However, by expanding the scope in television drama, style can become diffuse precisely because it draws upon a narrative mode, sometimes spanning many weeks. This complicates ideas about a unifying authorship by the showrunner. Rather, it acknowledges a greater engagement of the audience due

---

[9] Ryan, *Avatars of Story*, 23–5.
[10] Joel Brinkley, *Defining Vision: The Battle for the Future of Television* (San Diego: Harcourt Brace, 1998).
[11] Caldwell, *Televisuality*, 73–102.

to the capacity of serial drama to nurture loyal viewers, as well as its ability to provide a range of other pleasures, including the play between dramatic modes and generic codes over multiple episodes.

Televisuality

This book, therefore, attempts to do two things. The first is to understand style through its various discourses. Chapter 1 draws upon a historical approach to television that is similar to Noël Carroll's critique of cinema, seeking to find the historical tools for identifying the conditions for the production of types of film.[12] Discourses about textual complexity and original content are explored in Chapter 1 to make sense of the initial stylistic features in the TV shows that follow. To this extent, high-end television is to be understood as practices that are highly variable, although they continue to be specific to a single medium. The second objective is to deploy a closer reading of style than is usual in television studies. Although various discourses are useful when discussing, for example, ideas about television's 'legitimate' style and cultural value, a reading of television's poetics further articulates wider issues about authorship. The complex processes of authorship and the decisions taken by showrunners, directors and performers demonstrate the importance of considering the style elements of high-end drama. In the eight shows of this book, the creation of modalities and the signification of textual meanings allied to authorship start to demonstrate the greater variability of high-end television, while maintaining a distinctive televisual praxis, including its interaction with film.

In chapters two and three, *Seeing It on Television* discusses techniques allied to the poetics of authored storytelling and stylistic command but goes further by exploring how they affect the viewer to create a greater emotional engagement. In Chapter 2, Paulo Sorrentino in *The Young Pope* seeks psychological and emotional insight of his protagonist in a blend of realism and fantasy. Moments of affect suggest several levels of engagement using complex style. This also goes beyond debates about past theories marking distinctions in spectatorship between the film image eliciting a concentrated, focused look as opposed to television's intermittent glance. Instead, an understanding of the protagonist in *The Young Pope* relies on Sorrentino's aesthetic vision.

---

[12] Noël Carroll, *Interpreting the Moving Image* (Cambridge: Cambridge University Press, 1998).

Chapter 3 examines *The Knick* as part of a canon of work from director Steven Soderbergh. As in Chapter 2, the use of an acclaimed film director, Soderbergh, suggests the possibility of growing convergence between film and television. If Chapter 3 explores correlations between practices in television drama and US independent film-making, it also explains how film practice has been reconfigured for the long-form television series. In Soderbergh's *The Knick*, an extended gaze becomes indicative of an intense viewing to form an intimate spectacle of the suffering and vulnerable body. Soderbergh further exploits generic codes from the hospital drama – a genre closely identified with television rather than from the cinema. The brutality of medicine at the turn of the twentieth century is represented using a style and genre that are specific to television to counterclaims about convergence between film and TV. If the suggestion exists that directors such as Sorrentino and Soderbergh represent a migration of film directors to television, motifs and a reconfiguration of style continue to engage with the television image, albeit influenced by aspects of film.

Other discursive unities such as a directorial canon in the high-end series chart the institutional contours of the television shows within chapters of this book. In many ways, the shift to a shorter serial form marks the realignment or perhaps, more accurately, an intensified reorganization of a dramatic form that combines a director-based with a producer-based mode. As this book demonstrates, a richer textual order is sustained by a mode of authority from directors and producers migrating from film to television and filling the role of showrunners. But Chapter 4 deals with the adaptation of *Fargo* the feature film to *Fargo* the television show. Dominic Lees, a television drama director, shows how this tension rather than a stable televisual form – including a constant drawing away from but also push towards a grand aesthetic design – finally complicates claims about highly valued forms of television becoming cinematic. For Lees, juxtaposing various production decisions about *Fargo* marks the specificity of the television series compared to the film.

Besides poetics, this book hopes to show how high-end television plays a distinctly different role to film by also referring to its hermeneutics. In Chapter 5, a system of allusion distinguishes the source films of the Spielberg-Amblin universe from the Netflix serial of *Stranger Things*. The serial sets social and aesthetic parameters, effectively limiting the Duffer brothers as writer-directors of a high-status primary text as it becomes more cultic and indicative of a televisual fan base. In *Stranger Things*, a complex genealogy of intertextuality traffics memories of earlier films, as well as the need to create a self-sufficient world without the need for recourse to Spielberg-Amblin as the serial's primary source texts. Nevertheless, an important aspect of high-end television drama is the role of the cinematic. Cinema has usually been a prior discourse for television, whose complex visual form is designed to hold the viewer from the beginning to the end of the show without interruption. The evocation of the cinema as prior discourse suggests why high-end drama can mark a growing tendency for an image to look like cinema. Such images are rich in detail by using camerawork and lighting without having yesteryear's minimalist set dressing. Yet, in chapters four and five, high-end television has reworked the Coen brothers or the Spielberg-Amblin film universe. In *Stranger Things*, the images produce an analogue nostalgia that reconstructs the mythology of the 1980s to generate a remembrance of televisual heritage.

Within the methodological use of a close stylistic reading, Chapter 6 takes a focused look at one element of televisual style: performance. In *The Leftovers*, a close reading of acting style reveals the clash of radically differing performance techniques and modes within a single ensemble of actors. A congruence of authorial factors can be identified, which permits a plurality of performance modes in high-end drama. The case study shows the ability of authorship in high-end television to incorporate variable modes of performance within a series, while maintaining its appeal as distinctive television drama.

Chapter 7 returns to ideas of style and visual pleasure in the series *Mars*, produced by Ron Howard. Televisual spectacle in *Mars* creates complex images which encourage haptic feelings about the alien landscape the astronauts wish to colonize. A Hollywood name like Ron Howard suggests the possibility of cinematic spectacle. But, unlike film, *Mars* is inflected with a sense of being-there that mobilizes television's historic capacity for live or simultaneous transmission. The impression is what the audience see is unfolding in the present. Using new aesthetic techniques, as much as *Mars* aspires to be 'beautiful television' and its equivalence to cinematic science fiction, it is equally a reminder of how the high-end series relies on television's specificity. The production and consumption of spectacular images are organized around the construction of immediacy and haptic sensation on an alien planet. As we will see, newer stylistic techniques such as colour grading for 4K ultra high definition meet goals of digital spectacle for the television screen rather than for film.

Recent higher production values have offered an increasingly filmic experience in types of television drama as the method of consumption of streaming demands an uninterrupted viewing, underlining a programme's authored status.

Yet, *Seeing It on Television* deals with the key issue of television specificity in the form of high-end drama. Discourses about Televisuality within the specific form of the high-status programme are used as tools to restructure television's relations with film. The high-end series attracts talent from theatrical film and commands budgets similar to mid-budget movies. Nevertheless, the high-end television series continues to play a distinctly different role from the movies. At the same time, this book hopes to demonstrate that such differences depend less on attempts to detect ontological medium specificities. Instead, an analysis of style in high-end television drama demonstrates how recent Televisuality invites unfixed combinations of technological facility and varying cultural patterns.

1

Reconfiguring Televisuality in high-end television

The high-end continuing series has been part of the US television landscape for more than three decades, including shows such as *Sex and the City* (1998–2004), *The Sopranos* (1999–2007), *Lost* (2004–10) and *Mad Men* (2007–15). The desire for high-end programming has been a major factor in winning subscribers to premier cable outlets such as HBO; as well as what were basic cable networks, such as AMC, Showtime and FX; and, more recently, streaming services such as Netflix and Amazon Prime. The world of subscriber-supported pay television has been the story of US television in the last few decades, and the financial model of individual projects satisfying a brand is likely to remain for the foreseeable future. However, the increase in budget allocation for content production, as well as the growth in the number of subscribers – at the time of writing the number of customers for Netflix is 190 million - tells us little about critical attitudes to style in the high-end series and the ability of Televisuality to innovate and introduce something new.

Work by John T. Caldwell and Greg M. Smith of finding the essential basis of Televisuality in 1980s and 1990s television has situated formal practices in historical contexts of production.[1] For Caldwell, television became stylistically exhibitionist due to its move towards a 'film look' when 'cinematic values brought to television spectacle, high-production values, and feature-style cinematography'.[2] At the same time, Caldwell notes that new combinations of existing ideas about style demonstrate not only the need to explore the use of high production values but how the industry legitimizes itself by overproducing

---

[1] John T. Caldwell, *Televisuality: Style, Crisis, and Authority in American Television* (New Brunswick: Rutgers University Press, 1995) and Greg M. Smith, *Beautiful TV: The Art and Argument of Ally McBeal* (Austin: University of Texas Press, 2007).
[2] Caldwell, *Televisuality*, 12.

and complicating such values.[3] In this way, scrutiny of the legitimization of the expansion of formal devices in contemporary high-end drama can be made to reveal the origin of meanings to do with televisual textual practices, as well as evaluate the process of stylistic innovation in complex drama. If narrative has aesthetic goals and desired effects on the audience member, the investigation of contemporary high-end television is useful because it not only analyses how narrative is shaped and transformed by style in high-end drama but also demonstrates how systems of value can be used to interpret the meanings created by style in contemporary shows.

This critical approach to television style is influenced by David Bordwell's approach to historical poetics, situating formal practices of film-making within contexts of production and reception.[4] Such an approach can be transplanted to demonstrate how television directors, showrunners and producers have used or otherwise defied methods of television production. Style refers to 'how' a production is expressed as much as 'what' it is, and the scrutiny of stylistic practices can show change, as well as stability. The technological, economic and social context in which a stylistic device functions as it gives form to content becomes the basis on which textual significance can be discussed.

It should be recalled that, historically, television has been regarded, in the decades before the 1980s, as 'textually anaemic', although Caldwell has identified many instances of a clear use of style in earlier shows and other scholars have written about style in the formative years of television.[5] Television was understood as a domestic appliance and, unlike cinema, not a symbol of mass culture, with an elevated status. In the 1990s, John Caldwell argued that the television programme had been written out of the history of the medium and was hopelessly general about forms.[6] However, recent studies of television style have demonstrated the value of building a television poetics that accurately characterize stylistic traits of particular modes of production during its history from studio-based drama to shooting on location. Such studies seek to promote an understanding of television that has developed both conventional and complex approaches to its programming, including drama. More recently, high-end television has evolved into a sophisticated dramatic mode by integrating

---

[3] Caldwell, *Televisuality*, 191.
[4] David Bordwell, *Poetics of Cinema* (New York: Routledge, 2008).
[5] For example, see Jason Jacobs, *The Intimate Screen: Early British Television Drama* (Oxford: Oxford University Press, 2000).
[6] Caldwell, *Televisuality*, 352.

earlier televisual modalities, as well as cinematic modalities. Yet, if television poetics was given little scholarly attention, as Jason Mittell has argued, recent scholarly work has not only identified stylistic characteristics at historical moments but highlighted 'how cultural meanings and assumptions are encoded in the program [and] we can see how these textual elements fit into larger cultural and generic categories'.[7] In this way, high-end television style in the past decade can be shown to be significant because its techniques are related to cultural-aesthetic concerns requiring further enquiry.

Since the 1990s, an increasing trend for complex drama has been to signal its originating network's ability to produce a show or even cluster of shows that are ambitious in terms of narrative and style. According to Deborah L. Jaramillo, branding in television is a matter of product differentiation, and a subscriber network like HBO needs to offer different yet familiar programming.[8] For example, about a decade ago, networks such as FX and AMC began to sell their original series, such as *Sons of Anarchy* (2008–14) and *Breaking Bad* (2008–13) to Netflix, which quadrupled its subscription base from 12.27 million in 2009 to 47.35 in 2013.[9] What was driving audiences to subscription video-on-demand (SVoD) platforms such as Netflix was original content, especially serialized drama. For example, a show such as *Fargo* (2014–2020) from the once 'basic' cable network, FX, represents the accelerating trend of constructing a network brand that incorporates a series with impressive pedigrees, which relies on crossover talents taken from theatrical film. *Fargo* the television series is a loose adaptation of the film of the same name directed by the Oscar-winning Coen brothers and includes A-list actors such as Billy Bob Thornton. Nevertheless, a loose adaptation of an earlier indie film, *Fargo* the television series, continues, in many ways, to be rooted in the particularities of television long-form drama. This is true especially in its use of serialized narrative, the extended biographies of its characters and even the representation of emotional states, as character psychological traits are developed across episodes.

By 2015, FX, which had started in a Manhattan apartment twenty years earlier, was no longer using repeats to fill its schedules but using a strategy centred on original content in shows such as *Sons of Anarchy* and *Fargo*, winning

---

[7] Jason Mittell, *Genre and Television: From Cop Shows to Cartoons to American Culture* (New York: Routledge, 2004), 122.
[8] Deborah L. Jarmillo, 'The Family Racket: AOL-Time Warner HBO, *The Sopranos* and the Construction of a Quality Brand', *Journal of Communication Inquiry* 26, no. 1 (2002): 59–75.
[9] Daniel Frankel, 'The Big Short', *Emmy*, 39, no. 10 (2017): 41–3.

27 Emmys and receiving nominations for another 163.[10] However, it is difficult to make aesthetic judgements about television programmes being 'excellent' or 'superior' compared to other drama, as might be, initially, assumed by the term 'high-end' drama. Other terms such as 'complex' or 'innovative' also remain problematic because they assume an aesthetic system, which relies on dominant cultural norms. Television Studies is less about developing a method of aesthetic judgement in which a cohesive system offers an argument about innovative formal techniques as 'good' or 'bad' programmes. Instead, analysis of the style of high-end drama can go beyond matters of taste. This book is not about mere 'formalism' that assumes, for example, cinematic style is superior to television, but it seeks to approach style in high-end television drama as the physical manifestation of complex themes and narratives by exploring how these, then, form a cultural, as well as industrial, logic of distinction.

Although there has been an accelerating tendency of using higher production values in television drama, Deborah L. Jaramillo strikes a word of warning by noting that what has happened in the cinema limits our understanding of television aesthetics. For her, 'Cinematic should be a contentious word in the field of television studies. It should raise the eyebrows of anyone who thinks and writes about television; instead it has become commonplace for scholars and popular critics to use the term as shorthand when discussing [a] complex visual and aural style in scripted series.'[11] A complex televisual style is not inherently cinematic. If Jaramillo is wary of, for example, how spectacle on television is referred to as cinematic because it includes 'artistry mixed with a sense of grandeur',[12] it can also be shown that, for example, in *Stranger Things*, visual style offers opportunities to create a specific form that extends earlier television style, while forming a crossover with some types of theatrical film. Similarly, rather than the use of spectacle normally found in theatrical film, it can be shown how increased spectacle in shows such as *The Knick* and *Mars* is linked to the narrative complexity of character and story, which has been influenced by the development of a recent televisual aesthetic.

A mode of television that can be identified as 'high-end' demonstrates that aesthetic practices have been reconfigured as technology and economics are

---

[10] Anon, 'How Many Networks', *Emmy*, 37, no. 2 (2015): 32–8.
[11] Deborah L. Jaramillo, 'Rescuing Television from the Cinematic: The Perils of Dismissing Television Style', in J. Jacobs and S. Peacock (eds), *Television Aesthetics and Style* (London: Bloomsbury, 2013), 67.
[12] Jaramillo, 'Rescuing Television', 67.

rapidly changing. Since the beginning of the noughties, televisual textuality has altered from modes associated with network television to the full complement of cable/satellite TV options, including, most recently, streaming OTT services.[13] A mode of high-end television and its principles of textual composition need to be explained as practitioners of contemporary television drama follow, modify or reject older stylistic methods to communicate narrative information. At the same time, stories continue to mobilize a range of television poetics that are watched on a popular, domestic medium. The case for analysing contemporary style's existence and its increased visual exhibitionism relies on understanding its ability to finding solutions to the problems of telling a complex narrative and how it commands attention.

Value within original programming

One of the most notable features of high-end drama is its fulfilment of the demand for original material. Originality in complex serial drama can be described as one of the basic requirements for viewers to notice content in a cluttered media landscape of multiple, competing networks. Such competition has led to a repositioning of new and established broadcasting, cable and streaming networks to seek content that can take producers into the broad sunlit uplands of television's third golden age.[14] Unlike 'Least Objectionable Programming' during an older era of US television history, networks and producers take the types of risks that, historically, were difficult for a medium to be watched in the home, unlike cinema.[15] The desire for risk encourages strategies believed to bring success. In the 1990s, HBO became known for original programming, and its tagline of 'It's not TV' marked it off as distinct from network television content, in part due to its ability to deal with controversial issues, including sex and bad language, suggesting greater authenticity and insight about

---

[13] OTT stands for over-the-top and describes streaming services from companies such as Netflix and Amazon that use a SVoD platform.
[14] Albeit a contested term, the first US television Golden Age was in the 1950s. The second Golden Age ran from the 1980s to the 1990s. Contemporary drama is considered to be a third Golden Age.
[15] The term 'Least Objectionable Programming' (LOP) was used in the age of the three major US networks: ABC, NBC and CBS. It suggests a form of drama that, especially, during the 1960s and 1970s, was least offensive in terms of bad language, nudity, sex and violence to a majority audience assumed to be conservative in their viewing tastes. The term originates with Paul Klein while at NBC.

dramatic characters.¹⁶ As Horace Newcomb notes about HBO, its attitude to older television drama was a 'retro activation', which implied denigration of meanings about television that had hitherto existed.¹⁷ In the age of digitalization and globalization, this repositioning has evolved into a continuing strategy of branding a network as capable of taking risk while, at the same time, creating opportunities to produce original content. Simultaneously, programmes have become more of a marketable commodity, as well as a vehicle for the interests and concerns of writers and producers interested in shows that have enhanced moral or ethical insight.

It is important to recognize that with the possible exception of HBO, most audiences for cable channels such as Lifetime and USA Network in the 1980s and 1990s were not watching original productions but reruns of critically acclaimed, network-produced dramas such as *Cagney and Lacey* (1982–8), *Moonlighting* (1985–9) and *LA Law* (1986–94). These shows, which had been made by the networks and shown on prime time on the broadcast schedules, were popular with cable audiences. The length of the shows – an hour – was suitable for syndication on cable, which, at the time, had large gaps on their schedules to fill. At the same time, cable channels began to experiment with hour-long shows in the early 1980s when Showtime revived the *Paper Chase* (1983–6) – on CBS for one season – and ran it for several years to critical acclaim. But it was when independent stations began to make their own first-run hour shows that the cost became similar to the cost of a rerun of an expensive show such as *Miami Vice* (1984–90). For example, in the 1990s, MCA Television Enterprises teamed with independent stations such as KCOP in Los Angeles and WWOR in New York to experiment with a slate of original hour-long series. Although none of the shows produced such as *Shades of LA* (1990–1) received high ratings or lasted more than a season, the effort to produce original drama and attract audiences to something 'distinctive' was a strategy of legitimization of original content, which continues to this day in high-end drama.

From the 1980s, many critics claimed the start of a new golden age in US television based on the emergence of what became termed 'American Quality Drama' (AQD). Contemporary high-end television drama finds many of its

---

[16] Janet McCabe and Kim Akass, 'Sex, Swearing and Respectability: Courting Controversy, HBO's Original Programming and Producing Quality TV', in Janet McCabe and Kim Akass (eds), *Quality TV: Contemporary American Television and Beyond* (London: I.B. Tauris, 2007), 62–76.
[17] Horace Newcomb, 'This Is Not al Dente: The Sopranos and the New Meaning of Television', in Horace Newcomb (ed.), *Television: The Critical View*, 7th edn (Oxford: Oxford University Press, 2007), 574.

antecedents in shows that were considered to be 'serious' drama and might form a discourse of quality or distinction in the same way as AQD because they each deal with contentious or edgy scripts. In 1984, *MTM: Quality Television* was published as a critical history of MTM Enterprises, the company that made one of the most important shows of the 1980s on US television, *Hill Street Blues* (1981–7). The show was considered to be of higher quality than programming on the then-dominant network TV channels of NBC, ABC and CBS. A lobbying group at the time sought to define quality in TV:

> A quality series enlightens, enriches, challenges, involves, and confronts. It dares to take risks, it's honest and illuminating, it appeals to the intellect and touches the emotions. It requires concentration and attention, and it provokes thought. Characterization is explored.[18]

However, such claims appear based more on personal taste about what should be regarded as automatically 'good' rather than a cultural estimation about the worth of a text. Rather than talking about quality TV in the abstract, future debates attempted to identify particular characteristics of programmes that had been labelled as quality TV. The debate which followed found that the moniker referred more to a generic style that could be accurately 'read' by television audiences using narrative strategies rather than an aesthetic judgement about 'excellence'.[19] The issue of quality became best defined by not being 'regular' TV but drama that tended towards content that was controversial or whose transgressive tone aspired towards realism. At the same time, it often included a self-consciousness that functions as nostalgia about television history and included references to popular culture in shows such as the original run of *The X-Files* (1993–5) – a feature that continues to be used in shows such as *Stranger Things* (2016–present), looked at in Chapter 5. If original content suggests something not thought of before, although, crucially, not necessarily sui generis, issues of quality in the context of high-end drama can be better understood as an innovating process. High-end drama continues to re-combine television forms to introduce something new as it articulates the difference from television's past. In this way, original content suggests a set of values that are as much institutionally managed as artistic achievement.

---

[18] Quoted in Robert J. Thompson, *Television's Second Golden Age: From Hill Street Blues to ER* (New York: Continuum, 1996), 13.
[19] Thompson, *Television's Second Golden Age*, 16.

A signifying system in contemporary high-end drama continues to raise the vital question of what these exceptional programmes might offer the producers that create them. On the one hand, the need for brand enhancement by networks such as HBO has been to fix the lodestone for drama as 'not TV': it is neither predictable nor repetitive.[20] More specifically, the pleasures of 'risk' exist in shows such as *The Knick*, discussed in Chapter 3. In these ways, a high-end series may be equated with 'distinction' because it implies the ambition of its network, producer and writer. Similarly, other high-end drama such as *Stranger Things* is a reminder that the appeal of 'original' drama cannot be only because of qualitative differences to do with style. Rather, style is embedded into a wider discourse about production processes and cultural consumption that requires recognition of how formal systems encourage particular attitudes to contemporary television drama. These attitudes include the ability of a show to include dramatic strategies designed to be 'complex'. Attitudes to style reflect how the story and characters are presented to the viewer, that is, the way themes and characters may be deciphered. In these ways, formal strategies in a high-end series produce richer meanings.

At the heart of this criticism is the problem that innovation relies on the appropriation of style as cachet rather than as a sign of creativity – an emblem of value which, once recognized, underlines the cultural status of the viewer but, more certainly, the ambition of the producer. Consequently, underlying any discussion of style in high-end television drama is the realization that the process of innovation continues to rely on reconfiguring the relationship between the network and the producer, as well as between the show and the viewer. In these ways, the development of a distinctive style in contemporary examples of high-end drama is the creative response of programme makers to the need for complex images appropriate to the strategic goals of a network, as well as the integrity and passion of individuals producing shows such as *The Knick*, *Fargo* and *Stranger Things*.

Complex, high-end drama in its various discourses – economic, technological as well as cultural – maintains the idea that it transcends as much as repeats the same character formulas and variable stylistic elements as tone, while maintaining a less dogmatic idea of what its viewers want. If the serialized binge-fest of TV drama is repetitive – the act of watching multiple episodes of the same basic characters – the reward becomes how conventional signification processes

---

[20] 'It's Not TV: It's HBO' was first used as a slogan by the company in 1996 and lasted until 2009.

using camera, lights and other cues in television style are disrupted and used to inscribe creative choice. For example, composition in the first series of *The Young Pope* yields extra meaning about its main character of Lenny Belardo because it signals something novel.[21] In high-end drama, originality relies on a set of dynamic criteria of difference and repetition that fulfils the need for a predictable product that can be marketed, while simultaneously being disruptive of existing industry practices.

The contemporary relationship between the television programme maker and image is a feature of the expensive drive for originality, as well as the recent building of development deals that attract film talent before attempting a multi-series commission. More recently, high-end drama using its cachet of original content becomes more like forms of film that are visually exciting and cinematic, as it promises to deploy multiple locations and continuous movement. Equally, although high-end drama caters to a wide range of sensibilities, the overall aim of the network – itself fluid – and how it establishes as well as manages audience expectations about its shows are important.

Authorship and style

Televisual style marks the means by which authorship originates within the work itself. But there is a general difference between the style of high-end drama and other types of TV drama. This difference reflects not only the role of specific individuals such as the director and producer involved in the production but also different modes of production, varying from historic multi-camera production to the use of single-camera production on large sound stages in shows like *ER* (1994–2009) to finally shooting on location in television drama.[22] For early television directors, a style of naturalism or zero-degree style sought an image on television that privileged the actors. The reliance on dialogue – 'a preoccupation with people's verbal relationships with one another'[23] – would be the foremost narrative device. In this way, a story would be 'told' rather than 'shown', avoiding the creative agency of the director but relying instead on the actor's ability to deliver dialogue from a written script. Such a reliance on dialogue would also

---

[21] See Chapter 2.
[22] For more about historical modes of production, see Trisha Dunleavy, *Television Drama: Form, Agency, Innovation* (Basingstoke: Palgrave Macmillan, 2009).
[23] John Caughie, 'Progressive Television and Documentary Drama', *Screen*, 21, no. 3 (1980): 9–35.

require a fidelity to natural time more suited to a domestic medium in which the audience would watch it as if what was happening on screen was happening simultaneously with their act of viewing. For Troy Kennedy Martin, a BBC dramatist, since naturalism:

> evolved from a theatre of dialogue, the director is forced into photographing faces talking and faces reacting. The director faced with a torrent of words can only retreat into the neutrality of the two- and three-shot where the camera, caged from seizing anything of significance, is emasculated and only allowed to gaze around the room following the conversation like an attentive stranger.[24]

The aesthetic of naturalism limited the use of mise en scène, camerawork and editing.

Unlike early network drama, the deployment of realism on television in what became termed first-degree style allowed for the construction of a point of view using camera and editing, which did not rely on what was being spoken by the actors. At the same time, in network television – albeit with exceptions – personal style in first-degree drama was generally invisible to avoid a distinction between one show and the next or risk the disruption of a network schedule that had been built around the concept of an evening's worth of entertainment rather than discrete programmes.

More recently, second-degree style has been developed and informs much of high-end drama. This departs from an earlier realism which produces a 'heavily closed discourse'.[25] Second-degree style relies on the capacity for television narrative to find novel ways to interact with its viewers, as well as mark individual contributions that add value to a show. Second-degree style has a capacity to investigate, as well as demonstrate, the contingent nature of reality and truth. If outside the scope of this book, the possibility of forensic fandom, as well as fan fiction, exists in complex drama, encouraging producers of high-end television to take greater risks in shows where narration diverges from revelations offered within mise en scène and/or camerawork. Other commentators have realized that this demands from the viewer the ability to recognize the style of a show as establishing unreliability about the knowledge we hold about characters or

---

[24] Troy Kennedy Martin, 'Nats Go Home: First Statement of a New Drama for Television', *Encore*, 48 (March/April 1964): 21–33.
[25] Colin MacCabe, 'Realism and the Cinema: Notes on a Brechtian Thesis', in Tony Bennett, Susan Boyd-Bowman, Colin Mercer and Janet Woolacott (eds), *Popular Television and Film* (London: British Film Institute, 1981), 224.

the plot.²⁶ Authorial control and interpretative consistency of a text become less stable than in earlier television drama.

Nevertheless, since the beginning of the millennium, Matthew Weiner (*Mad Men*), JJ Abrams (*Lost*) and the three Davids – Chase (*The Sopranos*), Simon (*The Wire*) and Milch (*Deadwood*) – have exerted a screenwriter-producer power that suggests a more authorial influence on the dramas they are associated with. For example, *Deadwood* (2004–6) was a social problem drama whose dialogue was frequently referred to as 'Shakespearean', which Milch uses to draw attention to the class distinctions of the frontier.²⁷ Weiner, Chase, Simon and Milch are foremost writers, although Abrams was a producer, who also co-wrote some of his scripts. A theory of authorship in television has historically attributed the writer or the producer as the originator of a drama and within this authorship accords expressive autonomy.²⁸ Yet, it should be remembered, it was usual in US TV drama for a writer's storyline and dialogue to be rewritten by other staff writers at the bequest of a producer if a show was already established, although the script for a pilot would afford less interference.²⁹ Since the 1980s, the structure of the 'writers' room' has been a development of US drama as a way of devising episodes for shows like *Hill Street Blues*, initiated by Steve Bochco, its head writer and executive producer. The collaborative model of a writer's room with roles such as head writer or supervising producer to manage the writing of serials requires collaborative meetings between staff. The density of subplots in serial narrative requires team-writing.

However, in the case of high-end drama discussed in this book, this is not always the case, as writers like Noah Hawley and Paulo Sorrentino wrote not only the pilot episode but also the entire series.³⁰ On the other hand, the Duffy brothers have written the pilot but few other episodes of *Stranger Things*. Nevertheless, the collaborative role of the television writer has altered as networks become open to original material. In the case of high-end drama, it is difficult to say which writing model precisely predominates; the first series of *The Knick* was

---

[26] For more about fandom and the text, see Matt Hills, *Fan Cultures* (London: Routledge, 2002), 98–109.
[27] Joseph Milichap, 'Robert Penn Warren, David Milch and the Literary Contexts of *Deadwood*', in David Lavery (ed.), *Reading Deadwood: A Western to Swear By* (London: I.B. Tauris, 2006), 101–13.
[28] Graham Murdock, 'Authorship and Organisation', *Screen Education*, 35 (Summer 1980): 19–34. If the status of the writer for television varies from the United Kingdom to the United States, there are general similarities.
[29] Richard Levinson and William Link, *Off-Camera: Conversations with the Makers of Prime-Time Television* (New York: New American Library, 1986).
[30] Hawley wrote the entire first series of *Fargo*. Sorrentino wrote the entire series of *The Young Pope*.

written by three people, but the majority of its episodes were by the writing team of Jack Amiel and Michael Begler. The process of authorship in contemporary high-end drama highlights the fact that collaborative work continues to be important, but it has also declined as a characteristic, as a shorter season format of original content between eight and thirteen episodes began to be sold from around 2010. However, this should not ignore the problem of claims about a *télévision d'auteurs* in the United States.[31] Strict budgets and limited schedules will always be difficult to reconcile with the belief in the creative practitioner.

Yet, since the noughties, claims about authorship in works by David Chase, David Milch or Matthew Weiner do not only raise the status of particular individuals. High-end drama often destabilizes borders using stylistic variables that contrast innovation with convention and newer, more complex dramatic forms, including a form that is capable of both 'serious' drama and genre fiction in examples such as *Fargo*. Original programming from directors such as Paul Sorrentino (*The Young Pope*), Martin Scorsese (*Boardwalk Empire*) and Steven Soderbergh (*The Knick*) conflate an authorial process with an arc of development that demonstrates how style is the conscious intention to offer solutions to the problems of narrative. Style in high-end drama is used to distinguish recurring stylistic characteristics that serve as a signature of personal involvement. But, at the same time, the role of the writer or director is not a theory about how television authorship originates within the work itself – a semiotic immanence. In high-end drama such as *The Knick* it can be used more to map television drama's relationship to spectatorship and its ability to be flexible in its tonalities and textures.

Authorship may encompass the totality of a TV show and its operation of complex forces without it becoming a theory about the phenomenology of television. For instance, *The Young Pope* demonstrates that an authorial approach of finding textual borders only occupies one subsection of thinking about the making of a high-end television drama by the writer-director, Paulo Sorrentino. On the one hand, the role of Sorrentino is to operate as an artist and offer the expression of a vision. On the other hand, the drama deploys a textual form that presents a visual delirium and a set of associations between objects and gestures that suggests a different relationship to style as might be suggested by an authorial approach seeking clear resolution about the lives of the characters.

---

[31] The phrase '*télévision d'auteurs*' was first used by John Caughie to describe authorship within a possible art television in the UK. See John Caughie, *Television Drama: Realism, Modernism and British Culture* (Oxford: Oxford University Press, 2000), 31.

Recent televisual authorship can be a category that includes the import of an art house or indie aesthetic to the mainstream of popular culture, including in work by Scorsese and Soderbergh. However, it is important to note that an authorial approach in high-end drama is not the sole criterion of value. Rather, it is one method for making sense of the look of a particular series by incorporating other theories of cultural production about television that do not seek the idea of the author as a reliable source about the characters or story.

Showrunners

Perhaps because earlier networks such as ABC, CBS and NBC were more focused on volume, the calibre of producer during an earlier era was judged to be different. For example, since the 1960s, Esther Shapiro had worked on daytime soap before scripting several films made for television. Eventually, she teamed up with legendary television producer Aaron Spelling to develop *Dynasty* (1981–9). Shapiro has remarked that often in her career she realized there was a prevailing attitude from executives at the networks, which was 'Just get me through another season. Some network executives are really just looking for their way up – nothing comes from them, they're only there for the moment.'[32] In many ways, network TV and its executives worked hard to keep television drama 'safe' because of the temporary nature of their own status, without being deeply involved in producing projects.

Meanwhile, Steven Hewitt, executive vice-president of Showtime Entertainment Group at the time, has been described as an unusually creative executive as a precursor to the role of showrunner. His participation often helped to improve a project and he was drawn to working in cable.[33] From the 1990s, Hewitt's attempts to attract big-name actors, writers and directors were becoming more usual on cable, although it was an uneven process affected by attitudes to film and television and their separate capacities for storytelling. First used by *Variety* in 1992, as a way of describing a television producer, the term 'showrunner' was another intersection between various definitions and conceptions of television production and its operations. Its deployment signifies

---

[32] Quoted in Bart Mills, '*Dynasty*: All in the Family', *Stills*, April–May 1984: 26–9.
[33] Ann Hornaday, 'Channel Executive Seeks to Build Showtime's Slate of Original Fare', *The New York Times*, 29 August 1994 (Digital copy, unpaginated). Available at: https://www.nytimes.com/1994/0 8/29/business/media-business-channel-executive- seeks-build-showtime-s-slate-original-fare.html

how the borders between writer, director, producer and an executive producer like Hewitt have become steadily less rigid. The integration of what had, hitherto, been distinct formal professional boundaries was linked to the increased centralizing role of the showrunner. In 1995, *The New York Times* explored the idea of the showrunner in the case of John Wells, a television scriptwriter and executive producer of *ER* (1994–2009).

> At any one moment, Mr Wells is supervising the content and execution of at least four one-hour episodes in various stages of development – from script to filming to editing the post-production. . . . In the terms of trade, Mr Wells is E.R.'s show runner. For the last 10 years at least, the person with that unofficial title has been the true auteur of series television . . . a show runner makes all important decisions about the series' scripts, tone, attitude, look and direction. He or she oversees casting, production design and budget. This person chooses directors and guest stars.[34]

The role of the showrunner can be compared to a form of 'conspicuous authorship', but rather than a role akin to a novelist or film director, the showrunner combines several roles. Commanding a high-end project suggests more the role of a mogul like Jerry Bruckheimer, capable of attracting talent and making deals. At the same time, a showrunner who is predominantly a writer rather than a producer requires support. In this way, a showrunner such as Beau Willimon employed David Fincher for *House of Cards* (2013–18) to attract to the show Kevin Spacey and his co-star Robin Wright, a star who has been in several major films, including *The Girl with the Dragon Tattoo* (2011).

If conventional wisdom was that television creates its own stars of drama, avoiding talent drawn from theatrical film, it has been possible for film stars and directors to be attracted to working on a television series due to other trends. Once there was the stigma that if a film star was in television drama, their career was over. More recently, Jay Sures, co-head of the television department at the United Talent Agency, has observed that studios such as Disney continue to reduce the number of films they produce despite the success of theatrical films such as *Pirates of the Caribbean* (2003).[35] The result has been a migration of acting and directorial talent from cinema-to-television drama, encouraged by

---

[34] Andy Meisler, 'The Man Who Keeps ER's Heart Beating', *The New York Times*, 26 February 1995 (Digital copy, unpaginated). Available at: https://www.nytimes.com/1995/02/26/arts/television-the-man-who-keeps-er-s-heart-beating.html

[35] Jay Sures quoted in Jennifer Pendleton, 'Cinematech', *Emmy*, 28, no. 5 (September/October 2006): 73–4.

the attraction of its increased stature. A shorter series or arc also attracts A-list actors and directors. Television holds an appeal to such people because it avoids some of the 'development hell' of producing a film, with its protracted process of pre-production and the setting up of finance and distribution for films whose budgets run into the many tens of millions of dollars. A one-hour television drama usually costs between $2 and 3 million per episode, and development times are usually much shorter.[36]

Moreover, unlike earlier network television commissioning of twenty-two- or twenty-four-part shows, the number of episodes for a series looked at in this book is far less. The justification for large numbers of episodes was to fit a schedule in an era when US television required an autumn season for the upcoming television year. However, the notion of a season has declined in importance due to the availability of television on a pay-per-view basis.[37] The commissioning system in US television now has high-profile shows of fewer episodes all year round with bigger names which can be compared to the earlier practice of concentrating them in the advertising-lucrative autumn. Since the first decade of the twenty-first century, the developing concept of a showrunner has been used to reinterpret meanings about serialized drama that is often six, eight or ten episodes long. The high-end television series is not twenty-two or twenty-four episodes but lasts about eight to ten hours, although there are important earlier exceptions such as *Lost* (2004–10), which ran for twenty-five episodes in its first season.

These industrial trends did not create the role of the showrunner but further opened up the role. One key to success for a showrunner is not necessarily to be a good producer, director or writer but to understand what the network has ordered. In this way, a successful showrunner must interpret the critical function of the network by setting the creative tone of the future show. Creative tone can be understood as the detail in a project: a precise, singular vision of stylistic particularities that is designed to attract top talent. However, this also underlines the increased complexity in the relationship between a singular, highly motivated individual demonstrating leadership and a network on which they rely to enact their vision.

---

[36] Although there are exceptions, the budget for the pilot episode of *Boardwalk Empire* (2010) was $18 million.
[37] Syndication was also a consideration, and a series usually required 100 episodes to be successfully syndicated.

Unlike definitions of the showrunner as a 'heroic auteur' borrowed from cinema and their work constituting his or her oeuvre, the claim that a showrunner contributes an identifiable and distinct style to a show should not simply be understood as a protest against the industrializing process of television popularized in the press and in books.[38] If David Chase, the showrunner of *The Sopranos* has been widely reported for being egregiously critical of television drama because 'it trivializes everything',[39] Alan Ball has similarly been critical of working in film and opted to produce *Six Feet Under* for television. In fact, tensions within the role of the showrunner are not necessarily antagonistic. Shaun Ryan, the creator of the controversial police drama *The Shield* (Fox, 2002–8), puts it thus: 'It's the golden age of drama on American TV. The film industry has become so taken with the global market and simplifying things to sell around the world, that TV has filled a niche that film occupied in the 70s and 80s. . . . Alan Ball and *Six Feet Under* came out of that [film] world.'[40] The role of the showrunner can be understood less about raising the profile of an individual and more about raising the esteem held for television drama as a whole. In other words, a showrunner functions less as one person's vision or solitary artist but rather as the commercial strategy of product differentiation and marker of complex drama devised by networks such as HBO and FX.

In this way, Noah Hawley, the showrunner of *Fargo*, is used by FX to distinguish *Fargo* the television series from *Fargo* the film directed by the Coen brothers. If aesthetic unity within an author's 'work' exists within *Fargo*, this is not necessarily a personal style attributed to one person. Rather, the showrunner attracts talent – directors, star actors and writers. The trend has been for the showrunner to behave more like a film producer by attracting high-profile talent that can be vital for financing and sales. Michelle Buck, who produced the remake of *The Prisoner* (2009) starring Ian McKellen and was nominated for an Oscar for performances in *Lord of the Rings* and *Gods and Monsters*, explains: 'We're all trying to pull together the elements that will secure funding from broadcasters, screen agencies and rights distributors.'[41] High-profile film-makers can attract talent to major TV projects. Creative Artists Agency (CAA) agent

---

[38] A protest that becomes a leitmotif in books such as Brett Martin, *Difficult Men* (London: Penguin, 2013).
[39] Quoted in Virginia Heffernan, 'The Real Boss of *The Sopranos*', *New York Times*, 29 February 2004. Available at: https://www.nytimes.com/2004/02/29/arts/television-the-real-boss-of-the-sopranos.html
[40] Quoted in Glen Creeber, *Serial Television: Big Drama on the Small Screen* (London: BFI, 2004), 157.
[41] Quoted in Andy Fry, 'Shooting for the Stars', *Screen International*, April 2010: 22–3.

Michael Katcher explains that 'if Martin Scorsese or Todd Haynes is going to do something, it's going to attract talent'.[42] Other high-end productions capitalize on prestige-endowing theatrical talent, including Todd Haynes' version of James M. Cain's *Mildred Pearce* (2010), starring Kate Winslet. It was Winslet's first work since winning an Oscar for *The Reader* (2009).

It is worth noting that the rise of the television miniseries parallels the sharp decline in the mid-budget film sector. The arrival of greater mid-range film practices of shooting quickly on smaller budgets, which can be easily adapted to television, has meant that stars such as Matthew McConaughty and Woody Harrelson are receiving executive producer roles in shows such as *True Detective* (2014–19). For television audiences, the benefit has been a growing interest and investment in the style of a programme. For example, there is the cinematic sweep in *Mars* (2016–18), a tent-pole show produced by National Geographic and Imagine Entertainment. Imagine Entertainment is run by director Ron Howard and producer Brian Glazer, and *Mars* relies on the expertise of theatrical talent like Howard, the director of Oscar-winning films such as *A Beautiful Mind* (2001).

Any function of the showrunner within a theory of authorship suggests a need to recognize how paradigms of artistic excellence, including stylistic traits in contemporary high-end drama, are governed by aesthetic cultural systems that seek to attribute artistry to an individual. But the role of the showrunner cannot be clearly used to suggest authorship in the sense of creating a personal narrative. Instead, it should be understood to combine multiple roles, as well as promote interconnectedness between members of a team in the production. In these ways, the function of the showrunner in the high-end series in chapters of this book is both broadened and deepened.

Technology and image

Technical quality can function as the criterion for forming a category of value to be assigned to particular television programmes. Although the image capacities of film and television have historically differed, the higher degree of spectacle in many high-end shows suggests an adjustment in narrative structure that can accommodate greater visual pleasure. Many of the more recent changes of attitude

---

[42] *Screen International*, 20.

to spectacle in television drama can be attributed to Bruckheimer Television, whose show, *CSI* (2000–15), a police procedural, became known for its editing and special effects. If there has been a shift in the balance between spectacle and narrative in television since *CSI*, it can also be identified as a characteristic of high-end television. For example, Kevin Blank, *Lost*'s (2004–10) Emmy-winning visual effects supervisor, and his Digital Visual Effects (DVFX) team conjured up a fully rigged nineteenth-century British trading ship in the middle of the jungle, as well as created the plane crash of Oceanic Airlines Flight 815 seen in the pilot – a nine-minute sequence that required 125 VFX shots.[43] However, the use of spectacle does not in itself indicate a mode of high-end television. Geoff King's definition of spectacle is 'the production of images at which we might stop and stare'.[44] Meanwhile, Norman King's seminal analysis of the films of Abel Gance argues that filmic spectacle is that 'which arrests the spectator's look at the surface of the frame as opposed to what is within the frame'.[45] At the same time, as has been pointed by Shilo McClean, a clear distinction between narrative and spectacle raises problems because the same shot can be interpreted as 'pure spectacle' by some and by others as having a narrative function.[46] Moreover, if spectacle is equated only with values associated with the cinematic, it limits our understanding of television aesthetics.[47] Rather, as we will see in *Mars*, the aesthetics of spectacle when associated with high-end drama and a heightened visual pleasure are usually linked to the camera as narrating agency rather than a 'dazzling' display of the capabilities of any cinematographic technology.

The technological capacities of storytelling on television – digital cameras, sound recording and editing – have led to particular stylistic tonalities and plot textures, which inform screen modes in high-end drama. The latest cameras from manufacturers such as ARRI, Red and Sony are providing networks such as FX with the opportunity to emulate the picture quality of 35 mm film cameras and the look sought by cinematographers for greater contrast and colour control. For example, the ARRI Alexa camera has been used to shoot television's *Doctor*

---

[43] The ship Black Rock was first seen in *Exodus* and last seen in *Everybody Loves Hugh*, part 1, original TX 18 May 2005 and 13 April 2010.
[44] Geoff King, *Spectacular Narratives: Hollywood in the Age of the Blockbuster* (London, I.B. Tauris, 2000), 4.
[45] Norman King, *Abel Gance* (London: BFI, 1984), 201.
[46] Shilo T. McClean, *Digital Storytelling: The Narrative Power of Visual Effects in Film* (Cambridge, MA: Massachusetts Institute of Technology, 2007).
[47] Jarmillo, 'The Family Racket', 67.

Who and mooted to shoot cinema's *Avatar 2* (2021).[48] Moreover, matte and compositing shots – matching scenes that have been shot on the set with scenes that are computer-modified and refined with effects such as added light glows – serve the ideal of presenting spectacle on television. Often such effects take several weeks and a team of dedicated VFX artists. However, a media text's value, as Anthony Smith reminds us, is defined less by its formal qualities than its ability to be innovative in terms of storytelling.[49] In this way, the use of technological capacities in contemporary television drama should be understood as part of the new machinery of marking off today's high-end shows by a narrative reordering of the image. As we will see in shows in this book – for example, *Mars* – the development of VFX technologies of exhibiting space travel and landing on the Red Planet has been innovative because they augment the viewing experience of television by creating a fascinated gaze, as well as a narratological point of view.

Within high-end drama, the embrace of technology suggests the opening up of new trends in aesthetics that enable producers to destabilize older dramatic tropes. High-definition TV (HDTV) contributes to the production process and the breaking of rules about the storytelling process based on older tropes. A digital camera such as an ARRI Alexa re-creates a film look shot on 35 mm or indeed produces a sharper image. In this way, image texture, including the use of contrast and colour grading, creates enhanced visual tone that matches the vision of the televisual author. HDTV and the introduction of 2K and 4K images are a new innovation for delivering stories. Such sophisticated technology, and its crossover with the VFX industry, adds extra possibilities to produce more diverse content due to a complex texture. HDTV provides options for pictorial composition, although it should be recalled that technological constraints have led to creative solutions, including the aesthetic of minimal or low-key lighting in *The Knick* to create greater curiosity about the story and characters.

Digital imaging offers an expressive art but its aesthetic continues to promise authenticity about people's lives as complex stories on television are adapted to a richer visual vocabulary. At the same time, a parallel to draw here is with Jason Mittell's reference to an 'operational aesthetic' in complex drama. Writing about *Lost* (2004–10), Mittell argues that the series demands dual attention to both the

---

[48] Paul Watson, 'Arri Alexa in the Picture for Avatar 2'. Available at: https://www.tvbeurope.com/production-post/arri-alexa-in- the-picture-for-avatar-2
[49] Anthony N. Smith, 'Super Mario Seriality', in Roberta Pearson and Anthony Smith (eds), *Storytelling in the Media Convergence Age* (Basingstoke: Palgrave Macmillan, 2015), 21–39.

story and the narrative discourse that narrates the story.[50] Similarly, high-end drama draws attention to how the machinery of style works at an additional level of engagement beyond the storyworld itself. As narrative becomes less centred on causality, multiple points of view about character and other complex spatial and temporal structures come into play. Such structures include the possibility of role-playing seen in *The Young Pope* and the visual cues used to interpret the story. In this way, Televisuality in many of the shows in this book is a visual journey through uncharted territory that not only shapes the story but also navigates the narrative as a complex web of meaning to be negotiated.

Affective styles

In his study of film narrative, David Bordwell discusses 'the viewer's activity'.[51] For him, film style is constructed as a narrated language accompanied by a response from the spectator. At the same time, aesthetic theory and an understanding of interpretation of style have been difficult to apply to television because of a historically different form of viewing from film: television spectatorship has been argued to be distracted.[52] However, as we have seen, the bestowing of an author on a show such as *Fargo* or *Stranger Things* attaches itself to the romantic notion that the individual as showrunner is unique. Original content is, therefore, a sign of uniqueness: at once, both a definition of art and a criterion of its value. On the other hand, if the spectator is aware of the repetition of tropes borrowed from multiple forms of fiction, they may react to the show based on their past experience of television. In this way, a formal analysis of a television show emphasizes not only authorial control but the significance of the spectator's engagement with the image. Style in television becomes an expressive art as fictive emotions are tied to the diegesis, reinforcing the sense for the viewer of being present in the fictional world. In this way, quirkiness, ambiguity and strangeness in many high-end dramas in this book are presented as moods and feelings. In other words, specific elements in the text elicit an emotional response.

---

[50] Jason Mittell, 'Evaluation in Narrative Television', in Roberta Pearson (ed.), *Reading Lost* (London: I.B. Tauris, 2009), 130–1.
[51] David Bordwell, *Narration in the Fiction Film* (University of Wisconsin Press, 1985).
[52] John Ellis, *Visible Fictions: Cinema, Television, Video* (London: Routledge, 1992), 160–71.

Rather than a cognitive effort to reveal hidden meanings as might be expected in a ludic text, ongoing storyworlds in high-end drama can evoke multiple emotional responses without having a definite meaning. For example, Murray Smith suggests that 'identification' used to describe the relationship between spectator and character in film can be better explained by understanding the experience itself. For Murray:

> the behaviour of a person in a certain situation about which we have limited knowledge – as is often the case with a character in fiction – we imaginatively project ourselves into their situation, and hypothesize as to the emotion(s) they are experiencing.[53]

'Absorption' and 'empathy' can be used to examine the relationship between spectator and character. Structures such as 'levels of engagement' can further help to examine affective moments in, for example, *The Young Pope* that assume a spectatorship that is based less on the distracted televisual glance and more on a cathected gaze.

High-end shows often adopt a quirky sensibility that relies, in part, on the emotions affecting a character. Television as an emotional medium is achieved in high-end drama such as *The Leftovers* using an ensemble of characters. The ensemble will possess eccentricities, including the sense of tragedy felt by the character of Meg Abbott. Strangeness is revealed and quirkiness becomes part of the show's aesthetic achievements. Greg M. Smith approaches the understanding of emotion in drama through 'mood-cues'. He argues that 'the orientating function of emotion encourages us to seek out environmental cues that confirm our internal state'.[54] In *The Leftovers* and the character of Abbott, there is an indeterminate mood that constantly fluctuates between ecstasy and tragedy.

Similarly, for the spectator wishing to experience nostalgia, the re-circulation of genres and viewing experiences drawn from television's historicity often plays a key role. A symbiosis in shows such as *Stranger Things* and *Vinyl* reflects both the tastes of a popular audience and the evocation of earlier texts. In these examples, memory and remembering provide a connection to the past, which is used to generate forms of resonance, associative possibilities and allusive meanings, thus becoming spaces of reflection to find coherences in multiplying possible

---

[53] Murray Smith, *Engaging Characters: Fiction, Emotion and the Cinema* (Oxford: Oxford University Press, 1995), 97.
[54] Greg M. Smith and Carl Plantinga (eds), *Passionate Views: Film, Cognition and Emotion* (Baltimore: John Hopkins University Press, 1999), 113.

connections. For Smith, 'emotion markers' are 'configurations of highly visible textual cues for the primary purpose of eliciting brief moments of emotion'.[55] Audiences either accept the invitation to experience the same range of emotions within the text or reject them, although he adds: 'To accept the invitation, one must be an "educated viewer" who has the perquisite skills required to read the emotion cues.'[56] In these ways, in high-end drama, the textual process of a long-running story arc that includes personal memories, as well as action, is used to create powerful emotional effects.

Conclusion

This chapter traces some of the antecedents as well as the recent changes in critical perception – industrial, authorial, technological and cultural – without offering a totalizing representation of all high-end drama, especially around beliefs about quality in drama and its critical legitimization. As we have seen, such beliefs have often been an institutional goal as practitioners have sought to redefine the frontiers of 'safe' and 'risky' content. The search for brand building and enhancement primarily through the use of the miniseries is presently leading companies such as Showtime, HBO, FX, AMC and, most recently, Netflix, Amazon, Disney and Apple to show interest in high-end drama. Yet, the consideration of new modalities to do with enhancing the form is often less about controllable actions by either the institution or the showrunner or the use of technology and more to do with multiple influences on production.

The chapters in this book continue to chart changes in the critical perception of Televisuality. Its appearance in high-end drama is not so much a sign of vision by the showrunner but the cultural exchange between contemporary forms of television drama and television's past, whose formal boundaries continue to be re-negotiated. Other new tendencies in recent production do not mark an abrupt break in television production, albeit they appear as a significant disruption at times as high-end dramas attract film talent. Crucially, as we will see, high-end drama like AQD before it is better understood as an organizing set of principles for designating value that continues to draw on a successful

---

[55] Smith and Plantinga, *Passionate Views*, 118.
[56] Smith and Plantinga, *Passionate Views*, 12.

strategy first developed in the 1980s–90s. High-end US television has brought with it the continuing redefinition of frontiers of unpredictability, as well as ideas of an exchange between formal strategies of film and television production. In these ways, high-end drama is an indication of how value continues to be re-negotiated as television seeks further innovation.

2

Passionate realism

Paolo Sorrentino's *The Young Pope*

Contemporary high-end television drama defines new narrative territory, although it relies on continuity as much as it does on disruption of definitions of quality on television. If characterization is more complex, it continues to tend towards the controversial and aspires for 'realism'. However, the spectator's activity of seeing and believing can be disrupted as equivocal views of the action are presented. Instead of stylistic assumptions based on earlier ideas about realism, more nuanced understandings appear based on compositional motif, as well as how time and space are organized around degrees of subjectivity and objectivity that visually reveal psychological states. At the same time, narration in the television dramas discussed in the next two chapters recognize that they are addressing an audience using a method of controlled consumption that both works for and resists the notion of an authored text.

The Young Pope (2016)

The Young Pope was directed and written by Italian film-maker Paolo Sorrentino and produced by Sky Atlantic/ HBO and Canal+. It premiered on 3 September 2016, at the Seventy-Third Venice International Film Festival. Hitherto, other HBO series, *Olive Kitteridge* (2014) and *Mildred Pearce* (2011), had premiered at Venice. However, this was the first time in the history of the festival that a television series became part of the programme.[1] Festival director Alberto Barbera said thus about Sorrentino and the new series: 'He is a filmmaker who

---

[1] Ariston Anderson, 'Venice Film Fest: Paolo Sorrentino's The Young Pope to Get World Premiere', *Hollywood Reporter*, 9 July 2016. Available at: https://www.hollywoodreporter.com/news/young-pope-jude-law-tv-909582

dares to take risks [and who] ... tackles the language of television series, the new expressive frontier which many filmmakers – primarily foreign – have already tried their hand at.'[2] The show would be subsequently shown in five countries – Italy, Germany, Ireland, Austria and France – before airing in the United States. In 2017, it became the first Italian TV series to be nominated for a Primetime Emmy Award. The British actor Jude Law was cast in the titular role as Lenny Belardo and Diane Keaton as Sister Mary, who raises Belardo in an orphanage. Law had for much of his career been the archetypal leading man – a Hollywood film star – proving to be a mature, reflective actor and nominated an Oscar for Best Actor in a Supporting Role for *The Talented Mr Ripley* (2000) and Best Actor in a Leading Role for *Cold Mountain* (2003). Other top international talent in *The Young Pope* included James Cromwell (*American Horror Story*, *Six Feet Under*), who was cast as Cardinal Michael Spencer and Lenny's mentor. Italians such as Silvio Orlando and Cardinal Angelo Voiello made up the other cast members. Orlando was an actor who shared Sorrentino's own Neapolitan roots.

The decision by Sorrentino, a distinguished film-maker, to script and direct television drama raises issues about authorship and the use of a 'signature' style. In *The Young Pope*, Sorrentino uses framing, camera movement and editing to create subjectivities and a textual discourse that can be termed a 'psychological reality'. According to Sorrentino, *The Young Pope* forms a new 'creative paradigm' for television and accomplishes in that medium what has previously been done on the big screen.[3] Unusually, each of the episodes is untitled, suggesting a strategy of watching the series in one sitting or as an example of 'binge watching'. Binge watching suggests a mode of storytelling that has been labelled streaming poetics.[4] Rather than watching weekly episodes, the entire series can be watched by the viewer in one go. However, binge watching also suggests a lack of control and the offer of 'junk TV'. Yet, from about 2010, it was an economic strategy to differentiate itself from HBO that had led Ted Sarandos, chief content officer at Netflix, to remark that 'the goal is to become HBO before HBO becomes us'.[5]

---

[2] Liz Calvario, 'Jude Law – Starring TV Series *The Young Pope* to Debut at Venice Film Festival', *IndieWire*, 9 July 2016. Available at: https://www.indiewire.com/2016/07/the-young-pope-jude-l aw-series-debut-venice-film-festival-paolo-sorrentino- 1201704197/

[3] Antonio Cuomo, 'The Young Pope: Paulo Sorrentino e Jude Law tra provocazioni contraddizioni del loro giovane papa', 10 October 2016. Available at: https://movieplayer.it/articoli/the-young-pope-int ervista-a-paolo-sorrentino-e-jude-law-sulla-serie-sk_16462/

[4] Emily Todd Van Der Werff, 'Netflix Is Accidentally Inventing a New Art Form — Not Quite TV and Not Quite Film', *Vox*, 30 July 2015. Available at: https://www.vox.com/2015/7/29/9061833/netflix -binge-new-artform

[5] Nancy Hass, 'And the Award for the Next HBO Goes to . . .', *GQ*, 29 January 2013. Available at: https ://www.gq.com/story/netflix-founder- reed-hastings-house-of-cards-arrested-development

Netflix's ongoing engagement with HBO was leading to a method of distribution of borrowing from HBO its promotional language of exclusivity and cultural distinction. Moreover, Netflix was eliding notions of watching TV as 'junk food' for the eye and older estimations of television as culturally impoverished, while promoting binge watching as cutting-edge narrative. Altered viewing strategies were further suggested by Kevin Spacey, the star of *House of Cards*. When he was asked the question whether thirteen hours watched as a whole was cinematic, Spacey wondered whether it was really any different from a film.[6] Crucially, it was Netflix's intention to beat its rival, HBO, by offering other forms of consumption using its streaming services that has encouraged HBO and other cable operators to develop shows that can be easily streamed and watched continuously. At the same time, the notion of a 'society of controlled consumption'[7] can be combined with a discourse of 'conspicuous authorship' as a locus of experimentation, while attaining qualities of a televisual blockbuster. In this way, an industry strategy has led to a hybrid form, attracting new ways of watching as well as producing content.

In many ways, Sorrentino not only is the beneficiary of this trend but actively exploits the hybrid form in *The Young Pope* as something worthy of sustained attention by its audience. For Sorrentino, the new 'creative paradigm' for the show he envisioned would be at odds with a medium whose primary focus was on the everyday or domestic and had served older viewing practices on television.[8] Sorrentino would use what he had learnt from the cinema to focus television drama on the exceptional by creating an existential drama rooted in lush imagery, reimagining a cinematic blockbuster for television. Nevertheless, qualities of the quotidian in soaps and older high-end shows such as *The Sopranos* and *Six Feet Under*, which suggest less tight causal chains of events, continue to be loosely constructed in *The Young Pope*. It is important to note that Sorrentino deploys, at times, a mode of narration that discusses events before they occur so that characters reflect on their meaning afterwards. This method of recursive narrative is a way of allowing the viewer to formulate their own thoughts about Lenny and the others. For example, in episode one, in a series

---

[6] Quoted in Chuck Tryon, 'TV Got Better: Netflix's Original Programming Strategies and Binge Viewing', *Media Industries Journal*, 2, no. 2 (2015): 104–16.

[7] Ted Striphas, *The Late Age of Print: Everyday Book Culture from Consumerism to Control* (New York: Columbia University Press, 2009).

[8] Horace Newcomb is one of the earliest and best advocates of television as a domestic medium and its viewing practice as suitable to a medium being watched in the home. See *Television: The Most Popular Art* (New York: Anchor, 2004).

of talking heads, Voiella and fellow cardinals, including Caltanissetta, played by Toni Bertorelli, discuss how they might manipulate the new pope, preparing us for the various conspiracies that follow. Familiar methods of storytelling from older high-end drama – itself borrowing from older televisual forms such as soaps – are combined with techniques such as mise en scène and point of view (POV) that are reminiscent of experimental film-makers from directors like Fellini, raising the possibility of complex television as arthouse and capable of taking unfamiliar directions within its apparent realism.

Lenny Belardo is elected pope by the College of Cardinals, who they believe is an inexperienced, malleable man who can be controlled by them. However, Sister Mary says about Belardo, 'Everyone is afraid of you.' Belardo uses intimidation tactics, as well as gossip, to confront his detractors as the young pope. Nevertheless, Belardo is a complex man, as much troubled as he is sure of his relationship with God. A second-degree style allows the viewer to investigate the nature of reality and truth. Fanciful inventions abound in the show to disturb the viewer's sense of a predictive, unified world. The opening of the first non-titled episode begins with Jude Law in the role of Belardo crawling from under a pile of naked dead babies. Later, Belardo as Pope Pius XIII stares down a live kangaroo, a gift from Australia, and dons his splendid papal robes while LMFAO's 'Sexy and I know It' can be heard on the soundtrack.[9] As a complex, unpredictable pontiff, the miniseries invites the audience to feel equal measures of loathing and elation about him. Rather than outrage against a man who is a bully, unpredictability is the thematic core of the series and a curiosity about a man who resists easy categorization. In this way, the show fulfils the desire for original content that garners attention and minimizes, if not eliminates, pre-emptions about its main character. The ten episodes of *The Young Pope* are a reminder that this is not only a show disruptive of older ideas about programmes 'finding' their audiences as viewers dip in and out of it but a show that tests the boundaries of streamed television drama.

The Young Pope is a meditation on power, loneliness and faith. Belardo is abandoned as a young boy by his hedonistic hippie parents and placed in a Catholic orphanage. According to Law, 'He feels truly unloved in the deepest, most fundamental way. And he feels ignored by the one person that matters most – God.'[10] The desire for a highly conflicted, complex protagonist relies on

---

[9] LMFAO was an electronic American band that lasted from 2006 to 2012.
[10] Paula Chin, 'Have Faith, He Saith', *Emmy*, 5 (2017): 125.

the aesthetic vision from Paolo Sorrentino, who avoids making the character become too dark. By using wit, satire and absurdity, Sorrentino lends the show a poetic quality capable of disruption of older forms of televisual style but also capable of meditative interpretation.

Cinematic influences

High-end television has, at times, been regarded as 'cinematic'.[11] As we have seen in Chapter 1, the term 'cinematic' can be contentious and risk approaches to visual style that ignore the specificity of television and how it may be viewed unlike cinema.[12] Yet, during the second decade of the twenty-first century, the migration and willingness of theatrical talent to work in television has led to a 'film look' on television. However, this 'film look' differs from earlier television drama shot on 16 mm or 35 mm film.[13] Rather, as Robin Nelson notes, in high-end television drama, there has been an 'increased emphasis upon visual style, an aspiration to be as close to cinema as possible, increased dynamism of image and sound (and the two in relation to each other) and a new configuration of the tension between credible illusionism and textual playfulness'.[14] A high-end style has aligned viewing television drama with the experience of movies.[15]

Television has often preferred its own actors rather than those borrowed from theatrical film, but in high-end drama the appeal of stars has been used to attract its audience. For Jude Law, the opportunity to work in *The Young Pope* afforded the possibility of making a longer drama of ten hours rather than two on the big screen. His presence together with an international cast and the fact that the series was mostly filmed in Rome's Cinecittà's Studios – the Vatican interiors were recreated for the show – suggested it would enjoy worldwide distribution. Recently, the aspiration for a televisual equivalent to cinema has led to a growing interest in worldwide sales, as well as commercial and critical hits.

[11] Brett Mills, 'What Does It Mean to Call Television Cinematic', in Jason Jacobs and Steven Peacock (eds), *Television Aesthetics and Style* (London: Bloomsbury, 2013), 57–66.
[12] Deborah Jaramillo, 'Rescuing Television from the Cinematic: The Perils of Dismissing Television Style', in Jason Jacobs and Steven Peacock (eds), *Television Aesthetics and Style* (London: Bloomsbury, 2013), 67–75.
[13] See Max Sexton, 'The Origin of Gritty Realism: The Police Series in Special Branch', *Journal of British Cinema and Television*, 11, no. 1 (January 2014): 23–40.
[14] Robin Nelson, *State of Play: Contemporary High-End Drama* (Manchester: Manchester University Press, 2007), 109.
[15] Michael Newman and Elana Levine, *Legitimating Television: Media Convergence and Cultural Status* (New York: Routledge, 2012), 5.

The Young Pope was heavily trailed worldwide before its release as a challenging adult drama.¹⁶ Such campaigning further reveals the loss of a traditional prime time suited to national broadcasts and the transition to distribution methods more appropriate to streaming. Moreover, Sorrentino already possessed one of the highest international profiles for an Italian director. He had served his apprenticeship within the 'New Neapolitan Cinema' of the 1990s. His debut feature, *L'uomo in più* (2001), had been followed by *The Consequences of Love* (2004), the only Italian film to be screened in Cannes that year and the winner of numerous awards. *The Consequences of Love* was also the first of Sorrentino's films to receive international distribution.

It is important to note that Sorrentino acts as both director and sole writer on his films and exerts considerable control over their aesthetic. Mariapia Comand observes how Sorrentino's unpublished screenplays contain detailed description of settings, characters, gestures, editing strategies and music that correspond closely to his finished films.¹⁷ Similarly, the stylistic coherence that Sorrentino brings to *The Young Pope* points to the possibility of an authorial status on television as much as he has enjoyed at the cinema, together with his choice of the cinematographer, Luca Bigazzi, who had collaborated with Sorrentino in his films *The Great Beauty* (2013) and *Youth* (2015). Bigazzi has a strong interest in documentary, preferring a style that can be interpreted as 'realistic'. For him, films that document society, politics and contemporary issues are important, and he cites Silvio Soldini as a director he admires.¹⁸ A strong collaboration between the director and director of photography (DoP) goes to demonstrate how realist aesthetics in *The Young Pope* aspire to be an instrument for civic engagement about the role of the Catholic religion in the era of multiculturalism and tolerance of liberal-humanist values. At the same time, Sorrentino exploits the tension between the show's stylization and realism, which further suggests how the series can be understood as a complex piece of television drama, incorporating the experience of movies.

Sorrentino's directorial signature within the television series is remarkable and, in turn, reveals cinematic influences besides his DoP, including, most profoundly, Federico Fellini. Sorrentino acknowledges Fellini's influence in his

---

[16] For example, Sky Atlantic/HBO unveiled a giant sculpture by famed artist Michael Murphy, of Jude Law in Olympia, London. See the video available at: campaignlive.co.uk/article/event-tv-sky-atlantic-unveils-jude-law-sculpture-promote-new-tv-series/1413209

[17] Mariapia Comand, 'La matematica del mistero: Sorrentino narratore', in Vito Zagarrio (ed.), *La meglio gioventù-nuovo cinema italiano 2000-2006* (Venice: Marsilio, 2006), 189–95.

[18] Anon, 'Directors of Photography', *Italian Cinema*, 1, no. 1 (October 2004): 64.

films, as well as others such as David Lynch's use of lush invention and imagery.[19] Fellini as a key reference point offers clues about how dreams, in many ways, are more important than waking life in *The Young Pope*. The debt owed to Fellini is obvious, and Sorrentino's films echo many of the ideas from the director of *La Strada* (1954) and *La Dolce Vita* (1960):

> Dreams are fairy tales that we tell ourselves. They are the small and big myths that help people to understand. Of course, you shouldn't ask your dreams for instant or constant help in changing your daily behaviour. And you shouldn't abandon yourself to the pleasure of this night spectacle. The insensitive dreamer risks spending his days doing nothing, surrounded by brittle, evanescent things.[20]

Fellini was hostile to film-makers and critics who sought to brand a film with apparently objective meanings. Similarly, in *The Young Pope*, Sorrentino allows fantasy and reality to coexist, offering a wide range of images that can be used to interpret the metaphor of Belardo's adolescence – an expulsion from Eden – as well as his social background in the orphanage and Catholic education. Equally, much of *The Young Pope* is shot in the Roman streets at night or in chthonic spaces of the Vatican. The use of dream-like imagery reduces the viewer's understanding of Lenny to dispersed facts and phenomena that strain causality and become the entrance into a more evanescent, intangible dimension. Beginning at the end of episode one, Lenny appears several times at the top of the Vatican Basilica at night, which is repeated in other episodes, reminding the viewer that he is performing a perilous high-wire act as the familiar notion of reality is changed.

In many ways, *The Young Pope* is a dark comedy. Lenny barely eats, likes cherry coke and carries with him his father's pipe as part of a broader tapestry of baroque strangeness which is accommodated into a realist framework. If the TV series draws upon Fellini, it is also influenced by other film directors such as Bernardo Bertolucci and an understanding of how people are trapped not simply because of their flaws but by the rituals that they depend on and the claustrophobic worlds they inhabit. Lenny is trapped by the baroque surroundings of the Vatican, a miniscule city state where any sense of time appears to have stopped. He is also trapped by his keen observance of formal relationships, which he explains to his staff he prefers to ideals of friendship. Lenny is defined by the set of enclosures

---

[19] Jonathan Romney, 'Tragedies of Ridiculous Men', *Sight and Sound*, 17, no. 4 (April 2007): 40–2.
[20] Gideon Bachmann, 1964 interview with Federico Fellini (ed.) Bert Cardullo, *Federico Fellini Interviews* (Jackson: University Press of Mississippi, 2006), 23–34.

he has inhabited throughout his entire life, beginning with the orphanage, whose flashbacks parallel his life in the Vatican.

Point of view

Lenny as the new Pope Pius XIII plans to disrupt the superficial relationships that worshippers within the Catholic Church have with God. As he himself explains, 'I don't want any more part-time believers.' Lenny's rejection of ecumenicalism and the liberal philosophy of his predecessor are linked to the decision of his hippie parents to abandon him by placing him in a Catholic orphanage, thus giving them the freedom to pursue a hedonistic lifestyle. The promotion of identity politics is attacked by Lenny, who takes the decision to rid the church of homosexuality by banning gay priests, despite their being celibate. Sorrentino presents a character that is the antithesis of the 1960s-era counterculture movement, represented by Lenny's absent parents. As we will see, engagement with the character of Lenny – saint or sinner – as our main protagonist is problematized by his own radically conservative attitudes.

Nevertheless, Lenny is unsure of his mission to re-evangelize the Vatican and his own role as pope and confides in Monsignor and later Cardinal Bernardo Gutierrez, played by Javier Cámara, as master of ceremonies of the Holy See. Gutierrez is an emotionally fragile man, the holder of secrets because he is a homosexual and an alcoholic. However, to our surprise, their relationship recalls that of a patient and psychotherapist, and the unfolding confessional, as their deepest thoughts and anxieties about sexuality and gender are revealed, prepares the viewer for the visual delirium at various moments in the series. At these moments, the imagery signifies emotional release and, in *The Young Pope*, is associated with an individual's freedom of voice, which, at its most troubling for the viewer, has no limits and makes fresh demands.

The question of voice raises issues about narrative perspective and who is talking. In *The Young Pope*, narration is 'focalized' – a term borrowed from Gérald Genette[21] – through Lenny to a very large degree. However, POV and the idea of voice are not entirely congruent. If the images within the story are told from the POV of Lenny, a secondary issue is whether he is speaking in the first person

---

[21] Gérald Genette, *Narrative Discourse: An Essay in Method*, trans. Jane E. Lewin (New York: Cornell University Press, 1980), 11.

or whether the narrator is someone speaking for him in the third person. First- and third-person telling of the story reveals a deeper narrative schema between focalization and diegetic narration. It should also be noted that if the question of 'voice' depends on focalization, there are various levels of it, beginning with what Genette calls internal focalization when narrative is enunciated through the consciousness of the character. However, external focalization focuses on the character and how events are observed. In this way, a fictional text is a collection of descriptions of characters, and the function of a director like Sorrentino is to put into place a sequence of alternating perspectives within which the viewer can interpret the 'truth' of the story. This order depends on other concepts, such as time, space, causality and voice, which can be explored further to offer an insight into how Sorrentino transcends second-degree style normally found in realism to create a more complex, lived experience.[22]

The opening of episode one of *The Young Pope* is violent and fragmented, creating a puzzle from the outset by testing the limits between delirium and reality – whether dreams are only another aspect of everyday life. The disturbing if not repellent sequence starts with a baby crawling over a giant pile of dead babies. The camera tracks across the bodies to Lenny, dressed in his papal white robes, emerging from beneath the tiny corpses. He stands and begins to walk from the pile into a large square bounded by Romanesque facades. Shot at night, a multitude of lights twinkle within the Romanesque arches until a wide reverse shot reveals St. Mark's square in Venice and the dead babies piled high in front of its famous church, creating a stylistic intensity that is almost dialectical in its intent between beauty and ugliness.

Next, the montage cuts to Lenny waking in the papal bed followed by the quotidian rituals of brushing his teeth and preparing for the day. These shots demonstrate a powerful symmetry, not only within the composition of each shot – for example, Lenny is centrally positioned in bed – but between shots, as we cut between stasis and movement. The movement of the camera, which tracks behind Lenny as he brushes his teeth, is followed by a track-in into the papal apartment. The effect is an invitation to the viewer to observe Lenny closely and interrogate the meaning of the images. Each image and sound are counterbalanced by another image or sound to reinforce a sense of duality. This is made clearer by the use of mirrors: initially, Lenny reflected in the bathroom

---

[22] For more about second-degree style, see Chapter 1.

mirror followed by him opening his clothes wardrobe and a doppelganger of Lenny in the form of his clothes and a reflection (Plate 1).

From his bedside radio we hear soft classical music, but this is disrupted by static before Lenny disrobes to become naked and the observing camera retreats. The realism achieved by creating levels of focalization in the opening sequence invites access to the intensely private world of the pope. However, for the moment, the apparent mundanity of the waking, showering pope is at odds with the initial violent dream sequence of dead children.

The immediacy of the style and effect of verisimilitude takes the appearance of realism but, in the hands of Sorrentino, strongly contrasts with an earlier realistic style in television drama. In a general sense, television drama prefers to rest on narration emphasizing shifts in character POV for the purpose of creating the character interiority of psychological or emotional realism. The longing for an intimate style on television meant the preferred and frequent use of the close-up or two-shot rather than the long shot. Lillian Albertson notes: 'The camera . . . comes up close to the actor, and registers every fleeting expression.'[23] Hume Cronyn also emphasizes this technique in *Notes on Film Acting*: 'In close-up very little becomes very much; a whole new range of expression is opened to the actor.'[24] It was judged that the close-up was part of television's intimacy because the character's face could reflect a character's every thought and emotion. In this way, character-focused storytelling in television requires that the plot is the formulation of character. However, the preference in much of television drama for character at a deeper psychological level has come at the expense of plot and a distinctive visual style.

In AQD, performance continued to be a marker of an emotional experience, but acting was articulated using a marked increased emphasis on action and plot over character. Of course, any rhetoric of difference between plot and character is less invested in a dichotomy but more represents a cluster of narrative and visual values within the range of television drama. Such values can include spectacle – discussed in Chapter 7 – as well as other scenographic properties, such as verisimilitude and POV. *The Young Pope* is not a search for indexicality or concordance with reality, but, in the hands of Sorrentino, a 'hyperindex'. Rather than the aesthetics of realism, *The Young Pope* invites the remaking of causality through a multitude of sounds and images in order to deal with issues of social

---

[23] Quoted in Rhona J. Berenstein, 'Acting Live', in James Friedman (ed.), *Reality Squared: Televisual Discourse on the Real* (London: Rutgers University Press, 2002), 25–49.
[24] Quoted in Berenstein, 'Acting Live', 40.

experience and identity using a cluster of textual techniques. An interpretative thematic in high-end television drama distinguishes it and marks it as 'original content'.

After the opening montage, the credits roll and the camera cuts to track the young pope in slow motion amid the formal setting of the Vatican as he meets the various figures who will participate in the unfolding drama with him – cardinals and nuns – before becoming seated between two nuns holding their heads in deep contemplation. Lenny establishes the camera's eyeline by sitting between them before another cut and a near-naked young woman sitting by a river. Another cut shows a young boy – Lenny – looking at the woman before we cut back to the adult Lenny on the bench. The sequence cuts to several tableau shots of the cardinals, monsignors and nuns arranged to look back at Lenny. The effect of the juxtaposition and the fabulist nature of the sequence prepare the viewer for the liminal areas between delirium and reality made stronger by the fact that both Lenny and the camera are next put onto dollies and appear to float. This type of shot can be compared to Spike Lee's use of a double dolly shot when characters appear to be floating rather than walking and seen in *Malcolm X* (1992). Malcolm played by Denzel Washington glides through a medium shot to the site where he will be assassinated. The beatific expression on Lenny's face and the use of the double dolly are visually arresting as he approaches the papal apartment balcony dressed in a gossamer white curtain. The heavenly symbolism raises the philosophy of human destiny, and the anticipatory cue of death is made more striking by the sliding black graphic segmenting Lenny's face (Plate 2).

Lenny's appearance in front of the crowd in St. Paul's square, as he receives the adulation of the masses of the faithful on his anointment as pope, uses the gesture of stretching out his arms: the pose adopted by Pius XII, another highly controversial pope. He performs the legerdemain of stopping the rain falling on the masses gathered before him before the opening resolves itself by becoming a dream, confusing our sense of time and causing the temporalities of a mimetic realism to feel uncertain and fragmentary.

Hyper-subjectivity

The character of Lenny as the young pope is typical of Sorrentino's interest in ambiguous protagonists that are unsympathetic. As we watch *The Young Pope*, an ambivalent figure such as Lenny is not someone to easily identify with. Instead, the series creates an emotional and moral complexity that allows the audience to observe but also, crucially, experience more completely his character. Television's use of anti-heroes in complex drama has been a common trait since the early noughties. As we saw in Chapter 1, in the era of Least Objective Programming on network television, a protagonist such as Tony Soprano in *The Sopranos* (HBO, 1999–2007) would have been impossible because he aligns the viewer with dubious moral values and sociopathic personality traits. Yet, for cable channels within the era of 'original programming', such a narrative strategy can be sold to the audience as an example of controversial programming that is 'not TV' by further challenging its audience. According to Amanda Lotz:

> Where the strategy of the broadcaster is to erect a big tent that welcomes heterogeneous audiences with content unlikely to easily offend, niche entities such as cable channels succeed by developing programming that strongly interpellates narrower sections of viewers with content that connects deeply with their beliefs or interests.[25]

We have seen that a cable channel paid for by subscribers rather than by advertising is less likely to worry about presenting material that might be understood to be morally ambiguous or else encourages the audience to identify with a villain with predilections, as in the case of mafia boss, Tony Soprano, or meth cook, Walter White, in *Breaking Bad* (AMC, 2008–13). The strategy of 'perverse allegiance' in high-end television drama has foregrounded a type of 'hideous male' anti-hero.[26]

Drawing on cognitive theory, Murray Smith substitutes the usual 'identification' – considered to be too inadequate to describe the relationship of the viewer with a complex character – with the term 'engagement'. For Smith, engagement depends on several levels of comprehension, including alignment and allegiance. During alignment, the viewer is spatially and temporally attached to the characters and/or granted subjective access to their thoughts and feelings. Allegiance, on the other hand, is the emotional process that 'concerns the way in which a film attempts to marshal our sympathies for or against the various

---

[25] Amanda D. Lotz, *Cable Guys: Television and Masculinities in the 21st Century* (New York: New York University Press, 2014), 61.
[26] Jason Mittell, 'Lengthy Interactions with Hideous Men: Walter White and the Serial Poetics of Television Anti-Heroes', in Roberta Pearson and Anthony N. Smith (eds), *Storytelling in the Media Convergence Age* (Basingstoke: Palgrave Macmillan, 2015), 74–92.

characters'.[27] In this way, the screenplay and mise en scène in *The Young Pope* are carefully worked out to encourage storytelling techniques that encourage a constantly changing 'structure of sympathy'.[28] Such a strategy renders *The Young Pope*, at once, a fascinating but also frustrating drama. For Sorrentino, the world is not morally divided into good or bad men, as he seeks to create an existential drama about Lenny's troubled relationship with his faith in God and to his parents.

Under Sorrentino's directorial guise, Lenny is not an anti-hero in the same way as an ethically questionable character as Walter White from *Breaking Bad* or Don Draper from *Mad Men* (AMC, 2007–15). The portrayal of self-absorption is handled less to record a dwindling morality as happened in the arcs of those two shows. Nevertheless, similarities exist, especially in the handling of a serial character that over multiple episodes constructs a narrative that uses moments of affect to engage and hook the audience. In complex drama, audience identification with the main character as an anti-hero allows access to their knowledge or interior state but 'whose behaviour and beliefs provoke ambiguous, conflicted or moral allegiance'.[29] The emotional engagement with dubious characters using multiple plotlines has used styles such as extended close-ups and symbolic lighting to help the viewer favour an ambiguous protagonist. It can be argued that style must also be allied to narrative strategies to ensure a continuing emotional response to the protagonist. Such strategies consist of the perversity of the antagonists to encourage a more positive attitude towards the protagonist. Visually, *The Young Pope* consistently emphasizes repulsive, absurd characteristics, including the physiognomies of the cardinals and their shuttling gaits, as they discuss their actions on behalf of the Holy Roman Church against the young pope. Other dramatic strategies are the presence of family: Lenny enjoys a relationship with his adopted mother, Sister Mary. There are also acts of contrition, which Lenny performs, as well as the victimization of his character. In *The Young Pope*, style thematically allows the viewer to emotionally engage with a character seeking redemption in a changing world as Lenny seeks to protect the things he claims to want to defend, embodied by notions of the heterosexual, nuclear family.

If questions remain how exactly the show should be watched – either in a single session or weekly – the structure of the serial is able to align the viewer

---

[27] Murray Smith, *Engaging Characters: Fiction, Emotion and the Cinema* (Oxford: Oxford University Press, 1995), 6.
[28] Smith, *Engaging Characters*, 5.
[29] Mittell, 'Lengthy Interactions with Hideous Men'.

by offering revelations about Lenny and his adopted family using backstory: relationships to Sister Mary, his (father-figure) mentor, Michael Spencer and his adopted brother, Cardinal Bernardo Gutierrez, played by Scott Shepherd. The skeletons in Lenny's family closet are exposed as we watch various recollections of how his birth parents abandoned him, moving the viewer into greater allegiance with Lenny. Later, his feelings about family and children reach a climax as he watches the character of Esther, played by Ludivine Sagnier, having sex with her husband, a member of the Pontifical Swiss Guard.

Levels of engagement

To create a scandal and force Lenny to resign as pope, Cardinal Voiello arranges a young woman, Esther, who works as the pope's assistant, to attempt to seduce Lenny. Lenny, however, avoids her sexual advances, appearing morally exemplary to the shame of Voiella, who repents of his plans to discredit Lenny. Alignment is the first of what Murray Smith calls 'levels of engagement', a concept similar to Genette's focalization.[30] Near the end of episode four, perceptual alignment with Lenny is reinforced by the cut from a supposedly happenstance view of Esther becoming impregnated by her husband at home as Lenny walks past her window, to a dream sequence of Lenny in full papal robes touching Esther. At this moment, voyeurism is a sign of narrative agency, specifically the hyper-subjectivity of one man: Lenny Belardo. The use of alignment allows for external focalization: we observe Lenny and see what he can see. But there is another level of agency, using montage, allowing the viewer to experience the scene as internal focalization: we see what Lenny feels. Crucially, this is achieved by letting us directly experience the scene without a sense that we are being shown Lenny's emotions by Sorrentino – in other words, that someone else is speaking for Lenny. This is achieved by repetition of Lenny's POV, while, at the same time, creating the notion of a 'voice', where images are determined/directed by Lenny. The organization of the images becomes the equivalent of his thoughts.

In the dream-like montage sequence that follows, shot using low-key lighting, Esther becomes recumbent as St. Teresa of Avila, writhing in religious ecstasy as sculptured by Bellini, before another shot of Lenny in his papal robes touching her. The gesture is difficult to interpret: on the one hand, it is clearly sexual: he

---

[30] Genette, *Narrative Discourse: An Essay in Method*, 11.

desires the young woman and there is a mutual attraction. But on the other, the gesture is spiritual, impregnating Esther, as he invokes the Virgin Mary and the Holy Spirit. However, it raises the difficulty of Lenny comparing himself to God, his arrogance echoed earlier by his imperious attitude to homosexuality or disavowal of pleas for forgiveness from Voiella. Another cut and Lenny repeats the benefaction emulating Pius XII with arms outstretched. His demand that Esther becomes pregnant sounds less of a plea and more a self-command to work the same miracle that stopped the rain in St. Peter's Square in episode one.

The visual system of alternations of shot-reverse-shot and the relationships between character and space also present interpretations of the relationship between Lenny and Esther that continues to inform the viewer's alignment with the young pope (Plates 3, 4 and 5).

Formally, such a relationship establishes a false eyeline between them – how could they ever see each other if Esther is standing at her kitchen window and Lenny is standing at right angles to her – with the cutting from Lenny's POV used to disrupt spatial and causal relationships. It should not be forgotten that an eyeline match differs from a POV. Unlike an eyeline, the POV implies a space and distance tied much more to the presumed placing of Lenny in the scene. A POV is more restrictive than an eyeline because we are closely aligned to Lenny without the ability to share subjective viewpoints. The viewer's perception of the diegetic world is limited to what Lenny sees. In this way, the shots in the scene represent on screen an additional 'subjective' alignment with Lenny with the added effect that the almost entirely first-person account of space and time renders the author (Sorrentino) invisible behind the character's experience. Nevertheless, the development of space using the perception of Lenny using an improbable causality between him and Esther causes problems for the viewer and an interpretation of events. This is noticeable because Sorrentino by using editing does not use mise en scène or overlapping space to link Lenny watching Esther, adding to our sense of disorientation about the action. In fact, the sequence cuts from Esther apparently gazing at Lenny, who returns her look but never shares the same space as her.

For the moment, events prove baffling or only partially comprehensible and are followed by a follow-on shot from Lenny's POV of a maternity ward managed by nuns amid chapel-like surroundings. The camera reinforces alignment with Lenny by deploying shots of Lenny looking through a similarly cross-barred window frame through which we saw Esther earlier. His direct POV of a bed in the ward is intercut with another shot-reserve-shot between Lenny conversing with Monsignor Gutierrez, standing next to him. Now we have a shift of alignment to Gutierrez.

Sorrentino uses the opportunity to blend a greater degree of stylistic excess with hyper-subjectivity, lending the next sequence its emotional power. The extensive sequence drifts further into self-exploration but is no longer about Lenny. Instead, our perceptual alignment shifts to Gutierrez – a man who, hitherto, has contented himself living in the Vatican far from any emotional challenge. Gutierrez is alarmed to hear that he has been appointed the papal ambassador to the United States by Lenny, despite the fact that he has left the Vatican only twice, both times to go to hospital. Using POV as a mental projection, Gutierrez contemplates the mystery of his faith in God as the camera dollies towards him while he prays until hearing a woman's voice speaking Spanish and turns to observe a Marian vision. The childish dependence on the mother is made plain as the woman tells Gutierrez that 'the boy has become a man, but I will continue to protect the boy' (Plate 6).

The brief fantasy sequence is completed using a low-angle shot of the chapel Gutierrez is standing in. The Holy Spirit as the breath of life gusts across the floor before we return to Lenny, now sitting in the maternity ward, observing the nuns looking at pictures of children.

The meditation on woman-as-mother and the process of alignment with both Lenny and the gay Cardinal Gutierrez is a metaphysical examination of self, sexuality and masculinity. The subjective access to character demonstrates levels of engagement of alignment and allegiance that Murray Smith describes in film but are applied in a complex and unusual fashion in high-end television drama. The use of music also becomes instructive because it recalls a popular, nostalgic pop tune by a chanteuse: Senza Un Perché by Nada on a 1970s record player.[31] The shot of Lenny listening to the music is linked to a shot of an idealized image of his mother, naked, sun shining through her blonde hair: the perfect flower child. This is followed by a shot of Lenny looking out of the frame and a cut to his POV of a slow dancing woman whose sombre black clothes and Romanesque surroundings are juxtaposed with the song. Once again, the enigmatic ending defies decoding characters by inviting interpretation.

The viewer is normally led to sympathize with a character such as Lenny. However, rather than sympathy with a character, there is the more solid concept of allegiance, which suggests a greater causality than the flexible

---

[31] Senza Un Perché is translated as 'Without a Reason' and sung by Nada, the little chick of Gabbro.

notion of sympathy, and allies the viewer with a character, implying a long-term investment. As we have seen, it is not easy for the viewer to reconcile with the character of Lenny. If the elevation of the anti-hero has become a common thematic structure in complex television drama, in the hands of Sorrentino, it is extended to investigate the emotional inner lives of his characters. But if morally exemplary, Lenny is also capable of unpleasant attitudes. For example, in episode four, Lenny arranges for the sister of a nun to be buried in the Vatican only to berate her at the funeral for crying. His ambiguous attitude towards homosexuality also drives a young seminarian, after being refused admittance, to commit suicide in St. Peter's Square in episode six.

Not without charm, Lenny is affable but possesses moral shortcomings, including a Machiavellian intelligence that manipulates other people. Drawing upon Blakey Vermeule, Jason Mittell discusses how a character's mercurial intelligence is a trait suited to complex drama because of its 'high narrative reflexivity' and other tropes of complex TV such as allusions to games and puzzles. For Mittell, fascination with a Machiavellian character is a prime component driving the anti-heroic boom.[32] At the same time, high-end television acknowledges its own role as fiction by creating an operational aesthetic that makes its viewer aware that its anti-heroes are carefully crafted to be discussed and picked over. *The Young Pope* blends fascination about Lenny with hermeneutic puzzles that emphasize its status as original content, while Sorrentino uses mise en scène, camerawork and editing to create levels of engagement similar to but also distinct from serialized characters in other high-end drama.

Witnessing narrative space

If Sorrentino is able to use spatial relationships using editing in *The Young Pope* to unsettle causation that affects the viewer's interpretation of diegetic events, he also works within theories originally advocated by André Bazin, preferring the deep focus of on-screen space. For David Black, Bazin's theories are examples of a 'deductive realism' that emphasizes phenomenality.[33] Accordingly, a visual heuristic serves to document the diegetic world or possesses a quality of 'presence' on the screen. The idea of presence in the moving image, as a method

---

[32] Mittell, 'Lengthy Interactions with Hideous Men', 77.
[33] David A. Black, 'Cinematic Realism and the Phonographic Analogy', *Cinema Journal*, 26, no. 2 (Winter 1987): 40–2.

of theorizing spectatorship, returns to issues about medium specificity, as well as spectatorship, which can be briefly discussed here.

Historically, television has been live, whereas films have provided an illusion of a world captured in the instance within which it was recorded. Unlike film, television has the ability to transmit an event that is simultaneous with the act of viewing. If film is able to construct a 'perfect' illusion, television offers a boundless live transmission and an infinite vision of the world. In other words, television provides the central staging area of all reality because of its boundless ability to intrude into the private and public domain. According to Jeffrey Sconce, the emergence of television as the privileged surveyor of all reality implies a popular shift in media consciousness, 'suggesting . . . the seemingly infinite vision of television'.[34] In this way, televisual transmission has been argued to replace cinematic projection as the basis for thinking about subjectivity.[35]

At the same time, for Bazin, cinematic projection can offer spatial immediacy or a sense of being here now.[36] According to Julio Moreno, it is not possible to speak in the strictest sense of a narrator in film because cinema is too real to support a narrated subjectivity.[37] This sense of presence assumes that what is comprehended as 'real' in film is not confined to what is visible and audible. For example, the edited POV shot is not true to the nature of cinema because when contemplating images in a long shot, the spectator's eye is always superior to the camera lens:

> Just as the dramatic perceptions of everyday life lie beyond the optical scope of the eye, striking cinematic effects depend on what the spectator apprehends outside the scope of the camera. . . . Realistic utilisation of a movie camera, whether subjective or objective does not rely on the physical science of photography, but on the psychological science of human perception.[38]

This can be understood to mean that causality is not 'out there', but using a complex time scheme is a way of thinking, acting and desiring about characters that allows for the reordering of cause and effect into fresh affinities between

---

[34] Jeffrey Sconce, *Haunted Media: Electronic Presence from Telegraphy to Television* (Durham: Duke University Press, 2000), 183.
[35] John Ellis, *Visible Fictions* (London: Routledge, 1992).
[36] André Bazin, *What Is Cinema? Volume 1* (Berkeley: University of California Press, 1967).
[37] Julio L. Moreno, 'Subjective Cinema: And the Problem of Film in the First Person', *The Quarterly of Film, Radio and Television*, v7 (1952-3): 341-58.
[38] James P. Brinton, 'Subjective Camera or Subjective Audience?', *Hollywood Quarterly*, 2, no. 4 (July 1947): 359-65.

objects and people. For Christian Metz, this allows the viewer to be all-perceiving, and 'the cinematic spectator is separate from the film's fiction, able to judge and to assess; separate from the filmic image, which is absent whilst it presents itself as present'.[39] Theories of film spectatorship emphasize the cinematic experience as organized around the gaze. Televisual spectatorship, as we have seen in Chapter 1, can be organized around the difference between the gaze and the glance. On the one hand, television spectatorship depends on the glance, encapsulating a fleeting and intermittent attention to a smaller screen that suggests a disassociation from the subject rather than being productive of subjectivity. Yet, for high-end drama such as *The Young Pope*, a more concentrated viewing is required that permits a mode of television drama whose spectatorship is complicated by tendencies towards film-making but in other ways, as we will see, is televisual.

In *The Young Pope*, Sorrentino enforces the viewer's concentration on detail within the mise en scène by using extended viewing opportunities of spaces such as the papal office. The use of a long shot dramatically represents space and is used by the director to offer several clues about the characters shot inside the space. Here we have the possibility of 'deductive realism', which empowers the viewer to think about performance elements such as gestures and facial expression, as well as objects in the mise en scène. The use of deep space develops composition along these principles. At the same time, the shot is classically filmed; as the shot becomes longer, the more centred becomes the composition.

Lighting is from the windows to the left of the framing, which, moments earlier, we saw Lenny and Sister Mary converse in front of as curtains move in the strong breeze, revealing the wider world of the Vatican outside. This shot suggests back to the viewer that we are not in a built television studio but an actual place. Natural lighting from multiple windows underlines the forthcoming scene's greater authenticity and sense of the privileged gaze of a private space.

We have seen how Sorrentino is capable of blending subjective and objective views of Lenny to suggest a complex approach to televisual style and spectatorship with the aim of not showing, as we saw in episode four, what a character thinks but how they think – the thought processes revealed by mental images. Another strategy is to combine forms of spectatorship that complicate the viewer's understanding of the story. Midway through episode one, Lenny

---

[39] Christian Metz, *The Imaginary Signifier: Psychoanalysis and the Cinema* (Bloomington: Indiana University Press, 1982), 62.

discusses future church policy with Cardinal Angelo Voiello as he begins to cause upheaval in the Vatican due to his determination to reject the liberal philosophy of his predecessor. Sister Mary and Father Federico Amatucci retire to sit at the back of the room as witnesses of the scene about to unfold (Figures 1 and 2).

A long shot is composed to suggest a deep perspective (like a Renaissance painting and its fascination with vanishing points) but also hints that the viewer will act as a witness to interpret and judge the bruising encounter between pope and cardinal. The long shot cuts to a medium long of Sister Mary and Father Amatucci, followed by their profile close-up. The following POV shot represents

Figures 1 and 2 Witnessing the scene.

an apparent objective view of the encounter from Sister Mary and Amatucci's seated positions.

The conflict between Lenny and Angelo is filmed using shot-reverse-shot. Unlike the previous long shot, the composition avoids centring both figures perfectly and includes some dead space. We see in this 'dead space' a large crystal globe that suggests the worldliness of Voiello, but also his selfish motives. A reverse cut to Lenny reveals him to be less worldly; the dead space in the frame is predominantly white and left empty. The brittle dialogue between the men continues with some variation of camera distance within each shot-reverse-shot before the pope tells Voiello that the 'most pressing issue is for him to personally make him a cup of American coffee'. It should be recalled that if Sorrentino is concerned with a complex realist style in his films, he is also attracted to self-referential worlds and the rituals associated with them because social and political issues attract him. Other work by Sorrentino includes the study of Italian politics, football, music and the mafia. The request by Lenny, which becomes a command to make the coffee, demonstrates the power struggle between the men.

The handling of power in the mini-state by an individual charged with the moral imperative of the renunciation of power creates a sense of ambiguity and contradiction. On the one hand, the pope is a man capable of selfless love, but a struggle exists between the head of the Catholic Church and the stubborn resistance of Vatican courtiers perpetuating their own power. The struggle between Lenny and Voiella also demonstrates a Machiavellian embodiment of power: Is Lenny working for the good of the church or is he some sinister, self-obsessed individual searching for his own faith in God, which he has lost?

Interpretations that stress the social context of *The Young Pope* are sensitive to a drama that combines the use of long take, POV and so on and how they interact to concretize abstract issues such as hierarchy and power in the Catholic Church. The making of coffee is shot to emphasize the physical and psychological space between Lenny and Voiella. The long shot of Voiella standing to make coffee shows Lenny sitting at his desk in the distance on the other side of the room. As always, the shot is static by being crisply framed; we are invited to study the distance between them.

The next shot of Sister Mary and Amatucci is a reminder of how *The Young Pope*'s complex Televisuality takes on multiple views, beyond those established by Lenny and Voiella. Mary and Amatucci are witnesses to an extraordinary event that has a strongly intimate and private character, but, at the same time, the unfolding images on the screen are of a situation in which we, the audience, cannot intervene directly. The act of witnessing is of the inner drama of the two men and also helps to form the definition of presence on television. The positioning of Mary and Amatucci as witnesses creates an immediate contact with the audience, underlining an impression of a mode of presence and a sense of the scene as it really seems to be unfolding in the present.

Re-allegiance

Lenny's death at the end of *The Young Pope* is an emotional climax that restores our allegiance with a protagonist who has fallen from favour. Although not quite the anti-hero in other complex drama, the similarities suggest a changing 'structure of sympathy' that requires restoration before the closure of the narrative. The 'ars moriendi' in recent serial drama explored by Harrington implies that a death will be discussed and interpreted after the original series has reached a conclusion.[40] Prefiguring his death, Lenny suffers fits at various times, including in episode three, after a chance encounter with Esther. At the end of the series, the death scene takes place in Venice, in the same square where Lenny originally appeared in episode one to sermonize to a giant crowd. The use of space using a long shot of the square produces a great effect of depth as the camera sweeps over the crowd using a crane, as well as the use of sharp diagonals and lighting in the square itself to create volumetric perspective.

Scenographic depth is achieved by continued, extended camera movement. However, Sorrentino also achieves a sense of space using editing. We shift across a range of places and revisit characters seen earlier in the drama from Guatemala to Alaska to New York to the Italian prime minister, and a cross section of society from powerful politicians to prostitutes and farmers in Mexico watching the pope on TV. The montage suggests once again the 'infinite vision of television' and the associated intimacy of a public event.

Gutierrez gives the pope a small brass telescope, who, using an iris effect, views the crowd, suggesting his direct POV. The ability to see close-up the faces in the crowd and the training of a telescope on the crowd indicate a growing sense

---

[40] C. L. Harrington, 'The Ars Moriendi of US Serial Television: Towards a Good Textual Death', *International Journal of Cultural Studies*, 16, no. 6 (2013): 579–95.

of revelation. We are being shown these people and their reactions to Lenny as they see him as much as he sees them without withholding information about his own character for the first time. The telescope used by Lenny to scrutinize the crowd offers an expansive view that includes a superior degree of knowledge about Lenny's parents as they appear in the crowd. The camera as Lenny's POV through the telescope tracks past two aged flower children before tracking back to see them as they once were before a cut to Lenny and another cut back to his aged parents. They turn their back on him and walk through the crowd to disappear. The moment produces an emotional loss to Lenny, who staggers off the podium.

The series reaches its final moment of re-allegiance with Lenny as we watch him die. The moral sympathy demanded of the viewer is made possible by the suggestion that we have seen Lenny at every angle. His death in front of the crowd and on the world's television is handled using a high-angle shot that zooms out to become an aerial shot and a view of Venice on the lagoon. The volumetric use of space creates a hyper-reality and loss of the distinction between the real and the unreal as the camera continues to zoom out and becomes a spectacle of the Earth in space. Using a complex system of perspectives, the series has allowed the viewer to fully realize who Lenny was, while demonstrating how our moral evaluation has been manipulated to demonstrate an emotional complexity of alignment and allegiance.

Conclusion

The principle stylistic schema of *The Young Pope* relies on textual lushness. However, such lushness comprises of a broad variety of styles that range from spatial relationships constructed in deep focus to a contiguous space that is defined through glances and the POV shots that are used to gain a new emphasis and reveal more about either Lenny or one of the other characters. Importantly, for Sorrentino, narrative efficacy is not eschewed in favour of expressiveness, despite his reputation at the cinema for making films that prefer an excessive style. Rather, style is deployed to create a televisual sense of both presence and hyper-subjectivity using complex shots that often manipulate the viewer's varying allegiance with Lenny. In *The Young Pope*, Lenny wishes to remain anonymous – choosing to turn his back on the masses in St. Peter's Square as he sermonizes – and the manipulation of allegiance creates a sense of mystery about him. His subsequent actions raise only further questions by creating a stylistic schema that offers an unusual regiment of narrative engagement.

By using a complex style, Sorrentino allows the viewer to interrogate Lenny's character, to understand his alienation, as well as the rituals that imprison him and the others, so that we share their experiences and innermost thoughts. The show does not end with the rediscovery of hope, which would be expecting too much. Instead, we have a playful acceptance of life's assaults as Sorrentino represents and accepts all the contradictions in a faith in God. Sorrentino's achievement is not to represent Lenny's ennui but to replicate alienation in the viewer. The apparent death of Lenny at the end of the series is his reconnection with the world after his alienation. Lenny implores the mass he speaks to in Venice to smile before seeing his parents, who retreat from the crowd, leaving Lenny to transcend his alienation and experience an 'extraordinary death'.

3

Independent style

Stephen Soderbergh's *The Knick*

Prominent film-makers such as Paulo Sorrentino and Steven Soderbergh are finding their way to television drama. As they do, they bring their cinematic style to a medium whose use of the long-series drama raises new developments to do with storytelling, as well as realism. A trend for authored drama from a director must be measured against the rhetorical appeal of television realism and the audience's appreciation of it. If narrative techniques are extended in dramas with a renewed emphasis on thematic meaning for the viewer, how is style used for the viewer to socially engage in shows such as *The Knick*?

The Knick (2014–15)

Oscar-winning director Steven Soderbergh famously retired from film directing in 2013 after completing a corpus of movies, including the film that arguably changed the US independent cinema movement: *Sex, Lies and Videotape* (1989).[1] More recently, he has been responsible for Hollywood blockbusters such as the remake of *Ocean's Eleven* (2001) and *Traffic* (2000), which won him the Oscar for Best Director, and the film won Oscars for acting and best screenplay. Soderbergh's retirement from film was due to an increasing feeling of disenchantment with the economics of making a large film, leading him to claim that 'movies don't matter anymore' due to the trend of big-budget films for the foreign market.[2] For Soderbergh, narrative complexity and ambiguity had

---

[1] Guy Lodge, '*Sex, Lies and Videotape* at 30: How Steven Soderbergh Changed Independent Cinema', *The Guardian*, 20 August 2019. Available at: https://www.theguardian.com/film/2019/aug/19/sex-lies-and-videotape-at-30-how-steven-soderbergh-changed-independent-cinema

[2] Ben Child, 'Steven Soderbergh Retires from Film: Movies Don't Matter Any More', *The Guardian*, 30 January 2013. Available at: https://www.theguardian.com/film/2013/jan/30/steven-soderbergh-retires-from-film

become obstacles to the success of a film sold abroad. One of the consequences had been, he argued, a migration of the audience for the movies he had enjoyed making to television: 'The format really allows for the narrow and deep approach that I like. Three and a half million people watching a show is a success. That many people seeing a movie is not a success. I just don't think movies matter as much culturally.'[3] The retirement from film was a decision to no longer make a type of commercial film, but Soderbergh continues to work in and support independent film-making in the United States, encouraging indie directors such as Shane Carruth, Barry Jenkins and Amy Seimetz.[4] In *The Girlfriend Experience* (2016–19), a television show that he executive produced, Soderbergh, after working with Seimetz on an unreleased indie, *In God's Hands* (1998), was able to pair her with Lodge Kerrigan, another independent director. His role of executive producer/showrunner meant he was able to supervise the scripts, as well as draw on his experience as a director. The first four episodes of *The Girlfriend Experience* debuted at the Sundance Film Festival, indicating how the role of the showrunner is being adapted by film directors choosing to work in television.[5]

For *The Knick*, Soderbergh had the freedom to direct and shoot all twenty episodes in seasons one and two, as well as take the role of executive producer for the show. Soderbergh did not work with a DoP but, in similar ways to his films using the pseudonyms of Peter Andrews and Mary Ann Bernard, handled the cinematography, as well as editing. The production of *The Knick* also mimicked film production because the actors, including Clive Owen in the role of Doctor John W. Thackery, had access to the scripts months before shooting started in September 2013 in New York. It was also shot at a rate of five days per episode and cross-boarded with scenes from different episodes shot on the same day to maximize the sense of a unity of vision, as well as budget.[6] Each episode was not shot serially, but rather *The Knick* was delivered as an entire production. According to Soderbergh this required a 'lot of restructuring in the first half of the season, moving scenes from one episode to another and playing out through lines at a different pace and with a different structure than it was written . . . to

---

[3] Child, 'Steven Soderbergh Retires from Film'.
[4] Ricard Brody, 'Steven Soderbergh Dissects Hollywood', *The New Yorker*, 30 April 2013. Available at: https://www.newyorker.com/culture/richard-brody/steven-soderbergh-dissects-hollywood
[5] Nigel M. Smith, 'Steven Soderbergh on Turning The Girlfriend Experience into a TV Show', *The Guardian*, 8 January 2016. Available at: https://www.theguardian.com/tv-and-radio/2016/jan/08/steven-soderbergh-interview-the-girlfriend-experience-tv-show
[6] Tatiana Siegel, 'Personal Best', *Emmy*, 2 (2016): 60–5.

see the whole thing and make global changes'.[7] Soderbergh was responsible for hiring the writers of the show: Jack Amiel, Michael Begler and Steven Katz, with the former two writing the majority of the episodes. Katz was hired as supervising producer, a role responsible for the daily management of a show, including the writing room, and he wrote four episodes. The musician, Cliff Martinez, who had collaborated on multiple films directed by Soderbergh, would compose the oddly anachronistic electronic soundtrack in a period drama.

The Knick was not Soderbergh's first venture into directing television drama. Earlier in 2003, he had worked directing *K: Street*, the HBO's short-lived series about lobbyists and politicians in Washington. Each episode had largely been improvised to remain topical with current news events and became the inspiration for shows such as *The Thick of It* (2005–12) and *Veep* (2012–19). Soderbergh had used the opportunity to develop a new aesthetic, and although the show was cancelled, it became a useful experience for a director seeking retirement from films and finding work in television. As John Thackery presciently explains in *The Knick*, 'we now live in a time of endless possibility'. For Soderbergh, the ability to direct, as well as fulfil other functions of the showrunner, demonstrates a growing intersection between roles that have, hitherto, been separate in television production and its operations. The use of an acclaimed film director with a distinct aesthetic or style is not necessarily synonymous with claims about television becoming cinematic. However, as television shows have become shorter with the emergence of SVoD platforms and with the increased quest for brand power among cable channels, big-screen talent has been used to reconfigure film practices to the narratively concise television series.

The Knick was commissioned by Cinemax, the sister company of HBO, which began life as its answer to The Movie Channel, until announcing in 2011 that it would offer original programming.[8] The series was shot using handheld digital cameras, suggesting mobility, although camera movements are mainly controlled and steady, resulting, as we will see, in increasingly bravura long takes. Set in New York on the streets of Lower Manhattan at the Knickerbocker Hospital in 1900, Owen's John Thackery – 'Thack' to his colleagues – embodies one of the

---

[7] Teressa Iezzi, 'Bloody Hell: Steven Soderbergh Dissects His Modern 1900s Medical Drama, The Knick', *Fast Company*, 6 August 2014. Available at: https://www.fastcompany.com/3033915/bloody-hell-steven-soderbergh-dissects-his-modern-1900s-medical-drama-the-knick
[8] Michael Shain, 'HBO's Stealth Plan to Kill off Skinemax', *New York* Post, 14 February 2011. Available at: https://nypost.com/2011/02/14/hbos-stealth-plan-to-kill-off-skinemax/

show's main narrative modes of not so much a presentation of scientific facts about medicine and surgery but a cross between science and entertainment. Thematically, *The Knick* is concerned with invention and modernity as new surgical techniques at the Knickerbocker Hospital become harbingers of a social revolution. Yet, regardless of the scientific purpose behind the demonstrations of surgery, the voyeuristic pleasure experienced by the viewer watching the dissection of human viscera produces fascinating and lively entertainment.

Physicality and intimacy

Episode one of season one, 'Method and Madness', opens with Thackery in an opium den.[9] The shot is from his POV using stylized colour (red) that runs counter to the realism of the rest of the episode, but the colour symbolism – used by Soderbergh elsewhere in the series – hints at danger. It is followed by the brief authorial intervention of an opening caption announcing the place (New York City) and time (1900). The effect of the static camera is to observe Thackery, presenting the spectacle of his body in the grip of smoking opium, as well as the body itself becoming an object to be gazed upon by the viewer. The body is literally brought to light when Thackery exits the darkened den to step outside into daylight, before watching him inject cocaine between his toes, the close-up of the junkie shooting up prefiguring again the exhibition of the visceral. In this way, *The Knick* establishes that the starting point of the show is the body as a site that invites an intense gaze.

As his cab drives through the streets of New York, the opening sequence creates a conceptual space as it depicts New York and its people as fragments edited together: we have the 'real' city of the thronging multitude, the New York of the rich and the poor. A heady mix exists in the decoupage of electrically powered streetcars and a dead horse in the street inspected by a curious boy as passers-by happily ignore the rotting corpse. Equally, dramatic high- and low-angle shots navigate us through the city and the urban landscape provides a period pleasure. In *The Knick*, moments of heightened visual pleasure are mediated by the possibility of an engaged viewer, fascinated by the period detail and mix of modernity and historicism, but also its horrifying medical past.

[9] Original TX, 8 August 2014.

The setting of a television hospital drama is often tied to a city (Chicago in the case of ER and Chicago Hope). However, the foregrounding of the workplace within the hospital focuses attention not only on various medical practices but also on the social tensions between the characters. In *The Knick*, tensions are heightened by the tragic results for characters left alienated and the emotionally destructive effects of bad choices: for example, Thackery's failure to secure a loving relationship with Nurse Elkins (Eve Hewson) or with the socialite Abigail Alford (Jennifer Ferrin), leading to his ultimate death. At the same time, *The Knick* as in many hospital dramas:

> ultimately emerges as a character unto itself, and one, which is both harrowing and oddly inspiring to those who work there. For the characters in ER and NYPD Blue and the other ensemble workplace dramas, soul searching comes with the territory and they know the territory all too well. They are acutely aware not only of their own limitations and failings but of the inadequacies of their own professions to cure the ills of the modern world. Still, they maintain their commitment to one another and to a professional code which is the very life-blood of the workplace they share.[10]

In episode one, arriving at the Knickerbocker, Thackery walks into an operating theatre organized as the 'panopticism' described by Michel Foucault (Figure 3).[11] Rather than warders watching prisoners, there are unidentified men: it is never quite clear who they are, but we assume they are medical practitioners, establishing an institutional gaze as they sit and watch the arena below.[12] Extrapolating from Foucault, such a gaze alters the behaviour of patients, ensuring 'the automatic functioning of power',[13] a possibility which is used by Soderbergh to produce thematic concerns in *The Knick* about individuality, authority and institutionalization. Similarly, Helen Wheatley explains that operating theatres were constructed to be a form of entertainment in the nineteenth century:

> institutions like St. Thomas's Hospital in London were advertised in newspapers and surgeons might get a round of applause at the end of the procedures from the paying public. . . . Patients put up with having an audience at their time of

---

[10] Thomas Schatz, 'Workplace Programs', in Horace Newcomb (ed.), *The Encyclopedia of Television*, vol. 3 (Chicago: Fitzroy Dearborn, 1997, 1873).
[11] Michel Foucault, *Discipline and Punish: The Birth of the Prison* (London: Penguin, 1991).
[12] The show's medical adviser explains in a separate interview they are seated hierarchically, the most important and probably older medical professors at the front with assistant professors behind them and so on.
[13] Foucault, *Discipline and Punish*, 201.

distress (and threat to their life) because they received medical treatment from some of the best surgeons in the land, surgeons they otherwise could not afford.[14]

The notion of *circus* is repeatedly mentioned by Thackery. Regardless of the scientific purpose behind the Knickerbocker, the idea of a circus entertaining the medical profession reappears again and again in the series, culminating in season two, with the separation of conjoined twins who literally have been performers in a circus – Hubert's Freak Show – before arriving at the Knickerbocker.

Besides a panopticon, the sensory experience of a public exhibition in *The Knick* also exists as a form of 'body horror', an idea proposed by Simon Brown and Stacey Abbott, who identify the medical drama as a televisually specific form of horror with its 'spectacle of the grotesque body'.[15]

Dr Stanley Burns was the medical adviser for *The Knick* and is curator of an encyclopaedic archive of historical medical photography. He was on set from three to five days a week, and both the writers and director spent time researching from the photographic archive owned by Burns.[16] Burns would teach the actors, including Owen, how to use haemostats, clamp-like devices to

Figure 3 Panopticism.

[14] Helen Wheatley, *Spectacular Television: Exploring Televisual Pleasure* (London: I.B. Tauris, 2016), 160.
[15] Simon Brown and Stacey Abbott, 'The Art of Sp(l)atter: Body Horror in *Dexter*', in Simon Brown and Stacey Brown (eds), *Dexter: Investigating Cutting Edge Television* (London: I.B. Tauris, 2010), 205–20.
[16] Chris Higgins, 'Dr Stanley Burns, The Knick's Medical Advisor'. Available at: http://mentalfloss.com/article/58736/interview-dr-stanley- burns-knicks-medical-advisor

close off blood vessels and suture the latex tissue from the props department. For Owen, Burns would often call for a greater realism by insisting on more clamps and blood.[17] As Thackery enters the operating theatre for the first time, the Knickerbocker's chief surgeon, Jules Michael Christiansen, Thackery's mentor and friend, announces a procedure on a young woman who is experiencing complications from placenta previa, but he believes the procedure will save her life and that of her unborn child. Nevertheless, the rousing announcement hints at the presentation of spectacle for the delectation of the seated audience, as if the operation seeks to entertain a public hungry for knowledge but also craving sensation. Thackery is presented by Christiansen as an athlete about to enter a competition. As Christiansen describes the procedure that will be undertaken, the camera is positioned to take advantage of various low angles and fast movement, a manoeuvre usually associated with a threatening presence in horror films to create a suitable mode of observing the action but which here anticipates the operation's bloody failure.

Christiansen informs Thackery that they have 100 seconds to complete the procedure, creating the impression of athletes preparing for an attempt at an Olympic record. The mention of a 'hundred seconds' is followed by the sight of a scalpel slicing open the woman's pregnant belly, emphasizing the sheer physicality of the material body using a stylistic strategy of relentless detail. The stylistic tone changes as the editing becomes fast-paced as the surgeons become frantic, realizing that time is running out if they are to save the life of the patient. The baby is extracted from the womb and an attempt made to resuscitate it; they are also struggling to save the mother, who is by now bleeding copiously. The harrowing events are accompanied by the warning from the nurse that the patient's pulse is erratic. The reference to a patient's pulse becomes a familiar imprecation in the series, generating suspense around the possibility of survival and the creeping sense of finality in the spectacles offered by the various operations. The liminal threshold between life and death – the woman dies within seconds of suturing the copious bleeding in her womb – continues to add to the surgical 'body horror'. In *The Knick*, restraint and formal restrictions are displaced by gory images of the ruination of the body and its spectacle of death.

Jason Jacobs has documented how since the 1990s the hospital drama has encouraged 'a look of helpless compassion, horror, dread or morbid fascination'

---

[17] Ben Travers, 'Season 2: "It Gets Even Wilder"', *IndieWire*, 22 June 2015. Available at: https://www.indiewire.com/2015/06/consider-this-clive-owen-on-the-knick-season-2-it-gets-even-wilder-60755/

of the human body.[18] He describes this as 'apocalyptic' hospital drama that displaced earlier hospital drama and appropriated new forms of television realism that signalled voyeuristic interest in everyday life in 'reality TV' and workplace documentaries. Unlike earlier shows such as *Doctor Kildare* (1961–6) that 'embodied the aristocratic distance of the old medical priesthood',[19] hospital dramas such as *ER* (1994–2009) and *Chicago Hope* (1994–2000) deployed a morbid gaze, as well as themes of moral and ethical issues around the depiction of the extremes of human suffering and injury, that encourages audience proximity.

Equally, the reality TV formats of the 1990s popularized stylistic and aesthetic strategies that had been earlier developed in documentaries. They promoted the idea that televisual space was less necessarily a sense of contingent realism that could document the new subject material of raw emotion and authentic feelings. As John Caughie argues, television has had 'a metonymic relationship to reality ... [as] the objectivity of its camera [has disposed] it towards the observation of the real rather than the participation in it which the subjective camera gives to cinema'.[20] The participatory rhetoric of the handheld camera and the move away from the apparent passivity of observation narrate events from the standpoint of a participant and desire for greater immediacy, as well as intimacy. The style of *The Knick* can incorporate use of a handheld camera that resists the earlier fixed and fixing look that constitutes the 'object' of patients in a hospital. At the same time, for John O' Reilly, the deployment of 'virulently voyeuristic modes' of reality shows and new hospital and crime drama was an effort by their producers to meet a demand from viewers for 'anything that just might sate our desire to get up close to real events, raw emotion, and authentic feeling'.[21]

In *The Knick*, the use of camera is often about how 'In life or death situations the panic the camera conveys lets us know how shaky things really are'.[22] Soderbergh chooses formal strategies to create a critical realism of the camera in the thick of the action. The Red Epic Dragon camera was chosen because of its optic stabilization, contrasting with the earlier digital handheld cameras of reality TV and foregoing the formal strategy of shaky footage he had used in his earlier drama, *K-Street*. However, critical realism oscillates between observation

---

[18] Jason Jacobs, *Body Trauma TV: The New Hospital Dramas* (London: BFI, 2003), 68.
[19] Jacobs, *Body Trauma TV*, 6.
[20] John Caughie, *Television Drama: Realism, Modernism and British Culture* (Oxford: Oxford University Press, 2000), 122.
[21] John O' Reilly, 'The Real Macabre', *The Guardian*, 3 July 1995: 4.
[22] O' Reilly, 'The Real Macabre'.

and participation in such horrifying scenes as the death of a mother and an unborn child. Soderbergh's direction often indicates an awareness of the stylistic rhetoric of reality TV and deploys a traductive strategy, where the deployment of 'virulent voyeuristic modes' sheds light on perceived notions of aesthetics about truth and realism.

The Knick combines themes of social and physical abjection with a formal closeness of attention that demonstrates the fascination of bodies on television in hospital drama and other types of shows. However, its visual pleasures are in contradistinction to television's historical disregard of the spectacle associated with film. As we have seen in Chapter 2, television spectatorship has historically been explained using 'Glance theory', which appears, at first, to suggest only a casual engagement by the viewer with the image on television. But even early accounts of television spectatorship acknowledged the possibility of an intense gaze on some parts of the human body on screen:

> Whereas the cinema close-up attenuates the difference between screen-figure and any attainable human figure by drastically increasing its size, the broadcast TV close-up produces a face that approximates to normal size. Instead of an effect of distance and unattainability, the TV close-up generates an equality and even intimacy.[23]

Although the close-up can form a 'classic realism' that employs other techniques such as the reaction shot to render the camera an invisible presence, as we have also seen in Chapter 2, the close-up provides other possibilities to do with the sense of engagement of the viewer to television drama. Using a close-up shot, the viewing of the body in the apocalyptic hospital dramas, suggested by Jacobs, is indicative of the intensity of the viewing of an 'intimate spectacle'. In *The Knick*, a 'popular fascination with decay, death and the destruction of the body'[24] becomes an aesthetic that includes skin flaps and blood, and the brutality of medicine in 1900. Later, we become accustomed to close-up shots that reveal emotional as well as physical suffering, which ratchet up tension in the operating theatre but, elsewhere, produce an intense scrutiny of suffering, whose proximity is sensitive to delicate emotions of the viewer being moved.

The increasing use of the explicit and visceral in *The Knick* makes visible the unruly bodies of Thackery – addicted to cocaine and heroin – as well as other characters such as nurse Lucy Elkins, a woman who performs various sexual acts

---

[23] John Ellis, *Visible Fictions: Cinema, Television, Video* (London: Routledge, 1992), 131.
[24] Jacobs, *Body Trauma TV*, 1.

on unsavoury men. However, the ruination of the body as well as its intimate spectacle first manifests in the character of Abigail Alford (Jennifer Ferrin). In episode three of the first season, *The Busy Flea*, Alford, Thackery's former lover, comes to the Knickerbocker seeking medical help.[25] Once a beautiful socialite, she has been ravaged by syphilis contracted from her husband, who had an affair with a working-class woman in his office. She has been abandoned by her husband since the affair, and the syphilitic infection has destroyed her nose, leaving a disfiguring hole, which she disguises with a metal nose shield. Alford makes repeated references to her disgust with the disease, with her husband for infecting her and finally with her own physical deformation. Using the camera, initially, the closeness to her face points to a ruthless gaze of the details of her disfigurement, evoking 'compassion and horror', as well as morbid fascination.

Intriguingly, we first see Abigail from behind entering the Knick, followed by seeing her in shadow before she is taken into Thackery's office. Her mangled face is examined in an unsettling profile shot, as well as presented as spectacle for the engrossed viewer. Abigail remarks that because of the syphilitic infection and sensitivity to light, 'My eyes can't bear it'. The double meaning is obvious. The expectation of the monstrous would invite voyeurism. But the explicit voyeurism associated with the rise of reality TV and 'the aesthetic kick of the visceral' is de-aestheticized by Soderbergh's more nuanced direction.

Despite the grotesquery of Abigail's illness, the scene provides a distanced, critical view by linking emotional suffering with problems in wider society without a central spectacle whose offer is dangerous, disorderly worlds as voyeuristic entertainment. Instead, Soderbergh invites the audience to critically regard the characters in *The Knick*, and, in this way, Abigail's trauma, after she has been infected by her husband, allows us to understand that her suffering is a consequence of social inequality. Rather than presenting Abigail as strange and monstrous, the viewer is led to recognize her plight as a problem caused by the social and sexual inequalities of the age and, by implication, its critique of a society dominated by powerful men. Similarly, the relationship between patient and surgeon-doctor is complicated by one built on assumptions of exclusionary masculinity, without the possibility of female doctors. The culture of doctors and surgeons is shown to be controlling and, at times, in the case of surgeons such as Everett Gallinger (Eric Johnson), arrogantly confident; this domination is also reflected in other male characters such as Herman Barrow,

---

[25] Original TX, 22 August 2014.

the hospital manager, who abandons his wife in favour of the prostitute he has fallen in love with.

Abigail is escorted into Thackery's office by the ever-curious Nurse Elkins before a shot of Abigail walking towards her former suitor. Soderbergh de-aestheticizes the encounter by not using, for example, a musical score until the scene's closing moments. Small movements by the characters feel like an eternity in a scene shot to be 'dead-air', and the tone is kept flat and unemotional – an absence of affect that permits a more considered understanding of the pair by the viewer. The shot-reverse angles of Abigail and Thackery are framed with nothing between them as Soderbergh positions Thackery not behind his desk but on top of it. The framing omits a view of a desk with its clutter of microscope and other scientific objects – the accoutrements of his profession – visible a few moments ago when Thackery insists imperiously to Elkins that he is too busy to see anyone. Once the connection between the characters has been made, there is a cut to Abigail sitting in a chair as she prepares for Thackery to examine her. If the shots have until now hinted at their earlier intimate relationship, the close-up reminds us how the unruly body is controlled by the institutional gaze of the surgeon-doctor. As Thackery examines Abigail, her abject body ravaged by syphilis is ultimately made manageable, instilling her willing acquiescence to surveillance. Eventually, Abigail becomes an exhibit in a 'circus' when she undergoes a skin graft to cover her nose. Thackery attaches a flap of skin to her nose by attaching her arm to her nose to allow the skin to attach (Figure 4). At

Figure 4 Abigail becomes an exhibit.

last, Abigail chooses suicide rather than submit to her continuing status as a medical exhibit.

Her demise is symbolic of the Foucaultian notion of the medical gaze and a disciplined body.

The use of formal strategies and a critical realism in *The Knick* reflects a discourse about authority and the damaging control it ultimately exerts. The foregrounding of institutional but invisible strategies of authority and control is made concrete with the appearance of a movie camera in season two's episode one, 'Ten Knots'.[26] The camera is controlled by Cornelia Robertson's brother, Henry, who first marks out its ostensible purpose to reproduce reality to help the Knickerbocker's surgeons solve research problems. Cornelia is head of the Knick's social welfare office and the daughter of the head of the Board of Directors at the Knickerbocker. However, prior to its use in the operating theatre, the camera is used to shoot a stag film in episode four, 'Wonderful Surprises'.[27] Henry Robertson directs a nurse at the Knick, Daisy Ryan, to undress; she is unaware of what the camera can do. Later, it reappears in episode seven, 'Williams and Walker', to film a record of an operation to separate conjoined twins.[28]

The idea of the camera as entertainment and erudition is made stronger because the twins have performed in Hubert's circus. In its heyday, Hubert's was as well-known and frequented as Coney Island by New Yorkers seeking inexpensive thrills. Hubert's was the home to a series of 'freaks', such as Susie the Elephant Skin Girl and Prince Randion, the human caterpillar.[29] At the same time, the movie camera had been proposed by Thomas Edison as a scientific device that would 'do away with books in the school. . . . When we get the moving-pictures in the school, the child will be so interested that he will hurry to get there before the bell rings, because it's the natural way to teach, through the eye.'[30] During the operation to separate the twins, the camera exists as an omniscient gaze but also for a contemporary of Edison, Louis Haugmand, the moving image would be 'Bread and cinemas' after the manner of Roman bread and circuses.[31] Thackery announces that 'this will be the last day that they [the conjoined twins] will be a sideshow attraction and you their last circus audience'. However, in *The Knick*,

---

[26] Original TX, 16 October 2015.
[27] Original TX, 6 November 2015.
[28] Original TX, 27 November 2015.
[29] It also appears in a scene from *Midnight Cowboy* (1969) when Jon Voight strolls past it.
[30] Quoted in C. B. Brewer, 'The Widening Field of the Moving-Picture', *Century Magazine*, 86 (May 1913): 72.
[31] Quoted in R. Williams, *Dream Worlds: Mass Consumption in Late Nineteenth-Century France* (Berkeley: University of California Press, 1982), 80–3.

the facility of the camera of being able to record the real is explored alongside thematic concerns about the medical gaze even if Thackery is cast as one of the few characters whose own alienation disrupts his authority as a surgeon.

Guerrilla tactics and mobility

In *The Knick*, we have seen the importance of the close-up; however, this is counterbalanced by a kinetic style which complicates the rhetoric of the fixed or fixing institutional gaze in favour of the long take and mobile camera. Soderbergh had already taken full advantage of this mode of filming as an alternative during the making of *K-Street*, his earlier venture onto television in 2003. Yet there are important differences. In *The Knick* he would forgo the type of handheld DV cameras he had used in *K-Street*. Instead, he adopted a style that can be achieved using a larger camera without the sudden zooms and restricted views he had used earlier. Nevertheless, at important moments, he would continue to create the impression of capturing events as they unfolded rather than events that have been storyboarded and carefully staged for the camera.

Since the 1980s, camera mobility for television has been increasing since the development of devices such as the video assist, which allows a director or crew to observe what is being shot on a film camera, and cybernetic devices like jib arms and motorized cranes, which give a greater fluidity. Increasingly, television shots were no longer limited to the eye-level or the perspectival range of a human camera operator but could start far above the operator's head and offer extensive lateral, vertical and diagonal shots. This range meant that a director could offer a more autonomous approach to style rather than one anchored to the naturalistic aesthetic of an invisible observer watching a scene. As John T. Caldwell comments: 'This family of motion-control devices all do one thing for the television image: they automate an inherently omniscient point of view and subjectivize it around a technological rather than a human center.'[32] Due to a greater spatial fluidity, the camera was able to enter the space between the bodies of the performers, freeing directors from the older grammar of television drama: the master shot followed by the two-shot and ending with the close-up.

In earlier hospital dramas such as *ER*, a mobile camera strategy is visible when a Steadicam circles hospital beds and becomes the evolution of a style

---

[32] John T. Caldwell, *Televisuality: Style, Crisis, and Authority in American Television* (New Brunswick: Rutgers University Press, 1995), 80–1.

that can be shot economically while also seeking to convey people's experiences in more dramatic ways. Crucially, in addition to a more fluid use of camera achieved by robotics, digital cameras have brought other changes, including a less glossy 'cinematic' quality unlike the feature cinematography of television drama found in shows such as the Bruckheimer produced *CSI*, resembling a theatrically released film due to its high production values. Unlike *CSI*, technical innovations, including image stabilization with smaller cameras, have replaced the Steadicam with its extreme fluidity. Nevertheless, the cinematography in *ER* differed from other hospital dramas like *Chicago Hope*, premiering the day before *ER*. It was the use of the Steadicam, argues Jeremy Butler, which allowed *ER* to develop a kino-eye, drawing upon ideas first suggested by Dziga Vertov:

> I am kino-eye, I am a mechanical eye. . . . I free myself from human immobility, I am in constant motion, I draw near, then away from objects, I crawl under, I climb onto them. . . . I plunge and soar with plunging and soaring bodies . . . recording movement, starting with movement composed of the most complex combinations.[33]

Such mobility suggests how the camera can swiftly react to new events as they happen, lending invisibility to the craft of the cinematographer. On the other hand, *ER* favoured Steadicam shots rather than handheld shots, and this was used to create shots that lasted eighty seconds and longer.[34] It also suggested the cult of the professional camera operator and creation of a stylistic effect in its own right, drawing attention to the skills of the cinematographer.

Moreover, the Steadicam can be a marker of an aesthetic connoting a high-status text because of its cinematic antecedents in films from auteur directors such as Stanley Kubrick. Its bravura movements closely resemble tracking shots associated with theatrical film that glide unimpeded around the actors.[35] In this way, the Steadicam creates the expectation for the viewer of a 'filmic' disembodied gaze, floating and impersonal. Its limitation as a formal device is obvious: a strategy exists which tells the story as the director wishes it to be told, producing a signifying practice that creates a tension between authorship and the subject being filmed. In this way, the style of a Steadicam can be compared to the use of the long take and elaborate tracking shots found in films directed by

---

[33] Dziga Vertov, *Kino-Eye: The Writings of Dziga Vertov*, edited by Annette Michelson, translated by Kevin O Bien (Berkeley: University of California, 1984), 17.
[34] Jeremy Butler, *Television Style* (London: Routledge, 2010), 144.
[35] Jean-Pierre Geuens, '"Visuality and Power", The Work of the Steadicam', *Film Quarterly* 47, no. 2 (1993–4): 16.

Orson Welles and Jean Renoir, but as Michel Foucault stresses in his writing on authors, 'the subject should not be entirely abandoned'. Instead, he argues that a 'discursive practice' should raise questions not about 'who is the real author' but 'Under what conditions and through which forms can an entity like the subject appear in the order of discourse . . . what are the modes of existence of this discourse'.[36] Instead of the Steadicam with its inhuman presence penetrating space, a more participatory form is required that seeks to close the gap between people's experiences and how the story is narrated. We have already seen how the medicalized self through close-ups can signify not only an absolute objectivity but also institutional control of its subjects. Soderbergh was, therefore, to approach his subjects using, at times, a complex style that uses subtle signifiers of a schema seeking the critical viewer.

The digital option and the small-scale nature of newer cameras not only help shoot longer continuous takes but provide further advantages compared to the older Steadicam. Soderbergh was able to make use of the Red Epic camera and, with the help of an iPad and smartphone, communicate his directions to the crew to avoid having to shoot three or four pieces of coverage for scenes. 'Often the shot that ends up in the show is the first one that we got,' explains André Holland, playing Algernon Edwards, the Knick's acting chief of surgery.[37] The net result is for images to become marked as more spontaneous or shot in a manner that suggests a lack of planning. Stylistically, the sense of realism derives from earlier traditions of cinéma vérité that resists a fixed, wide-angle, surveillance style. The style adopted by Soderbergh for *The Knick* overcomes the problem of using the Steadicam, that is, the rehearsed feeling of characters entering the frame in time to meet the camera's movement. If the director has worked out the choreography of actors and cameras, character movement can seem to be positioning the actors to make best use of dramatizing the action in the narrative. A faster, more mobile use of camera not only equates to dramatic action, but in *The Knick* a balance between speed, motion and character development results in tensions between the requirements to simultaneously observe and aestheticize the images. By shooting with a scaled-down crew, on location and using available light, Soderbergh was able to allow his actors to move freely without the problem of having to hit marks for position, framing and focus. This economic guerrilla style of film-making was one that he had been already using to great effect, in the

---

[36] Michel Foucault, 'What Is an Author?', in John Caughie (ed.), *Theories of* Authorship (London: Routledge and Kegan Paul/BFI, 1981), 290.
[37] Quoted in Matt Zoller Seitz, 'The Binge Director', *New York Magazine*, 5 October 2015.

world of low-budget independent film but also in his bigger-budget films such as *Erin Brockovitch* (2000), *Traffic* (2000), *Che* (2008) and *The Girlfriend Experience* (2009), and that he would deploy again in *The Knick*.

The pace of production meant that 570 pages of script for season one of *The Knick* was shot in seventy-three days.[38] Using the Red Epic camera, most of the drama could be shot in the available light without augmentation. A guerrilla style, which Soderbergh had used since the days of his first film, *Sex, Lies and Videotape*, would mean that the shooting could progress quickly, helping the actors to remain focused and maintaining the emotional intensity required by Soderbergh for the characters. An iPad was patched into Soderbergh's camera via wireless to inform technicians and actors waiting on standby of how scenes should be shot. Aesthetic questions would appear on their screens: 'Where is the best place to begin'; 'Perhaps the first shot should both start and end with a close-up of medical instruments used in the procedure'; 'Maybe the shot should end further away from the actors, and then the next shot should pick up in close-up.'[39] The aim of Soderbergh was to immerse his actors in the New York drama and to forget that he was making a period piece. The method of guerrilla shooting served to create a sensation of presence or the immediate time of the image without elaborately composed long shots that had taken many hours to shoot in older drama on the networks. For *The Knick*, Soderbergh shot the most complex long takes in less than two hours.[40]

According to one of the writers of the series, Jack Amiel, both seasons were shot in about 150 days, less time than was required to usually shoot one large-budget movie.[41] The speed of shooting and the use of a guerrilla digital-video shooting style to enhance the realism of the performances also suggest 'sustained shots that go on forever', suggesting again, as Heath and Skirrow observe, 'Like the world, television never stops, is continuous.'[42] Rather than visually arresting period textures producing historical verisimilitude, style in *The Knick* is designed to build a sense of the unending flow of images to craft the impression of immediate, intimate and continuous contact with a chaotic Victorian New York. The ability to make 'direct' contact with the past with its signifiers of immediacy suggests a permanently alive view on the world of hansom cabs and gas lamps,

---

[38] Iezzi, 'Bloody Hell: Steven Soderbergh Dissects His Modern 1900s Medical Drama, The Knick'.
[39] Seitz, 'The Binge Director'.
[40] Seitz, 'The Binge Director'.
[41] Seitz, 'The Binge Director'.
[42] Stephen Heath and Gillian Skirrow, 'Television: A World in Action', *Screen*, 18, no. 2 (Summer 1977): 54.

as well as its visceral racism. Soderbergh shot with the handheld Red camera as he was pushed by grips on a small wheeled platform that he called 'a dolly du derrière'. This allowed him to participate in scenes with the actors as if enjoying instantaneous contact with the scene rather than, as he explains, '[being] 50 feet away, behind the monitor. I like the intimacy of that, and the actors like knowing how close I am.'[43] The immediacy of the image was made to offer the illusion of a more unmediated 'reality' unusual for period drama.

As another example of playing on the impression of realism, *The Knick* uses natural lighting as much as possible. Standing sets are lit with visible or practical lighting – from desk lamps, chandeliers and even candles in the case of Edwards operating downstairs in the basement of the Knickerbocker. Downstairs, he even uses a match to light the scene. In season two, Cornelia Robertson moves through a house with a candle without extra lighting. However, the use of very low lighting registers shifts between *vérité* and expressive effects. It should be recalled that low lighting without the aid of filler lights can indicate noir or a style that uses shadow and visual stylization. Rather than a specific visual schema, subtle shifts between styles exist. For example, *The Knick* eliminates highly stylized shots that exceed the requirements of narrative exposition. At the same time, the apparent objectivity of the camera is not left unproblematic: even when a scene is illuminated by a naked light bulb or a match, the minimalism of the basement Edwards is forced to occupy expresses his feelings of humiliation amid the surrounding squalor.

The sheer physical presence of dirt and grubbiness in New York's streets and tenements – so often contrasted to the sterile whiteness of the operating theatre – is something that Soderbergh clearly wished to include in his period drama, separating it from other television dramas, such as *Boardwalk Empire* (2010–14). The aesthetic perfection of *Boardwalk Empire* had led some critics to suspect that 'the show was trying just that bit too hard to tick all the boxes . . . [and] there was something rather lifeless about it'.[44] Here style was used to create historical verisimilitude in an example of prestigious television on HBO, as part of a corporate strategy of creating economic and cultural value. However, a guerrilla style that has been prominent in Soderbergh's work since the film *Traffic* suggests his break from notions of value established by Cinemax/HBO in its use of artistic and financial risk taken in *Boardwalk Empire* and other prestigious drama. Rather than the epic flourishes of *Empire*, cycles of violence in

---

[43] Seitz, 'The Binge Director'.
[44] Cynthia Littleton, 'HBO Lays Big-Bucks Bet on *Boardwalk*', *Variety*, 7 August 2010. Available at: https://variety.com/2010/tv/features/hbo-lays-a-big-bucks-bet-on-boardwalk-1118022673/

episodes such as *Get the Rope* (season one, episode seven) create an impression of catching the action as it happens.

In *Get the Rope*, an incident of racial violence provokes a riot.[45] An off-duty Irish policeman, Phinny Sears, mistakes a black woman for a prostitute, accosts her only to scuffle with her boyfriend and is stabbed before being rushed to the Knickerbocker. However, the surgeons are unable to save him and he dies, provoking a riot by the Irish against African Americans. New York is a brutal and, at times, chaotic city, whose long, seething tensions to do with race and class conflict are likely to bubble over, resulting in another violent cycle. Although the next scenes are violent and brutal, the composition moves back and forth between efficient storytelling, expressive characterization and authorial commentary. The initial stabbing is soon followed by a scene of a white mob dragging a black man off his bicycle, which is filmed from a distance, an image that is intense in its recording of a violent confrontation. Sears's mother demands vigilante justice by insisting African Americans are brutally attacked, and the use of a long shot on a handheld camera in available light maximizes the look of documentary realism.

This is followed by the point of view of a bystander in the crowd of Irishmen gathered around Sears's mother in the grounds of the Knickerbocker to suggest the act of bearing witness of an event and the illusion of unmediated reality (Plate 7). At the same time, the quality of the light in the sequence flattens the image despite its long focal length to signify a harsh immediacy and the fact of being present in a brutal world.

A few seconds later, the camera tracks laterally, viewing further attacks on African Americans (Plate 8), the shot continuing to offer the direct experience of a witness, replacing the subjective eye of the artist in its rawness. Next, the footage is shot through the iron fencing surrounding the Knickerbocker. The blurring of the shot and overall effect is to maintain a sense of the camera responding to events as a black man is beaten to the ground and kicked.

The attacks outside the Knickerbocker constitute the first of three acts of violence in *Get the Rope*. Footage during the three acts is shot as objective truth but, at times, includes a touch of the journalistic seeking to investigate events while adopting the rhetoric of liveness. The racism affecting Algernon Edwards in earlier episodes manifests viscerally in *Get the Rope*, but the violence is not glamorized as explicit movie violence: there is no slow motion or bloody squibs.

---

[45] Original TX, 26 September 2014.

Indeed, the violence is on screen for a few seconds, but the sense of *vérité* that encompasses those seconds uses one or two camera angles at the most. In this way, a single take is shot, and it can be claimed that Soderbergh has learnt from Steven Spielberg's use of one minute or so long takes. These follow the action without the audience noticing the length of the take. However, the significance of the take in *The Knick* is at odds with Spielberg's creation of a sense of wonder in films such as *Raiders of the Lost Ark* (1981) but belongs to a tradition established by Orson Welles in films such as *The Trial* (1962) or *Chimes at Midnight* (1965).

In *Get the* Rope, Edwards hides under a sheet on a hospital gurney pretending to be a corpse as the others smuggle him out from the Knickerbocker. Filmed during early morning, with the sun shining through the branches of tall trees, lighting becomes unbalanced to the point that it appears stylized. The expressive effect of natural lighting is put to good effect to suggest an overexposed exterior shot that seems bleached out and is similar to shots in Soderbergh's film, *Erin Brockovich* (2000). The bleached-out look also has a yellowish tint used in *Traffic* (2000), suggesting a remembrance of other work by Soderbergh and a clue to his appeal for audiences, attuned to his status as a film director of distinction and, in turn, to other directors such as Welles. To the viewers of high-profile television drama, these distinctive stylistic flourishes signal a director who made his name in the independent film sector and has been redeployed to high-profile television drama while continuing a stylistic schema that includes minimalist formal practices, as well as bravura flourishes. For example, the sequence of Edwards under the gurney is shot with remarkable economy, relying on two basic shots of seeing Elkins pushing the gurney along the road to cutting to Edwards under the sheet. When the gurney is stopped, we hear the conversation between Elkins and a cop. We do not see them as Elkins convinces the policeman that there is no one under the sheet except a badly beaten corpse. Instead, the camera remains on Edwards for the length of the scene, which is about a minute long.

Other examples of the long take exist in the second episode of the first season, *Mr Paris Shoes*.[46] This starts as Soderbergh shows all the series' major characters arriving at the Knickerbocker, tracking with them as they walk until Thackery strides into frame – an action which matches his assumed authority over the others. Next, in the same episode, new electric lights have been installed, and the camera follows the group led by Thackery of Bertie, Edwards and Gallinger as they visit patients in their beds and the lights flicker in the ward, causing

---

[46] Original TX, 15 August 2014.

Thackery's rising irritation. Barrow, the hospital administrator, is deeply in debt to a gangster called Bunky Collier, and the electric wiring has been cheaply and unsafely installed. The lights go out, leaving the shot in semi-darkness, forcing Barrow to open the screens on the windows. The lights flicker again, causing Thackery to lose his temper so that he grabs hold of a fire axe and uses it to demolish the fuse box on the wall. The entire take is much longer than the violent scenes in *Get the Rope*, lasting over two minutes compared to twelve seconds, but the running time is adjusted for its emotional effect: the slow building of tension until Thackery loses his temper.

Other approaches to realism

The mode of shooting with a minimum of shots is a reminder of Soderbergh's indebtedness to a type of filming that he describes as 'emotionally honest and immediate'.[47] On the other hand, this is not restricted to one style, and approaches to realism can be at odds with the sinuous long takes, echoing the Steadicam used in key moments in *The Knick*.

Instead, handheld digital-video imagery, echoing Soderbergh's own work within independent film, is deployed when Edwards provokes a brutal fight in an African American-only bar. The fight is the culmination of the emotionally destructive racism surrounding Edwards and his own bitter alienation from the other surgeons at the Knickerbocker. Forced to live in menial circumstances in a roach-infested rooming house and forbidden to operate by Thackery – scornful of the notion of a black man performing surgery – his alienation becomes a self-destructive impulse. The fight scene develops as Edwards sits at a bar and gives spleen to the romantic affection shown by a man to his girlfriend sitting next to him. The following cut to the fight outside the bar is an instance of style that takes an extraordinarily gritty turn that is as *direct* as it can possibly be by siting the camera just behind Edwards. The tight framing, as well as jarring perspective, creates a sense of unprecedented physical intimacy as the camera follows every movement of Edwards's head as he absorbs his opponent's punches.

The unorthodox visual perspective is attenuated by slowing down the action, following the use of a SnorriCam. A camera rigged to the body of the actor

---

[47] Soderbergh quoted in Anthony Kaufman, *Steven Soderbergh Interviews* (Jackson: University Press of Mississippi, 2002), 145.

so that it faces them directly creates a viewpoint that is both intimate with the character of Edwards and able to de-familiarize the viewer's customary proximity to character using mid-shots and close-ups. The effect is that when the actor walks, they do not appear to move but everything around them does. The SnorriCam has been used by other film-makers such as David Aronofsky as a method of anchoring subjective experience to an expressive formal device. However, at the same time, as Geoff King points out, mainstream commercial cinema's use of unconventional form tends to be 'restricted to the expression of individual consciousness or experience'.[48] The requirement for expressive characterization in *The Knick* avoids becoming more avowedly experimental or dispensing with narrative efficacy.

Nevertheless, in *The Knick*, style, as well as editing, can be understood as signalling the presence of an author, as well as connoting a sense of greater authenticity. Shifts in formal strategies in film is, as King also observes, 'an effect in its own right, drawing attention to the form of the work or the skills of the creator, rather than being subordinated to any other rationale'.[49] If the use of mobile camera in *The Knick* suggests verisimilitude, heavily stylized moments draw attention to themselves as formal-artistic devices. This is evident again when Edwards after achieving victory in his first fight confronts a champion boxer in the same bar. *Crutchfield*, the final episode of the first season, deals with the aftermath of the doomed relationship between Edwards and Cornelia Robertson.[50] Here editing rather than the use of camera makes other types of connections offered by montage with quick cross-cutting.

Like the earlier fight scene in *Mr Paris Shoes*, Edwards unnecessarily provokes his opponent. This time his opponent appears sitting in the bar with the sign behind him visible through a window: 'The Black Cat' (Plate 9). We realize this man is likely to be a formidable challenge as the narration exploits the double meaning of the sign. The next shot is carefully composed: Edwards's upper-class dress and the fact he is standing single him as the outsider. The light from an unseen source may be an affirmation of his heroism in the face of adversity, but he is disconnected, alone, and the world of the shot is an expression of his alienation.

There is a cut to a new narrative space and the exterior of the church where Cornelia will be married. The sombre tone of the music offers an ambiguous

---

[48] Geoff King, *American Independent Cinema* (London: I.B. Tauris, 2005), 129.
[49] King, *American Independent Cinema*, 82.
[50] Original TX, 17 October 2014.

meaning about the wedding. Other shots follow that exhibit the New York bourgeoisie in their finery and comfortable in their self-assured privilege for the viewer to realize that the wedding represents a dynastic alliance of money between Cornelia and Philip Showalter, the scion of another wealthy family. Cornelia was pregnant with Edwards's child, but she preferred to have an abortion rather than be ostracized by the privileged class she owes everything to but will eventually destroy her. As the sequence develops, the two narrative spaces are crosscut but linked temporally, as well as graphically, revealing parallels. The main parallel is between the site of the fight involving Edwards and the interior of the church (Plates 10 and 11).

The graphic parallelisms in the mise en scène signal Soderbergh's ability to add expressive techniques that draw attention to his status as author and, by showing class and race conflict in America, the political dimension of *The Knick*. At the same time, the editing avoids the characteristics of overly rapid intercutting found in the montage of Soviet cinema and continues to act as a narrating agency, maintaining a pace that allows the viewer to critically assess the images. For example, the choir's beatific song is intercut with Edwards being savagely beaten, the cutting back and forth between Edwards losing the fight and Cornelia marrying Philip Showalter eventually becoming jarring.

The montage of the violent pummelling of Edwards and Cornelia's wedding can be compared to the infamous baptism scene at the end of *The Godfather* (Francis Ford Coppola, 1972). In *The Godfather*, cross-cutting draws a parallel between Michael Corleone baptizing his son in church and several murder scenes as his rivals are wiped out by his henchmen. In the same way, scenes in the sequence in *The Knick* start in the same way: Edwards prepares for a fight, while Cornelia prepares to be married. As the wedding finishes, the fight finishes too. Allusion to an older film not simply draws on the talents of Soderbergh but reinforces notions of his auteur celebrity status. *The Knick* demonstrates an ability to refashion televisual narrative in the high-profile drama using borrowed formal elements and use of complex authorial style.

Conclusion

A possible third season of *The Knick* was abandoned by Cinemax allegedly because Soderbergh planned to shoot it using a radical shift in style: anamorphic black and white. In March 2017, Cinemax confirmed it would not be renewing the series as Soderbergh explained he had planned for season three to be set in 1947 with a new ensemble cast but continuing to be centred on the methods and value of medicine.[51] Such a difference in style illustrates the show's relationship back to the personal preferences of the director. At the same time, the minimalism in *The Knick* defies the assertion from John T. Caldwell that Televisuality depends on an excessive or decorative style. Writing about the Televisuality of the 1980s and 1990s, Caldwell claimed, '*The new television does not depend upon the reality effect or the fiction effect, but upon the picture effect* [Italics in the original].'[52] By 'picture effect', Caldwell was referring to television's proficiency at producing pictures amid a postmodern culture. However, as we have seen, far from TV textuality possessing a wealth of allusiveness, the power of much of *The Knick* derives from a diegesis that feels lived in. A simulated liveness in much of *The Knick* using, for example, low-key lighting, the long take and other formal devices represents the reality of locations in New York at the turn of the twentieth century, which the audience visits and experiences as actuality. Yet, despite claims about *vérité* to record the integrity of performances, the show yields to images that are more abstract and stylized at other moments. The net effect is that the discovery of a signature directorial style as a point of cultural and commercial worth is troublesome in *The Knick*. Unlike *Boardwalk Empire*, the show mostly fails to produce Televisuality that clearly flaunts itself as an 'art-object'.

At the same time, Soderbergh's tactics of fast-paced shooting are more relational than oppositional to a level of innovation and creative freedom, suggesting variants on high-end practice in *The Knick*. A notion of realism should be understood as a directorial schema that comprises flexible rules about period drama on television, as well as the new hospital dramas identified by Jason Jacobs. Rather than a 'picture effect', it is probably more accurate to regard *The Knick* as a locus for more overt assertions of style in high-end television drama within a desire to provide alternative understandings of realism and social engagement as demanded by the director.

---

[51] Zack Sharf, 'The Knick Ended Because Steven Soderbergh Wanted to Shoot Season 3 in Anamorphic Black and White', *IndieWire*, 7 July 2017. Available at: https://www.indiewire.com/2017/07/steven-soderbergh-knick-cancelled-season-3-details-1201851975/
[52] Caldwell, *Televisuality*, 152.

4

Fargo

Adaptation of a cinematic text

The four seasons of *Fargo* (FX, 2014–20) represent what Matt Goldberg has described as 'a fool's errand – a TV adaptation of one of the Coen brothers' best movies without their involvement'.[1] The statement immediately invokes complex questions of television authorship. The highly successful show was based on the 1996 feature film by Joel and Ethan Coen, one of the most lauded of their extensive canon, and one that sits among the American Film Institute's '100 Greatest American Movies'. With the television adaptation, the Coen brothers are credited as executive producers on all four series; however, they played almost no part in the creative work of delivering the forty episodes. Indeed, the critical and commercial success of the anthology series is attributed to its prolific writer and showrunner, Noah Hawley. In this chapter, a discussion of the complexities underlying the show – how Hawley's production leadership interweaves with the cinematic precedent set by Joel and Ethan Coen – will illuminate issues of adapting style in recent high-end television drama. Throughout his work on *Fargo*, Hawley was engaged in a constant negotiation between his own original work and his filmic forebears, Joel and Ethan Coen.

Noah Hawley as scriptwriter

Hawley's stated project was to preserve the qualities of the 'Coen brothers world': the adaptation would be centred on the principle of honouring a well-known, authored cinematic style within TV drama. He expressed his intentions thus: 'With *Fargo*, I'm going to tell you a story, and it's going to feel like you're

[1] Matt Goldberg, '*Fargo*, Season Four in the Works for 2019 on FX', *Collider*, 5 January 2018. Available at: http://collider.com/fargo-season-4-premiere-date-2019/

watching a Coen brothers movie.'² There was commercial sense in this approach; although the film was released eighteen years before the airing of season one, it enjoyed a huge critical reputation.³ From the inception of the FX channel's development of the project, executive John Landgraf reassured *Fargo*'s fans that the TV show would remain 'remarkably true to the film'.⁴ This commitment would be reinforced in the promotion of the first series (Plates 12 and 13).

The creators of the series thus positioned *Fargo* as an exercise in convergence between the two media: the tagline for the TV show, 'Aw jeez, here we go again', emphasizes direct continuity with the feature film. This concept, however, sits easier in the mind of television executives engaged in promoting a new show than in an analytical discussion seeking to understand the frequently cited phenomenon of the convergence of cinema and television in high-end drama.⁵

The adaptation of *Fargo* was not the only cinema-to-television project at this time. HBO announced *Westworld* (2016–20) in the summer of 2013, just as Noah Hawley had finished drafting his ten scripts for *Fargo* and the show commenced pre-production. However, the status of Joel and Ethan Coen as authors of a distinct brand of independent cinema surpasses the authorial signature of Michael Crichton, who wrote and directed the feature film of *Westworld* (1973). Moreover, HBO's decision to appoint Jonathan Nolan as co-creator of *Westworld* was a choice to bring the creative influence of an internationally famous Hollywood screenwriter (*The Dark Knight*, 2008; *Interstellar*, 2014) to bear on a forty-year-old text. Michael Crichton's original provided a concept from which Nolan and co-creator Lisa Joy would make their own very distinct television drama, thus simplifying issues of authorship in the series. With *Fargo*, however, FX had a relatively inexperienced creator in Noah Hawley. *Variety* reporter Daniel Holloway characterizes Hawley's status before *Fargo* as 'that guy with two failed broadcast dramas'⁶ – *The Unusuals* (Sony, 2009) and *My Generation* (ABC, 2010) – though Hawley had also scripted episodes of *Bones* (Fox, 2005–17). The public perception of the *Fargo* adaptation project would be, initially, dominated by the creative status of Joel and Ethan Coen.

---

² Quoted in Daniel Holloway, 'Mind Games', *Variety*, 334, no. 16 (24 January 2017), 48–53, 51.
³ For example, see William G. Luhr (ed.), *The Coen Brothers' Fargo* (Cambridge: Cambridge University Press, 2003).
⁴ Catherine Shoard, 'Coen Brothers to Adapt *Fargo* for TV Channel FX', *The Guardian*, 5 August 2013. Available at: https://www.thguardian.com/film/2013/aug/05/coen-brothers-fargo-fx-television-channel
⁵ John T. Caldwell, 'Welcome to the Viral Future of Cinema (Television)', *Cinema Journal*, 45, no. 1 (Autumn 2005): 90–7.
⁶ Holloway, 'Mind Games', 50.

With Noah Hawley's intention to tell stories as if we are in a 'Coen brothers world', his primary task was to craft teleplays to reflect the writing style of Joel and Ethan Coen, whose screenplays have a remarkable distinctiveness developed through their practice of intense partnership in the writing process. Hawley was not the first scriptwriter to attempt the task. In 2003, MGM Television produced a TV pilot, scripted by Robert Palm and directed by Kathy Bates, which aired but was not picked up for a series. Palm's adaptation held to the original characters, with Edie Falco playing Marge Gunderson and Bruce Bohne reprising his Officer Lou from the Coen brothers' film. The script follows Marge's investigation of a new crime, but Palm's intention was clearly to adhere as closely as possible to the *Fargo* storyworld that the audience would remember. There would have been multiple reasons for the decision not to develop a series from this pilot, but certainly not its closeness to the original film. Ten years later, Warren Littlefield (now working as an independent producer) returned to the project, but instead of re-engaging his old collaborator, Robert Palm, he hired Noah Hawley to write a new pilot. They caught the interest of FX, which was prepared to invest in the project, but the company made one stipulation: the new series would not feature Marge Gunderson.

This response from FX contains an interesting insight. The executives understood that although a *Fargo* series would draw a TV audience thanks to public familiarity with the feature film, any opportunity for viewers to make close comparisons would undermine the response to the TV show. This had been Littlefield's concern in 1997. Frances McDormand had won her first Oscar for her performance as Marge Gunderson: her droll interpretation and Minnesota accent were some of the greatest pleasures of the film. As Carolyn T. Russell has commented, 'McDormand's Marge may be the single most important reason why *Fargo* has been able to attract a wide audience.'[7] Removing her character from the television adaptation would insulate the project from like-for-like comparisons with the Coen brothers' movie.

Significantly, the result of this decision was that the project would no longer be an adaptation of the movie, insofar as the Coens' characters and storyline would not be reworked for television. Noah Hawley would write completely new plotlines and create his own characters. The justification for the project being called 'Fargo' would come from locating the series in the same Minnesota/ Dakotas region of the United States, and – of critical importance – the show

---

[7] Carolyn R. Russell, *The Films of Joel and Ethan Coen* (Jefferson: McFarland, 2001), 139.

would inhabit the Coen brothers' storyworld. For Joel and Ethan Coen, the balance was acceptable: 'We're not big fans of imitation', they told Hawley.⁸

Nevertheless, a form of pastiche is exactly what Hawley relied on in the first series. Robert Hanks has noted that his scripts were a constant reflexive exercise in referencing the Coens: 'Noah Hawley's script lets slip a sly glee in borrowing from the film, and from pretty much every other Coen brothers picture – Orthodox Jews straight out of *A Serious Man* (2009), a boneheaded personal trainer out of *Burn After Reading* (2008).'⁹ While Hanks makes a valid point about characters, the broader significance of the Coens' *Fargo* was that it marked a break from their earlier films, including the ones that he cites. Carolyn R. Russell has written of how 'the Coens' previous films feature storylines that click along toward a startling inevitability with the precision of a digital Rube Goldberg device; they are studies of the relationship between cause and effect as might occur in a universe only the Coens can imagine'.¹⁰ Yet, in *Fargo*, the writers break with their own narrative tendencies. Joel and Ethan Coen stressed how, whereas their previous movies had been purely fictional, this project was driven by an interest in the 'real'. However, the stated commitment to realism was complicated by the imaginative ways in which Joel and Ethan Coen handled their material. Although the story may have been inspired by the real-world murder of Helle Crafts by her husband in 1986 and two separate stories from Minnesota, the film's opening title card is intentionally misleading: 'This is a true story. The events depicted in this film took place in Minnesota in 1987. At the request of the survivors, the names have been changed. Out of respect for the dead, the rest has been told exactly as it occurred.' Needless to say, none of this is actually true.

Noah Hawley adopts this framing device, with the year changed for each of the seasons of his TV show. It is the beginning of a strategy of negotiating both similarity with the Coens' *Fargo* and his own original role as writer-showrunner for the television series. Hawley's original work in scripting *Fargo* was not based on any storylines from the Coen brothers, but from the beginning of season one, he draws his audience into a game of comparison with the movie. The first

---

⁸ Neal Justin, 'Coen Brothers' "Fargo" Comes to Television: The Coen Brothers Classic Finally Makes It to the Small Screen', *Minneapolis Star Tribune*, 14 April 2014. Available at: https://www.startribune.com/coen-brothers-fargo-comes-to-television/254818201/
⁹ Robert Hanks, 'Fargo' (review), *Sight and Sound*, 24, no. 12 (December 2014): 100.
¹⁰ Russell, *The Films of Joel and Ethan Coen*, 140.

shot of the TV series is a direct reference to the feature film. Once again it is a lone car, traversing the huge snow-covered plains of the northern Midwest, although this time at night. In the film, the identity of the driver remains hidden, but in episode one, 'The Crocodile's Dilemma',[11] we immediately meet Lorne Malvo (Billy Bob Thornton), an assassin whose collision with a deer on the road unleashes two storylines. First, the mystery of the man in underpants who breaks out of the trunk and runs off into the night to meet his frozen death. Second, Lorne's minor head injury that leads to his chance encounter with Lester Nygaard in a hospital waiting room. Each of these plots bear the hallmark of the Coen brothers, narratives that combine the bizarre and the criminal, providing the collision between a witless lummox and the forces of senseless violence. Characters in Hawley's *Fargo* are presented in order to carefully position the audience into seeking references with the movie. Replacing the car salesman, Jerry Lundegaard, is insurance salesman Lester Nygaard. Molly Solverson, leading the police procedural storyline, reminds us, because of her gender, of Police Chief Marge Gunderson in the movie. We are drawn into the strategies of comparison and difference (Figures 5 and 6). Molly is single and younger than Marge; Lester is childless and has additional family influences – his brother and sister-in-law – that pressure him towards crisis.

Hawley offers stark differences in character when he presents his antagonists. In the movie, the qualities of Carl Showalter (Steve Buscemi) and Gaear Grimsrud (Peter Stormare) – villains hired by Jerry Lundegaard to kidnap his wife – function as representatives of violent criminality, as well as working as a comic double-act of clashing personalities. Importantly, their violence is portrayed as senseless and incomprehensible to Brainerd's experienced police chief, Marge Gunderson. The TV show's Lorne Malvo, however, comes from a very different character type of evil – the intellectually brilliant villain. He takes delight in his malevolence, concocting baroque means of terrifying and brutalizing his victims, such as his handling of the supermarket entrepreneur Stavros Milos (Oliver Platt), where he exploits the businessman's religious faith. In episode three of the first season, 'A Muddy Road', Malvo rigs his plumbing so that blood gushes on Milos in his shower, and infests his supermarket with locusts.[12] In her review of season one for *The New Yorker*, Emily Nussbaum notes

---

[11] Original TX, 15 April 2014.
[12] Original TX, 29 April 2014.

Figures 5 and 6 Female protagonists lead the police procedural in *Fargo* (1996) and *Fargo* (2014).

that the nature of Lorne Malvo's evil character 'ties the show to a set of cable-TV conventions, making Malvo the sort of philosophical assassin who spools out speeches about predators and apes and women raped by Rottweilers'.[13]

---

[13] Emily Nussbaum, 'Snowbound: The Minnesota Noir of *Fargo*', *The New Yorker*, 16 June 2014. Available at: https://www.newyorker.com/magazine/2014/06/23/snowbound-2

In the Coen brothers' storyworld, evil is incomprehensible and pointless, and we are not asked to speculate further. In reconfiguring *Fargo* for television, Hawley allows evil to fascinate as baroque and Machiavellian. The audience is invited to admire the brilliance and even absurdity of criminal minds, giving the audience elements of Grand Guignol and melodrama. The stylist exuberance of their screen violence becomes a key televisual pleasure, as violent possibilities elicit a range of emotions that signify a prestigious production.

Noah Hawley as showrunner: Establishing the style of the show

Noah Hawley's imprimatur was visible before pre-production began for season one. The scripts for the ten episodes were completed by Hawley as sole writer before the production got underway, albeit the drafts were also approved by Joel and Ethan Coen. This situation is more reflective of feature film production, where production only begins with a completed screenplay, whereas in television drama, a showrunner will start hiring key crew while co-writers are still in the midst of drafting episodes. Noah Hawley entered pre-production in the summer of 2013, and his intention of creating a series that looked and felt different from older television drama inevitably drew attention to a production culture within a changing television industry.

In casting the show, Hawley accepted the only suggestion made to him by the Coen brothers: to appoint casting director Rachel Tenner, who until this point had worked almost exclusively in features. Together, they made two key decisions that signalled a commitment to changes within the television industry. The first was to cast Billy Bob Thornton as Lorne Malvo. Thornton did not just have Coen brothers' pedigree (*The Man Who Wasn't There*, 2001) but was a star of US indie cinema (Sam Raimi's *A Simple Plan*, 1998; the Bret Easton Ellis-scripted *The Informers*, 2008). Hawley used the anthology structure of his show to enable his star to appear in *Fargo* for the ten episodes of series one, not requiring Thornton to sign a contractual commitment to any forthcoming series (a previous industrial norm in TV production that can disrupt the career path of a performer). The second decision was the unusual choice of Allison Tolman to play the central role of Molly Solverson. Tolman was a trained actor but almost completely unknown: such a risky choice was extremely rare in television, but familiar in the world of indie cinema, where directors have frequently asserted their independence from commercial constraint by choosing non-actors or low-profile performers to play leading roles.[14]

The structure of the production was based on pairs of episodes, a system in which Hawley would hire five directors, each working on two consecutive episodes to be shot back-to-back. The first two episodes of the series would be the key to establishing the visual style of *Fargo* and to the success of the whole enterprise. Noah Hawley chose Adam Bernstein to direct, a decision that put the opening of the series in the hands of a solid television director who was known for his multiple episodes of *Breaking Bad* (AMC, 2008–13), as well as comedies such as *Scrubs* (ABC, 2001–10) and the innovative prison drama, *Oz* (HBO, 1997–2003). The choices of production designer and editor were also individuals with impressive television careers – John Blackie and Skip Macdonald. Only in the appointment of one role, DoP, was Hawley prepared to step outside the stable of TV industry regulars: Matthew J. Lloyd was hired to 'lens' the first two episodes of the series. This was a remarkable choice and a statement about the intentions the showrunner had for *Fargo*. Lloyd had almost no experience as a TV series DoP: at this point in his career, he had lit just one episode of *Alpha House* (2013–14). The most recent credit that Lloyd brought to Hawley was his feature film, *The Better Angels* (A. J. Edwards, 2014), an art house piece produced by Terrence Malick and shot in monochrome, about Abraham Lincoln's harsh Indiana childhood. Beyond this, Lloyd had also shot one other feature, the more regular *Robot and Frank* (Jake Schreier, 2012), and a host of short films and music videos. Hawley was clearly prepared to take a risk, encouraged by his director, Adam Bernstein, who had worked with Lloyd on *Alpha House*. As a result, the showrunner chose a relatively new but creatively ambitious cinematographer, whose principal work and influence were from the world of feature film production. While the other key heads of department would be highly experienced television professionals, the person responsible for building the lighting and camera style of *Fargo* would be a newcomer, unencumbered by the cinematographic techniques of style in US television.

However, Matthew J. Lloyd worked on only two episodes of the series and was never hired again. The reason is unclear, but it may have been linked to his relationship with Adam Bernstein, whose episodes he shot and who

---

[14] Cynthia Baron and Yannis Tzioumakis, 'Acting and Aesthetics in American Independent Cinema', in *Acting Indie: Industry, Aesthetics and Performance* (Basingstoke: Palgrave Macmillan, 2020), 45–73.

likewise did not work on any further episodes of *Fargo*. Instead, it was the television stalwart Dana Gonzales (thirty-four episodes of *Pretty Little Liars*, 2011–13) who became the dominant DoP for the series, shooting all the remaining eight episodes and a further twelve episodes across the second and third seasons. Hawley's confidence in Gonzales was proven after he chose him as cinematographer when he directed the opening episode of season four. Gonzales won a Primetime Emmy for his work on *Fargo*'s first season and his influence persisted alongside the four directors with whom he collaborated. The failure of Matthew J. Lloyd to have more impact on the visual style of *Fargo* complicates assumptions about the ease of movement of professionals from feature film production into even large-budget, high-end television drama. Although Lloyd has, subsequently, established himself as a cinematographer working across both film and TV, his impact on *Fargo* was overshadowed by a DoP whose primary skill was to already have worked within the structures of television drama.

Fargo's storyworld

The sense that the TV show's audience feels located within a 'Coen brothers world' has been invoked both by the creators of the series and by critics. Nevertheless, if the term is used to express the unifying qualities of the film and TV show, its general looseness suggests scope for reconfiguring the textuality of the TV show. One UK newspaper reviewer described the experience of watching *Fargo* series one:

> There's something almost dreamlike about the experience of watching it. Like revisiting a favourite old childhood haunt; a funfair, perhaps, because the original Fargo was so joyful. Some of the rides have moved, or been changed, or updated, but the feel of the place, the look and the sound, the terror and the laughing, is the same.[15]

The 'Coen brothers world' continues to be an important programme format and one that carries meaning for many spectators and critics. Significantly, if this world suggests a primary or Ur source, the implication is not only the successful

---

[15] Sam Wollaston, 'What Could Have Been a Disaster Is a Respectful Homage', *The Guardian*, 20 April 2014. Available at: https://www.theguardian.com/tv-and-radio/2014/apr/20/fargo-tv-review-disaster-or-homage

importation of film style into television drama, but a reconfiguring of aesthetic forms. By defining the storyworld more closely, an analysis of sequences from the series illustrates continuities and disparities of composition between the film and TV show.

The original physical setting and the thematic structure of *Fargo* transport the audience to an extraordinary world. The film's opening shot presents a snowbound prairie landscape, a geography bearing the metaphor of limitless expanse, its flat white horizons merging into pale overcast skies, and arrow-straight roads extending into nothingness. Contrasting with the vast exterior, the world of the character drama is mostly trapped in interiors, restricted environments where people huddle against the hostile climate. The Coens have described their native region of the United States as 'Siberia with family-style restaurants',[16] and they build a storyworld that carefully exploits these qualities, reflecting both the brutal and the cheery aspects of the place. The snow creates a sense of timelessness: when watching the film, the characters' daily existence – heavy winter clothing and tyre chains – seems to be the permanent state of affairs. We never stop to consider how the life of these people in Brainerd, Minnesota, would differ in midsummer. This snowbound world creates a context in which the story's characters are intimately bound together – their culture of deliberate cheeriness belying the friction that inevitably ensues in such conditions. The original storyworld is a superbly successful construction of filmic otherness. This wintery portrayal of the mid-Northwest has rarely been seen before by the audience and affords the Coen brothers a limitless dramatic canvass. Within an unfamiliar, unbounded environment, anything can happen, a feature that is key to narrative unpredictability.

It is not just the physical environment that builds the uniqueness of this storyworld. The characteristics of this region's social culture are emphasized to provide a sense that although we are in the United States, this is an utterly different America from any of the cinematic depictions which the audience are familiar with. The Coens were brought up in Minnesota and their film expresses their detailed knowledge of its people, as well as a warm fondness for the curious particularities of their behaviour. The key feature of this is described as 'Minnesota Nice', an irrepressible cheeriness and gentility that characterizes social behaviour in the region. As Emily Nussbaum notes, this can hide true

---

[16] Quoted in Jeffrey Schwartz, 'Minnesota Nice', Special Features, *Fargo*: Special Edition, MGM Home Entertainment, 2003.

character: she describes Jerry Lundegaard as a 'watery-eyed lummox who wears a mask of Minnesota nice'.[17]

A second defining feature of the region's particularity is accent. This Midwestern region of the United States was settled by immigrants from Scandinavia, in particular Swedes. The lack of opportunities, beyond agriculture, meant that very few other groups of migrants followed them here. The Coens are exuberant in their exploitation of how the region has frozen certain characteristics of Sweden in its local culture. The heavily accented English spoken by the locals is unlike any other American accent audible on screen. Cinema and television have brought a dozen versions of American English, from southern drawls to Boston twangs, but the lilt of the Swedish accent in *Fargo* is a new cultural experience. It also reinforces a sense of otherness, effecting a distanciation as enjoyment of the accent's musicality gains another level of appreciation when watching the movie. Jerry Lundegaard becomes a subject of humour, his accent emphasizing his 'nice' personality, out of his depth in the world of kidnapping.

Thus, the Coen brothers emphasized key features in *Fargo* that created its distinctive storyworld, including their engagement with a playful realism in presenting the crime drama, the snowbound physical environment and a regional social context that features the artificial gentility of 'Minnesota Nice' and a peculiarly accented English.

Noah Hawley's *Fargo*, season one: Continuities and disruptions of visual style

Of all the series of *Fargo*, it is the first that struggles hardest to maintain a continuity of style with the Coen brothers' storyworld: we have already seen that this was a stated aim of its creators. Social environment, landscape and character structure are all used to blend the spectator's experience of Hawley's *Fargo* with memories of the Coen brothers' original. This stylistic strategy extends to the extent of the physical blocking of a sequence. A key early scene in the first episode, 'The Crocodile's Dilemma', is a clever mimic of the famous 'morning sickness' scene from *Fargo*, providing shifts in the character structure, while faithfully adhering to the visual qualities of the Coen brothers'

[17] Nussbaum, 'Snowbound: The Minnesota Noir of *Fargo*', *The New Yorker*, 26 June 2014.

originating sequence. In both versions, a crashed car is situated off-road in the snows, with police attending. A local police chief arrives to join their junior colleague in assessing the scene: in the Coens' *Fargo* this is Marge Gunderson meeting Officer Lou; in Hawley's version it is Chief Vern Thurman meeting Molly Solverson. Genders are swapped but the structure of the scene is similar, with matching moments of banal banter that establish the closeness of personal and professional relationship. The viewer experiences familiarity and engages in a game of guessing what else Noah Hawley will change from the original.

In *The Crocodile's Dilemma*, director Adam Bernstein and cinematographer Matthew J. Lloyd studied carefully the technical choices made by Joel and Ethan Coen with their cinematographer Roger Deakins. Bernstein's directing of *The Crocodile's Dilemma* frequently encourages comparisons with the feature film, but each time made with subtle alterations. When Chief Vern Thurman takes a bedside phone call, he and his wife are in the exact same bedroom clinch as we saw in the case of Marge and Norm in *Fargo*, although the gender roles of the police protagonist are reversed. In the first scene in Lester Nygaard's office, the insurance salesman sits opposite a married couple: through the large window behind them, vehicles stream past. The direction reflects the film's first office scene with Jerry Lundegaard, but with the blocking reversed: the car salesman's back is to the window, likewise with heavy traffic being visible. Roger Deakins describes in the *Fargo* DVD commentary that this was an idea that the Coen brothers specifically wanted: the world is passing by Jerry. The film's link between the visual environment of the scene and character is not relevant to the TV show's Lester Nygaard, whose motivations are different from Jerry's need to make his mark on the world. Lester's character arc springs from his need to kick against maltreatment by his wife and by Sam Hess, the old school bully who confronts and humiliates him again. Bernstein blocks his office scene not to reinforce meaning within his narrative but to simply draw elements of similarity with the film. These examples help define a directing strategy for the first season of Hawley's *Fargo*, one that titillates the viewer with references to the movie, while simultaneously emphasizing the show's differences.

In the movie, to achieve a sense of ordinariness during pre-production, Joel and Ethan Coen established a creative principle for their team: 'blandness' would be the theme of the film's environment. Ronald Bergan quotes production designer, Rick Heinrichs, as saying his brief was to find 'soul-deadening, flattened' locations, while Joel and Ethan Coen's design instruction was 'Less color, less design, less kitsch. . . . We wanted no design. Absolutely nothing.'[18] The Coen brothers' carefully constructed bland visual style is attempted in the TV adaptation, but we see that the programme makers struggle to maintain this design principle throughout the first season. Production designer John Blackie established the show's style in the first two episodes, creating for Hawley and Bernstein a range of sets that reflect the subdued tones of the film's locations. Vern Thurman's house interior is completely bland, with its pale cream wall colours, varnished wood fittings and simple décor. The home of Lester's wealthier and arrogantly patronizing younger brother, Chaz Nygaard, is richer but also strikingly bland. The interior of Lester and Pearl Nygaard's house, however, lacks the colour-drained style that Rick Heinrichs achieved for Jerry and Jean Lundegaard. The living room has deep-coloured, patterned wallpaper and the set dressing is more detailed. Although the kitchen has similar wood-effect cabinets to the film's location, the TV show offers us an image of the Nygaards in a wealthier and better-designed environment. By the time the drama takes Lorne Malvo (Billy Bob Thornton) to the bar where he stakes out his victim Sam Hess, the show has altogether abandoned the principle of blandness. Unlike the drab interior of the movie's bar where Jerry meets his hired hoodlums, Carl and Gaear, the TV series presents us with a bar complete with pole dancing and neon lighting.

Costume decisions in the show also make a break with 'bland'. Lester wears a dark suit, blue shirt and tie; his winter coat is orange, a radical shift from the beige of Jerry Lundegaard, and so bright that the Hess boys tease him for looking like a pumpkin. Lorne Malvo is deliberately styled as an outsider, dressed in urban chic: dark blazer and black high-necked sweater. Similarly, his haircut makes him stand apart from the Midwest locals.

Camera movement was minimized and camera style carefully restrained in Roger Deakins's work for the Coen brothers' *Fargo*. This fitted with the bland aesthetic in the movie, as Deakins describes: 'There is not a lot of fast tracks, and flowery camerawork and camera moves. . . . You don't need to add visual pyrotechnics to gloss it up, because this very bizarre story . . . [is] more bizarre because it's played so straight.'[19] This approach was attempted but soon proved unsustainable after Noah Hawley's pilot episode. Although Matthew J. Lloyd deliberately chose similar lenses to those used by Roger Deakins, the stylistic link extends little further than this. Lloyd swiftly breaks from his forebear's visual simplicity: the second sequence of *The Crocodile's Dilemma* begins with a shot of a clunking washing machine in

---

[18] Ronald Bergan, *The Coen Brothers* (London: Orion, 2000), 175.
[19] Roger Deakins, DVD Commentary, *Fargo*: Special Edition, MGM Home Entertainment, 2003.

the Lundegaards' cellar, only for a rising crane movement to pass up through the ceiling of the room and into the kitchen above, to find the couple who are eating lunch. Such visual extravagance is unthinkable in the visual language of the Coen brothers' *Fargo*. It signals a departure from the film-makers' intention to create a more 'realist' form of cinema in *Fargo* with a pared-back camera style. Rather, in the TV show, the crane movement of Lloyd's camera crossing through spaces foregrounds the artificiality of the studio set. Equally, less flamboyant but un-*Fargo* camera movements occur in the episode. The key scene where Lester meets Malvo in a hospital waiting room opens with an extensive dolly movement, starting from a close-up of Lester and resolving on a two-shot of Lester and Malvo positioned at either end of a row of seats. Later in *The Crocodile's Dilemma*, during the motel sequence where Malvo mischievously incites a dispute between the staff, the camera moves are used frequently with Malvo entering his own moving POV and tracking movements across the car park. The message presented to the television audience is clear: although the show will include many similarities with the movie's storyworld, the adaptation will develop a visual language of its own, whose textual strategies suggest it to be an example of high-end TV.

Performance style in Noah Hawley's *Fargo*: Limitations of exhibitionism

In the Coen brothers' *Fargo*, the accents delivered by the cast were central to the fascination of the audience, and web tutorials can still be found that teach fans how to reproduce the Swedish-inflected American English heard in the film. Joel and Ethan Coen hail from Minnesota so their knowledge of the local accent is first-hand. If there was anything 'exhibitionist' about their movie's style, in comparison to the expertly crafted blandness of the visual representation, it was the accent and performances of their cast. In the transposition of the film to a high-end TV series, we can evidence important changes in the registers of the new cast's performances that complicate an understanding of issues of adaptation within the Televisuality of this drama.

In preparing for the TV series, Noah Hawley was aware of both his own unfamiliarity with the northern Midwest and the potential significance of accent in the reception of his show. He appointed the highly experienced dialect coach Tony Alcantar to closely train the cast in the regional accent. Alcantar remained a constant presence throughout the first three seasons and was instrumental in shaping a coherent regional accent across the show. To interrogate the dissimilarities with the movie, a close analysis of voice and performance will be used to compare the 'Morning Sickness' scene in the movie (at 34'22") to the parallel sequence from *The Crocodile's Dilemma* (season one, episode one), when the police chief arrives to investigate a crashed car beside the side of a snowy country road.

In the 'Morning Sickness' sequence, pregnant chief investigator Marge Gunderson inspects a triple-homicide crime scene. Actor Frances McDormand's performance emphasizes the relaxed local behaviour pattern and charming bonhomie ('Minnesota Nice'), chatting with her lower-ranking police colleague, Lou (Bruce Bohne), who matches her strong Swedish American accent. These performance choices provide the spectator with layers of pleasure: light comedy and cultural exploration, successfully elaborating an otherwise-routine crime genre scene of a police investigation. The actors' accents establish an ironic friction with the seriousness of the grisly scene, pushing the spectator to watch as observer with an almost anthropological interest in the characters. The screenplay's dialogue works together with the vocal performance to support this strategy. Marge describes her observations to Lou and maps out a scenario for the crime, concluding with:

> MARGE: And I tell ya' what, I'd be very surprised if our suspect is from Brainerd. From his footprint he looks like a big fella.
> (*She bends down and looks at the ground beside the car.*)
> LOU: You see something down there, Chief?
> MARGE: No . . . I just think I'm going to barf.
> LOU: Jeez! You okay, Margee?
> MARGE: Yeah, I'm fine. It's just morning sickness.

Dialogue and performance are deployed together to imbue the scene with a sense of the absurd, creating ironic distance for the spectator. Bruce Bohne's accent is emphasized more than McDormand's in all their scenes together, a careful choice by the Coens that aligns the character with the dim sidekick stereotype, echoing the double-acts of comic film.

Beneath the YouTube clip of this scene is an interesting comment on accent left by a blogger: 'Fake accents! I'm from South Dakota and I've met people young and old from Duluth to Rochester and never once have I heard any Minnesotan have that accent.'[20] The comment illustrates the Coen brothers' careful and

---

[20] Available at: https://www.youtube.com/watch?v=kPHbIyDTPHU

deliberate directing of their actors' vocal performances, allowing the cast to go beyond a natural Minnesota accent in order to achieve a dramatic effect. They encouraged a form of performance exhibitionism that, although distressing for some spectators familiar with the region, delighted the wider audience.

We have already seen how, in *The Crocodile's Dilemma*, television director Adam Bernstein uses elements of visual style to carefully link his scene with that from the movie. However, reversing the apparent initial referencing of similarity between the TV show and the movie is the different approach to vocal performance. When comparing the two scenes, it is the accents of the actors that provide the greatest divergence. McDormand and Bohne deliver their lines in lilting Minnesotan, with their accent and the Scandinavian gaps and hesitations 'hiccuping' the dialogue. Alison Tolman (Molly Solverson) and Shawn Doyle (Vern Thurman) speak in a simple and clear accent, with only a hint of regional character. In this way, the sequence is transformed. What Bernstein achieves is distinctiveness from the original *Fargo* movie. While his choices of visual style take the audience into the storyworld of the Coen brothers' movie, his direction of vocal performance establishes a distinct televisual alternative.

The softer approach to the Minnesotan accent is central to the stylistic tone of the TV series and the creation of its characters. Voice is key to the protagonist Lester Nygaard's professional persona: he is a salesman, and his 'sales patter' is his livelihood. Freeman's vocal performance provides lightness – an innocence to the character, reinforcing his status as a loser within a thoughtlessly macho culture. The TV show's decision to deploy a gentler quality of Minnesotan accent even extends to the bear of a man who confronts Lester in the street, the former school bully Sam Hess (Kevin O'Grady) who tormented Lester decades ago: this is not the deep, full throat voice of an American Alpha Male. The vocal delivery of O'Grady is relaxed despite his confrontational role in the scene; his use of the 'Minnesota accent' is as light as that of Martin Freeman. This delicacy of voice appears to be a deliberate performance choice. When we first hear a non-Minnesotan accent, in the hospital where Lester first meets the assassin Lorne Malvo (Billy Bob Thornton), the outsider's voice is gentle, almost soft, while questioning the protagonist. Thornton suggests a wolf in sheep's clothing with his voice, while his eyes reveal the amoral assassin that lies beneath.

Further elements of performance in the TV show reinforce the restrained quality of acting style. By analysing the secondary characters in season one, a clear choice of naturalism in the performances becomes noticeable. Keith

Carradine plays Lou Solverson, Molly's father, an ex-cop who runs a diner: his performance is a model of naturalistic screen acting, his calm demeanour reinforcing the wisdom of the older character. Equally, the domestic scenes played by Julie Ann Emery and Shawn Doyle, as Ida and Vern Thurman, are a gentle portrait of a married couple expecting their first child, the actors carefully downplaying the lighter moments of friction over the colour of the baby's bedroom. In these scenes, the performers adopt a restrained version of the Minnesotan accent, with some players delivering dialogue with only a trace of regional identity. The difference of approach to performance style between the film and the TV show is particularly pronounced if we compare parallel characters, such as the wives of the protagonists. In the Coen brothers' *Fargo*, Kristin Rudrud as Jean Lundegaard delivers a heightened performance with a strong dose of comedy, imbuing her character with 'Minnesota Nice' and a heavy accent. In Noah Hawley's *Fargo*, Kelly Holden Bashar as Pearl Nygaard plays down any comic sensibilities and reduces her accent to a fraction of Rudrud's.

A decision by Hawley and his directors is evident: the performance of the TV show must be less pronounced than in the Coen brothers' film. Tony Alcanter worked to coach the huge cast in the regional accent, but the actors were not expected to reach the heightened delivery that so famously characterized Frances McDormand's Marge Gunderson. The dominant feature of the performances in Noah Hawley's *Fargo* is restraint. There are certainly some big characters in the show, such as season three's Emit/Ray Stussy played by Ewan MacGregor, but they are frequently surrounded by secondary characters performed with the restraint familiar in other high-end dramas such as *Breaking Bad* (AMC, 2008–13) and *The Handmaid's Tale* (Hulu, 2017). Although Hawley's *Fargo* allows its audience to enjoy the otherness of the Minnesota culture, the naturalistic sensibility to directing performance is common across the series. In this stylistic divergence between the televisual and the cinematic *Fargo*, the original movie seems brash in comparison to its offspring. It could be argued that the performance in the TV show is linked to traditions of naturalism in the medium, yet we have identified how Hawley's version of *Fargo* – in terms of visual style – deploys an increased exhibitionism compared to the Coen brothers' film. Instead, Hawley adopts a strategy of investing heavily in certain aspects of exhibitionism and not in others. Two stylistic domains exist, but Hawley's *Fargo* TV show is autonomous from work by Joel and Ethan Coen.

Violent exhibitionism

In season one of Hawley's *Fargo*, Glenn Howerton plays the personal trainer Don Chumph. The visual handling of the sequence in episode six, 'Burridan's Ass', when Chumph meets his death, is a further example of the distance between Joel and Ethan's movie *Fargo* and the TV adaptation.[21] It is an example of Hawley's interest in an exhibitionist depiction of screen violence. The sequence highlights some extra features of televisual style in contemporary US high-end drama.

The sequence is a triumph of the character Lorne Malvo as a psychopathic genius. We watch him as he composes an elaborate mise en scène by taping the gagged Chumph to an exercise bike, where he must die. The set-up is akin to a ghastly art installation: the bike is positioned in front of the door and Malvo tapes a shotgun to his victim's hands. The vanity of the personal trainer's profession is represented by the exercise bike that he now cannot escape. The use of backlighting creates a super-stylized image of Don Chumph facing his personal hell (Plate 14).

Malvo has rigged an outdoor tripwire that is connected to two semi-automatic weapons inside the house. When his tip-off leads to armed police being scrambled to the scene, choral music begins, recalling a Requiem Mass. Police approaching the house trigger Malvo's automatic weapons and a mass of return fire from police gunmen pours at the building. The sound design mutes the gunfire, with the use of slow motion to create an otherworldly feel as extreme violence is blended with sacred music. The message is one of inevitability, and the death of Chumph is embedded into a mystical narrative of certain slaughter. When armed police breach the front door and see the silhouetted Chumph holding a gun, they open fire: countless rounds are fired at him by five officers in an extended sequence. The shooting continues for twenty-one seconds of screen time, framed by the reverberating choral voices, with squibs bursting from Chumph's chest and shoulders. The victim, bound to his stake, could almost be a modern-day Saint Sebastian, lacerated with bullet wounds instead of arrows. The scene ends with a dark and artistically framed close-up silhouette of Chumph, his dead body slumping, drips of black blood falling in slow motion from his nose, while the repeated musical patterns swell in a form of modern melodic Gregorian chant.

[21] Original TX, 20 May 2014.

The violence in this scene is stylistically indulgent and presented as horrifying, although made memorable due to a sense of beauty. This sequence carefully follows the tropes of the police procedural in its depiction of the arrival and deployment of armed police, but then it deploys style decisions that raise the scene above the familiar. Hawley and director Colin Bucksey (who received an Emmy for this episode) adopt a mode in which technique is observed and can be admired in how it has been staged and filmed. The violence is ghastly, tragic, inevitable and yet always memorable. The creators of *Burridan's Ass* have abandoned the realism that works so well in the feature film in favour of an exhibitionist style of violence, mayhem, sadism and murder that is more redolent of melodramatic blood and thunder, with its violent possibilities.

Season two: Rupturing style

While Noah Hawley conceived of threads to link the seasons of his *Fargo* (for instance, Molly Solverson appears as a small child in season two), he was also emphatic in creating difference between each ten-episode run. In this, he took advantage of prevailing conditions in the television industry that created the space for his anthology structure. As Anthony N. Smith has discussed, the ten/ thirteen episode structure of high-end drama narratives was an innovation by HBO in the 1990s taken on by its cable rivals: 'The shorter season form that HBO popularised has at least the potential to result in the type of coherently and artistically structured season that critics often valorise [. . .] thereby potentially raising each channel's value to advertisers and cable providers.'[22] This suited Hawley well, and for him the logic of creating a completely new story scenario for the second season responds to the meanings and pleasures about originality in the shorter season form. Talking to *Variety*'s Geoff Berkshire, he commented that 'every *Fargo* season begins with the question, "What would the Coens do?" – Joel and Ethan Coen never made the same film twice'.[23]

To signal the separation of the second-season narrative from its predecessor, Hawley opens the first episode, 'Waiting for Dutch', with a bold and hilarious break from the audience's memories of the first season.[24] Shooting in

---

[22] Anthony N. Smith, *Storytelling Industries: Narrative Production in the 21st Century* (Basingstoke: Palgrave Macmillan, 2018), 110.
[23] Quoted in Geoff Berkshire, 'Noah's Arc', *Variety* 329, no. 10 (2015): 58–9.
[24] Original TX, 12 October 2015.

monochrome, the camera dollies across a battlefield in the Great Plains to find a lone survivor standing: a Native American chief. Only the theme music from the first season links us to *Fargo* as we know it. The sequence abruptly segues into a mockumentary format, as an assistant director enters to apologize that the star, Ronald Reagan, is late: the prosthetics department is still embedding arrows in him for the scene. Both dialogue and visual style reinforce the ludic quality of the sequence, with fake splice-edit effects, visual noise and a camera position that is now locked-off, as if the crew have given up but left the camera running. The scene provokes a sense of delight in the unexpected comedy and the speculation: What function can this sequence possibly play in a *Fargo* storyline? The referencing bears no relation to the Coen brothers' feature film: Noah Hawley has cut us adrift, wondering where his storytelling will lead us.

The narrative that follows bears no relation to the bizarre opening. It is set in March 1979 and follows the story of Peggy Blumquist (Kirsten Dunst) and her husband Ed (Jesse Plemons) as they try to cover up her hit-and-run on the son of a local crime family, the Gerhardts. Visual style is deployed abundantly to distance the new season from the original. The 1970s theme is developed with archive newsreel featuring President Jimmy Carter, split-screen imaging in period style and lavish costuming (Figure 7).

Figure 7 1970s period male costumes in *Fargo* season two.

The ludic exploitation of period style is a feature of Joel and Ethan Coen's film-making, but Hawley seems to be exceeding his antecedents in his show's expressions of style and narrative playfulness. At the same time, Hawley is consistently trying to maintain the characteristics of the Joel and Ethan Coen world view in *Fargo*, despite the ever-greater distancing of his narratives from theirs. The Waffle Hut shootings in *Waiting for Dutch* provide a case study of how Hawley maintains this debt to the original film and, more generally, the Coen brothers' pictorial oeuvre. In a sequence where the young gangster Rye Gerhardt (Kieran Culkin) confronts and threatens Judge Mundt (Ann Cusack), Hawley deploys the Coen device of unpredictability in a series of plot surprises. The judge has patronized Rye and sprayed him in the face with bug killer and he pulls a gun:

- *Surprise 1*: The Waffle Hut chef bursts into the scene brandishing a heavy pan; he races towards Rye, the visual effect of slow motion preparing us for him to despatch Rye – but instead he is shot dead. The waitress screams and is also shot.
- *Surprise 2*: Judge Mundt stands up behind Rye and stabs him in the back; Rye is injured, but he turns and shoots her.
- *Surprise 3*: When Rye turns back around, the waitress is not a corpse on the floor: she has disappeared (a reference to the Coen brothers' *Blood Simple*). Rye exits the Waffle Hut and finds her staggering across the snows. He shoots her.
- *Surprise 4*: A UFO appears in the sky; Rye watches it, transfixed in the road.
- *Surprise 5*: A car comes suddenly down the road and hits Rye at speed. It stops, pauses and drives slowly away, Rye's body still on its bonnet.

The sequence carries the Coen brothers' sense of comedic violence and their love of unpredictable plot twists, but Hawley multiplies the layers even further than in their scripts. He invests in the unpredictability of plot and the ludic quality of his storytelling, but the bland visual style of the Coens' *Fargo* is abandoned altogether. This point is key to understanding adaptation in this example of contemporary high-end drama: it does not need to conform to the visual style of a primary text such as *Fargo*. Rather, it seeks to create its own visual culture, as well as remediate value within stylistic difference.

In this way, Hawley also continues to complicate concepts of authorship. As showrunner, he was personally able to take charge of the distinctive visual style of season two. Dana Gonzales brought Hawley his ideas for the look of the series, based on the 1970s colour images of photographer William Eggleston:

I showed that to the production designer [Warren Alan Young] and Noah Hawley [executive producer/writer/showrunner] and we all agreed. We attached ourselves to that era and used only the colors from that period.²⁵

Later, in post-production, Geoff Berkshire reports how Hawley led the continuing search for the season's style:

> the visual style – an ode to '70s cinema complete with split screens, freeze frames and an overall grittier aesthetic – was born in the editing room. 'It takes time to find it, the identity,' Hawley says. 'We discovered that cinematic language was not part of the scripted conception.'²⁶

The image of Hawley as showrunner is one of complete control, in which he wrestles with the creative outcome of the series in a series of one-to-one dialogues with key personnel. It should be noted that Hawley directed episode two of the second season and later the opening episodes of the third and fourth seasons. Yet his engagement with visual style and period detail recalls the Coen brothers, whose films such as *O Brother, Where Art Thou?* (2000) exploits the design of its 1930s setting, and *Miller's Crossing* (1990) is a lovingly recreated image of the Prohibition era. Hawley's depiction of the 1970s in season two of *Fargo* and the 1950s in season four follows a logic of representing cultural and regional identities in the same manner as the Coens, even as he departs further from the style of the feature film.

John T. Caldwell pointed to a developing exhibitionism in visual style in late-twentieth-century US television, and in several respects, Noah Hawley's *Fargo* is a continuation of this older trend. The exuberant violence, the heavily stylized period detail and costumes in the first two seasons demonstrate elements of what Caldwell called 'a manic rollercoaster of overwrought telling'.²⁷ In the third season of *Fargo*, highly stylized formal techniques continue to encode the programme as valuable. The first episode, 'The Law of Vacant Places', takes us to 2010 and the twenty-fifth anniversary party of the successful businessman Emmit Stussy (Ewan MacGregor).²⁸ In an upstairs office, Emmit grants a five-

---

[25] Quoted in Debra Kaufman, 'The Winter of '79: The Evocative Noir of Fargo', *Creative Planet Network*, 4 January 2016. Available at: https://www.creativeplanetnetwork.com/news/news-features/winter-79-evocative-noir-fargo-612406

[26] Geoff Berkshire, 'Fargo Showrunner Noah Hawley on Season 2 and Thinking Like a Coen Brother', *Variety*, 16 September 2015. Available at: https://variety.com/2015/tv/features/fargo-season-2-noah-hawley-1201594337/

[27] John T. Caldwell, *Televisuality: Style, Crisis, and Authority in American Television* (New Brunswick: Rutgers University Press, 1995), 192.

[28] Original TX, 19 April 2017.

minute audience to his underachieving younger brother, Ray, who wants to borrow money for a wedding ring. Ray is also played by Ewan MacGregor. In a bravura shot of DVFX, the opening of this encounter pans from one character played by the star to another. Next, this cuts to a wide profile two-shot, centred on a large leather-topped desk with Ewan MacGregor sitting on both the left (as Emmit) and the right (as Ray) of the frame. In the guise of two different characters, he is looking at himself. Using an expressive style, the confrontation between the brothers is illustrative of an internal confrontation within Emmit Stussy. It is also gimmicky and an intertext reference to other cases of one actor playing more than one character. In the case of two brothers, perhaps, the closest is *Dead Ringers* (David Cronenberg, 1988).

Conclusion

While *Fargo* is, apparently, an example of the adaptation of a film to television, it is more useful to understand the stylistic choices of Noah Hawley's *Fargo* as an example of high-end drama than its fidelity to the film. The excesses of Hawley's visual style are encouraged by the context in which he works: the requirement of FX to stand out among its rivals through its exhibitionist style and the parading of its authorship, as a sign of cultural value. Nevertheless, the countervailing impulse towards relatively naturalistic performances by most of Hawley's cast complicates our understanding of televisual exhibitionism but may also be attributed to similar industrial requirements. As an overtly flamboyant product, Hawley's *Fargo* displays a mode of performance from its actors, which is part of the process of constantly seeking new means of marking its difference from the film. This marking of difference gives the series its value. It also has a direct impact on our understanding of Noah Hawley's position as showrunner in relation to the Coen brothers. If there is an industrial requirement for each successive season to be different from the last, then it will stray progressively further from the original film. Noah Hawley's position as showrunner develops autonomies – precisely to achieve 'distinction' – with each new season that he creates. As Luca Malavasi comments: 'In this way, the film ends up becoming part of the TV series, not the film from which a television series is drawn.'[29]

---

[29] Luca Malavasi, 'Da *Fargo* a *Fargo*', *Cineforum*, 564 (2017): 67–70.

5

A wealth of allusiveness

Stranger Things, *Boardwalk Empire* and *Vinyl*

We have seen how realism as a style has been reinterpreted for high-end drama. Its ability to allude to a single author, in the case of Sorrentino and Soderbergh, encourages arguments about the importance of the director and their alternative visions of the Roman papacy or fin-de-siècle New York. However, as we have seen in previous chapters, style can be understood as less the act of enunciation by an author and more a map that can be learnt to be used by the audience to read and interpret a narrative. This chapter is about the use of allusion in its many varied forms and the tension that exists between the quest for a single point of origin and the relative autonomy of the text in high-end television.

Stranger Things (2016–19)

Created by brothers Ross and Matt Duffer, *Stranger Things* became acclaimed as Netflix's homage to 1980s genre fiction soon after its debut on 15 July 2016. The success of the show led to the invitation of its child actors to President Obama's White House music festival in October of that year. Child actors Finn Wolfhard, Caleb McLaughlin, Noah Schnapp, Millie Bobby Brown and Gaten Matarazzo, as well as older stars such as Winona Ryder, helped the show gain surprise wins for best drama ensemble at the Screen Actors Guild Awards (SAG).[1] The show also won awards from the Producers Guild of America beating *Game of Thrones*.[2] According to Google, *Stranger Things* was the most sought-after show

---

[1] SAG Awards Nominations 2017, *Entertainment Weekly*, 28 December 2016. Available at: https://ew.com/article/2016/12/14/2017-sag-awards-nominations/
[2] Jeremy Kay, 'Westworld, Stranger Things Earn Producers Guild of America TV Nods', *ScreenDaily*, 5 January 2017. Available at: https://www.screendaily.com/news/westworld-stranger-things-earn-producers-guild-of-america-tv-nods/5112575.article

of 2016 around the world, becoming a pop-culture phenomenon and streaming to 190 countries.³ The reception of *Stranger Things* demonstrates the appeal of nostalgia and throwback to an earlier type of screen horror with heroes, villains and monsters. In *Time*, Daniel D'Addario would observe:

> The show's tone, giddily indulgent of both small-town cliché and monster-serial oddity, is so backward-looking that, on first blush, it's hard to imagine how the show could succeed, artistically or commercially, in our more ironic age. And yet *Stranger Things* is an unqualified success – a show whose fondness for its own source material makes its nostalgia warm and inclusive.⁴

The inexplicable, parallel world of *Stranger Things* about five children was to take advantage of television's interest in cultural specificity and the resonances of memory, coupled with the economics of long-form television on streaming services such as Netflix. The specificity in *Stranger Things* was a derivative range of 1980s artefacts and culture – a mediated world of children in peril and the themes of an absent father borrowed from the films of Steven Spielberg and the books by Steven King against a pastiche of intertextual references. It was also a world specific to ideas of 1980s America within an era of network peak TV that heavily relied on allusion in its many forms.

Stranger Things builds a solid suspense story with themes about child abduction and unethical practices inside a secret research laboratory set in the small town of Hawkins, Indiana. Familiar storylines about abducted children recycle themes set by bestselling writers from the 1980s such as Stephen King and Dean Koontz. Similarly, mind-control research using human subjects as guinea pigs for experiments revives storylines in books such as *Firestarter* (1980) by King. In *Stranger Things*, one of the subjects is Eleven, played by Millie Brown, whose outstanding gifts of psychokinesis and telepathy make her especially valuable to the experimenters led by Dr Martin Brenner (Matthew Modine), who she perversely addresses as 'Papa'. The mind-control abilities of Eleven are developed so she can contact a monster called the Demogorgon. The alien world which the monster inhabits is referred to using the folkloric-sounding sobriquet of 'Upside-Down'. When Eleven escapes from the laboratory, she befriends three boys – Mike Wheeler (Wolfhard), Dustin Henderson (Matarazzo) and Lucas Sinclair (McLaughlin) – who share her adventures as she seeks to evade various

---

³ Available at: https://trends.google.com/trends/yis/2016/GLOBAL/
⁴ Daniel D'Addario, 'Stranger Things Is Nostalgia That Works', *Time*, 14 July 2016. Available at: https ://time.com/4406854/review-stranger- things-is-nostalgia-that-works/

agents sent by Brenner to recover valuable government property. Meanwhile, the disappearance of Will (Schnapp), the younger son of Joyce Byers, played by Winona Ryder, leads Jim Hopper (David Harbour), as the chief of Hawkins Police Department, to attempt to thwart Brenner.

For the Duffer brothers, *Stranger Things*, ostensibly set in 1983, was envisioned as a theatrical movie, the homage to two Steven/Stephens – Spielberg and King.[5] However, the lack of interest from Warner Brothers led them to write the script for television. Although, as they admit, an interest in Spielberg and a lifelong obsession for films such as *Close Encounters of the Third Kind* (1977) and *E.T.* (1982), as well as Peter Weir's *Witness* (1985), would mean that writing for television would be a major adjustment in terms of narrative and style. As Stanley Cavell points out, 'an immediate difference presents itself between television and film. . . . What is memorable, treasurable, criticizable' in television 'is not primarily the individual work, but the program, the format'. For Cavell, television works aesthetically according to a serial-episode principle.[6] However, it was HBO's *True Detective* (2014–19), directed by Cary Fukunaga, which encouraged the Duffer brothers to continue to write *Stranger Things* for television, although as an eight or ten-hour film.[7] It can therefore be said that at the same time that television seasons have become shorter, films have become longer. One interesting antecedent to *Stranger Things* is the linking of horror and television, which was visible in 1980s films: *Poltergeist* (1982) and *Videodrome* (1983). These films hint at the history of horror on US television and its appearance not only within the anthology series, including shows such as *Night Gallery* (1969–73), but in the made-for-television movie. As we will see, hybrids between film and television are not without precedents. It further raises interesting questions about assumptions to do with televisual form as being essentially serial that Cavell and others such as Christopher Anderson have argued is a sign of how television technology has been developed as a domestic medium.[8]

---

[5] Emma Thrower, 'Stranger Things: The Duffer Brothers Share the Secrets of Their Hit Show', *Empire*, 20 July 2016. Available at: https://www.empireonline.com/movies/features/stranger-things-duffer-brothers-share-secrets-hit-show/
[6] Stanley Cavell, 'The Fact of Television', in *Themes Out of School: Effects and Causes* (San Francisco: North Point Press, 1984), 239, 242.
[7] Tom Grater, 'Emmys 2017: The Duffer Brothers Talk "Stranger Things"', *ScreenDaily*, 30 June 2017. Available at: https://www.screendaily.com/features/emmys-2017-the-duffer-brothers-talk-stranger-things/5119204.article
[8] Christopher Anderson, 'I Love Lucy: US Situation Comedy', in Horace Newcomb (ed.), *Encyclopedia of Television*, 2nd edn (New York: Routledge, 2013), 1158.

Commissioned by Netflix, *Stranger Things* was shot on a Red Dragon camera to be streamed and binge-watched. Christopher Ives, the cinematographer on *Stranger Things*, planned the visual style with the shot listings in blocks of episodes at a time. The aim was to shoot it not like 'regular television' but as 'an event'.[9] Lenses more often used to shoot theatrical film were chosen, as well as shooting in 4K and the footage extracted at a high bit rate for remastering in post-production. Another feature of shooting with the Red camera was that within post-production, it was increasingly possible to zoom in. With the Red camera, productions could zoom in to about 800 per cent in post.[10] This allowed Ives to composite using DVFX without blowing up the image and losing part of it. It also meant that if the actors did not hit their marks, they could be re-composited inside the image. Finally, the camera was able to film at very low-lighting levels, although by series two, a new type of Red camera meant that this had been increased markedly to shoot in virtual darkness.[11]

If broadcast TV has, historically, been shot mostly one episode at a time, two episodes of *Stranger Things* were cross-boarded and shot every twenty-one to twenty-two days before the dailies were passed onto the editors.[12] An editor's cut was completed in a further five or six days, unlike a normal television schedule of shooting an episode every eight days and taking four days to edit it.[13] The producer of *Stranger Things*, Rand Geiger, tried to make the workflow for the editing reflect the working practice of cutting a film so that all the episodes had sound and visual effects added at the end of the post-production:

> We basically treated the entire series as this big feature film that we broke up into what was considered back in the old days 'reels'. For us, it was great because we did all our mixing and color-timing on the back end once all the episodes were locked and completed and all the visual effects were done. It allowed us that flexibility of being able to watch the entire series and go back into respective episodes and really fine-tune this basically eight-hour movie, which I think paid huge dividends in the storytelling.[14]

---

[9] Matt Grobar, 'Stranger Things: Cinematographer Tim Ives on Shooting the Upside Down', *Deadline*, 26 August 2017. Available at: https://deadline.com/2017/08/stranger-things-tim-ives-duffer-brothers-cinematography-emmys-interview-1202141889/

[10] Anon, *British Cinematographer*, 4K Special Report. Available at: https://britishcinematographer.co.uk/special-report-4k/

[11] Anon, *British Cinematographer*.

[12] Steve Hullfish, 'Art of the Cut with the Editors of Stranger Things'. Available at: https://www.provideocoalition.com/art-cut-editors-stranger- things/

[13] Hullfish, 'Art of the Cut with the Editors of Stranger Things'.

[14] Fred Zimmerman quoted in Hullfish, 'Art of the Cut with the Editors of Stranger Things'.

Creative flexibility, especially the ability to spend time experimenting before 'locking in' the final edit, was to have a significant effect on the production process. Since the 1990s, the ease of accessing shots from digital storage has eliminated the need to wait for video to roll before playing or editing. The post-production phase has been the most affected by digital technology, with time savings, as images can be arranged, rearranged and manipulated faster, as well as options in effects such as colourization. In high-end drama such as *Stranger Things*, the overall result is that editors can make decisions while focused on a particular scene. The attention paid to the editing, as well as other style elements overall, would allow for a more subtle and poetic approach while maintaining simplicity in the mise en scène.

Allusion and intertext

In the 1980s, Noël Carroll identified a growing use of allusion in Hollywood.[15] For him, allusion was a collective noun for many types of practices, including quotations, the memorialization of past genres, the reworking of past genres, homages, the recreation of 'classic' scenes, plot motifs, lines of dialogue, themes and gestures from film history.[16] An allusion to film history meant that informed viewers would recall past films while not taking this as plagiarism but as the 'expressive design of new films'. In this way, it was possible for a film-maker to allude to the iconography of an older film-maker such as Howard Hawks to form a symbolic structure that distinguishes the present from the past. In *Stranger Things*, the reworking of meanings creates a tension between the old and the new so that technology associated with a pre-digital age is regarded in the show as capable of breakdown and frustrating to use. For example, Mike and Nancy's father, Ted Wheeler, struggles to adjust the rabbit-eared TV set in episode one of the first season. There are also continual references to the 1980s within the mise en scène, including film posters from the time such as *Risky Business* (1983) in Nancy's bedroom (Mike's sister) and the mention of the role-playing fantasy game Dungeons and Dragons, played by Mike, Dustin and Lucas.

The ambition of the Duffer brothers was to create a storyworld based on allusion, whose hermeneutics derive from the semiotic excess in *Televisuality*,

---

[15] Noël Carroll, 'The Future of Allusion: Hollywood in the Seventies (and Beyond)', in *Interpreting the Moving Image* (Cambridge: Cambridge University Press, 1998), 240–64.
[16] Carroll, 'The Future of Allusion', 241.

as defined by Caldwell, as well as a reworking of the Spielberg-Amblin film universe. If a personal, authored vision of the world of *Stranger Things* exists, it relies concomitantly on an audience able to follow and tease out the mythologies contained within both the fantastic and the more domestic elements in *Stranger Things*. The tension between a personal vision and an audience selecting and emphasizing, as well as having an analytical perspective, complicates an understanding of the series. For Julia Kristeva, intertext is the notion that original or authorial meanings are reproduced from earlier texts.[17] For Mike Riffaterre, intertextuality is 'the perception ... of the relationship between a work and others that have either preceded or followed it'.[18] Television can be thought of as the quintessential postmodern medium that relies on recombination, re-functioning and pastiche. John Caughie remarked, 'In television studies, there seems to be a creeping sense that television is so thoroughly a technology of postmodernity – perhaps even the defining technology which makes the decisive break with the "modern age" and reshapes everyday life as postmodern – that all its forms must be *ipso facto* postmodernist.'[19] Within intertextuality, examples consist of intentional meanings that audiences are meant to recognize and that can be defined as 'works' belonging to the author. Such works invite decipherment of references drawn from past texts and can be aligned with poetics. In this way, allusion in *Stranger Things* is a type of intertext that operates as an exchange between producer and audience that animates his or her reading practice of the 'work'.

A possible mutuality between the Duffer brothers and the audience is used to create a 'cultural game': to display the signs of pop culture and knowledge that can be read as a subtle anti-literalizing device that attributes the meaning in *Stranger Things* to its creator. Pastiche is a distinct textual mode that closely resembles another text and the features of an author, genre or style. In richer texts, it can be argued, the enjoyment for many people is tied to the fact that the gaze of the cultivated, sophisticated arbiters of culture, for example, a 'media literate' audience, is attracted to the pastiche element in *Stranger Things* due to its complex style. This is not to say that there is a foregrounding of style over narrative but style marks the means by which authorship originates within the work, as well as summoning specific, extra-textual knowledge about the 1980s.

---

[17] Julia Kristeva, *Desire in Language: A Semiotic Approach to Literature and Art* (New York: Columbia University Press, 1980).
[18] Quoted in Gerard Genette, *Palimpsests: Literature in the Second Degree* (Lincoln: University of Nebraska Press, 1997), 2.
[19] John Caughie, *Television Drama: Realism, Modernism and British Culture* (Oxford: Oxford University Press, 2000), 163.

Analogue nostalgia

Vinyl records, cassette tapes, single-speed bikes, ham radio, walkie-talkies and Yoda action figures are a cognitive map to the series. The task of the style is to reconstruct the mythology of the 1980s, as part-explained by a remembrance of televisual heritage. Remembrance and reflection are made to operate within a cultural game as allusion becomes pastiche. The focusing by the Duffer brothers on textual meanings again suggests the role that authorship has in the formation of the show. However, the ludic appeal of *Stranger Things*, and its concentration on signifiers of the 1980s, is not only part of the increased stylization in high-end drama but also the creation of a common cultural heritage. Using allusion – specifically pastiche – is part of a desire to establish a community with its myths about government secrets labs and abducted children that uses display and spectacle to represent further tropes of pastiche.

Lynda Reiss, the props master, on *Stranger Things*, explains that TV is now of 'movie quality' and it's what people expect and she had to deliver. At the same time, she adds that she didn't 'want to do a nostalgia-tinged product.... I want it to be the '80s. I don't want it to be what everyone thinks is the '80s. Our baseline was the reality of the Midwest in 1983.'[20] The difficult challenge of finding original objects from the 1980s to go into the show began with items such as the Panasonic boom box to play cassettes. Other items such as Dungeons and Dragons books were replicas. One of the show's art directors handed Reiss his old books, which she scanned and copied for the show. The reliance on 'authenticity' of the objects demonstrates how much of the mythology of the series perfectly fits the streaming age of high-end drama. Unlike older drama and the earlier model of the mass audience, smaller niche audiences are loyal champions of ancillary products and secondary distribution windows contributing to profits.[21] Such audiences expect high production values, but, without a mass audience, companies such as Netflix have to operate what Caldwell refers to as 'tiering' or catering to a wide range of niche taste cultures.[22] If outside the scope of this book, the net effect of this means the reliance upon the lure of branded loyalty is to generate a distinct identity that can lead audiences to other media. Detail

---

[20] Tom Moynihan, 'The Stories Behind *Stranger Things* Retro '80s Props', *Wired*, 27 July 2016. Available at: https://www.wired.com/2016/07/stories-behind-stranger-things-retro-80s-props/
[21] Amanda Lotz, *The Television Will Be Revolutionized* (New York: New York University Press, 2007), 128.
[22] Caldwell, *Televisuality*, 124.

within the production design and its objects are one sign of this strategy that have led to the development of a multi-platform franchise of *Stranger Things* across four series.[23]

If Reiss was opposed to 'doing period' but wanted the show to have a physical texture – an indexicality going back to the original artefacts – it was lo-fi analogue redolent of particular feelings.

Yet, as we have already seen, aesthetic decisions to do with cinematography and editing create a tension between the pre-digital world and *Stranger Things* that raises issues about past and present works. Richard Dyer has sought to rescue pastiche from postmodernism.[24] Rather than a phenomenon belonging to late capitalism as a way of understanding recent history and culture, he argues it has existed in many historical periods, enabling form to article types of cultural heritage.[25] The use of nostalgia in *Stranger Things* suggests a sincerity of purpose to make it possible to experience the historicity of feelings for the 1980s. For Dyer, pastiche can 'recognize and mobilize the structure of feeling it perceives'[26] and both act as a celebration of older-screen entertainment and be a source of regret because the moment has passed when it was made. The moment of regret is, according to Jason Sperb, 'most intense during periods of dramatic cultural and technological upheaval, whereby the perceived reassurances of a simpler past anchor our perception of an uncertain present (and future)'.[27] Pastiche is, therefore, eminently historical, and its historicity raises awareness of an earlier stylistic mode, as well as a relationship between pastiche and affect.

The amount of nostalgia on television has increased greatly, and in the same year as the release of the first season of *Stranger Things*, reboots of 1990s shows such as *The X-Files* and *Full House* became zeitgeist hits. The rise of nostalgia is also visible on shows such as *Riverdale* (2017–20) and *Emerald City* (2017), as well as the first two seasons of *Fargo*, the Noah Hawley homage to the Coen brothers, looked at in Chapter 4.[28] All these shows have in common an underlying nostalgia that reveals the change in the television experience that

---

[23] The fourth series is to be released in 2021.
[24] Richard Dyer, *Pastiche* (London: Routledge, 2007), 131.
[25] For one of the best and earliest accounts on postmodernism as a manifestation of late capitalism, see Fredric Jameson, *Postmodernism: Or, The Cultural Logic of Late Capitalism* (Durham: Duke University Press, 1991).
[26] Dyer *Pastiche*, 130.
[27] Jason Sperb, *Flickers of Film: Nostalgia in the Time of Digital Cinema* (New Brunswick, Rutgers University Press, 2016).
[28] See also Max Sexton and Dominic Lees, 'Fargo: Seeing the Significance of Style in Television Poetics?', *Critical Studies in Television*, 14, no. 3 (September 2019): 343–61.

has been replaced by the digital, as television content is consumed on multiple platforms such as Netflix, Amazon but also YouTube and Vimeo. Older shows are re-watched online and the ghost of television's past is made to appear again. If shows are remade, standards of authenticity in nostalgic drama might require a rewind in technology to the broadcasting technology of the time complete with recording onto 4:3 tape and period lamps. However, *Stranger Things* is another reminder of the re-negotiation of value in style in screen entertainment. Certain films such as the neo-noir biographical crime movie *American Gangster* (2007) hearken back to an analogue era, whose texture uses, for example, super saturated colours. But this quality is absent in *Stranger Things*, and neither does the show reflect upon the physical experience of either going to the movies or watching television on tape by using humanizing elements that represent the mistakes of camera or lighting with analogue equipment. A recent experiment by the BBC of using vintage television cameras to shoot a comic horror episode of an anthology series came to the realization that the colorimetry of a tube-based camera was hard to fake in post-production, making it all the more poignant that the moment when drama could be shot and later enjoyed in certain ways has passed.[29] If shooting on a digital camera in *Stranger Things* offers a beautifully crisp image, it is too clean to create a sense of analogue authenticity and replaces it with the notion of a digital experience. This realization led Tim Ives, the show's DoP, to fit the Red camera with lenses that were softer and flatter than contemporary high contrasts – ignoring the preferred look for drama today – for a pastiche look.[30]

A complication to aesthetics in the show is the added fact that the Duffer brothers sought to emulate their favourite 1980s films, especially those from Amblin. However, the films were not watched at the cinema but on a home video recorder. If cinematic standards of cinematography and digital VFX compared to photochemical compositing exist in *Stranger Things*, the watching of film on video is an alternative remembrance. As well as past television, its historicity is a combination with other analogue media platforms that define the cultural landscape on which the show is based. The monster in the show, the Demogorgon, is familiar because it borrows not only from past television. According to the Duffer brothers, 'We grew up on genre films. . . . We're specifically thinking about Ridley Scott's Alien, John Carpenter's The Things

---

[29] Adam Tandy, 'Resurrecting the Ghost of TV Past', *Broadcast*, 16 December 2016: 24–5.
[30] Grobar, 'Stranger Things'.

and Clive Barker's Hellraiser.'³¹ Such memories foster feelings about a diverse heritage that validates the medium but one that incorporates watching films on videotape, reruns of films on television and finally other types of content specially for television, including the made-for-television film.

In this way, the series is a signifier of questions to do with aesthetics and textuality so that, if set in 1983, *Stranger Things* is also a twenty-first-century production, whose editing, as well as cinematography, can be set firmly against the look of a pre-digital world. Vinyl records and cassette tapes are reminders of a lack of clarity, especially tapes with 'hiss' in the sound. Similarly, the analogue exists as a sign of television heritage – a world of standard-definition 4:3 television without the benefit of home cinema with surround sound. The drawing of attention to obsolete technology appears in episode two, 'The Weirdo of Maple Street', when Mike boasts to Eleven about his family possessing a 22-inch television set.³² However, the slickly edited images are a continuing reminder of *Stranger Thing*'s method of production unlike anything that existed in 1980s television. In the show, the negotiation of value and quality in television drama draws on historical comparison in its pastiche of 1980s technology, fashion, bikes and board games. At the same time, the loss of clear formal distinctions between cinema and TV is a reminder of the tension in the show between its re-creation of the mythologies of a pre-cell, pre-computer graphics world and the use of digital cameras and VFX composition.

In these multiple ways, style in *Stranger Things* has to be as much judged by contextual and cultural factors as well as seeking its 'artistic qualities'. As pastiche, its place within television historiography tends to less privilege the authors of the show – the Duffer brothers – and their heroic story of bringing *Stranger Things* to the screen.³³ Instead of the strategy first pioneered by HBO in its attitude of delegitimizing older television, Netflix capitalizes on a televisual heritage that acknowledges the medium's metamorphosis. In *Stranger Things*, a type of period detail within its mise en scène is presumed to be more expressive as an indicator of artistic quality, as well as its more complex and detailed editing. For example, the production designer, Chris Trujillo, chose to 'craft' a 'vivid' period aesthetic

---

[31] Will Roberts, 'The '80s Movie That Most Inspired Netflix's "Stranger Things"', 31 January 2018. Available at: https://www.cheatsheet.com/entertainment/80s-movies-inspired-netflixs-stranger-things.html/
[32] Original TX, 15 July 2016.
[33] See the chapter 'Things Come Together', in *Stranger Things: The Official Behind-the-Scenes Companion* (London: Century, 2018), 19–45.

for the series.³⁴ For him, the colour palette would generate verisimilitude strictly in photographic terms. The palette would be autumnal rather than the garish colours he associated with the 1980s. 'I see Indiana as being fall-colored – rusts and rich yellows and the oranges and red brick and the creamy whites. . . . We wanted to feel the green of the forest, your tree-trunk browns, and that [sense of the town is] all hemmed in by nature.'³⁵ Such an approach complicates the moment of pastiche of the 1980s in the show as not part of the memory of images from the era but a broader desire by the show's makers for photorealism.

The fact that *Stranger Things* refers to a variety of cultural influences, including role-playing board games, novels, music and clothing, has to be understood as the effort to construct not only verisimilitude but part of a larger effort to evoke new cultural relationships between television and film. This includes the canon of private film-viewing experiences within the home, as well as the domestic repetition of the theatrical Amblin universe once it had reached TV. In *Stranger Things*, the setting of the story in Indiana anchors shots to be evocative of a photorealistic Midwest, but its cross section of American suburban life as it follows the Mike Wheeler and Joyce Byers families exists within a complex system of allusion.

Screen monsters and heritage

If the Duffer brothers' first experience of popular films was from television – including watching in 1989 ads for Tim Burton's *Batman* – the re-circulation of the mythologies of horror on television existed before the 1980s. In *Stranger Things*, the reworking of the King books and Spielberg films matches what Noël Carroll refers to as memorialization. For Carroll, if already visible in Spielberg's *Raiders of the Lost Ark* (1981), memorialization is not a replica of earlier B films and theatrical serials but a reverie 'on the glorious old days . . . heightening the excitement of *Raider's* potboiler prototypes [so] that they are finally as breathtaking as we want to remember them.'³⁶ Pastiche in *Stranger Things* relies on the prototypical features of authors and styles from 1980s pop culture but also a sense of the 'Golden Age' of television, as it has become mythologized

---

³⁴ Gina McIntyre, *Stranger Things: The Official Behind-the-Scenes Companion* (London: Century, 2018), 49.
³⁵ Quoted in McIntyre, *Stranger Things*, 51.
³⁶ Carroll, 'The Future of Allusion', 248.

by its creators as an age of innocence. At the SAG awards, David Harbour's acceptance speech was to extol how the show's values coincided with making America great again, 'where we are more accepting of . . . people being flawed and weird and strange'.[37] The odd pairing of the idea of making America great again with an older, more humane society was overlooked as it went viral, but it should be recalled that the sources for the prototypes of *Stranger Thing*'s 1980s heroes, villains and monsters were themselves indebted to 1950s prototypes.

After Universal's rights had lapsed, the *Flash Gordon* serials first appeared on US television in 1951. Later, the growth of a specific form, the telefilm, meant that television deployed a heterogeneous aesthetic in the 1950s and 1960s that ranged across many types of material, although the dominant rhetoric was borrowed from the cinema, consisting of framing, lighting and editing. But on television, such rhetoric was affected by the size of the smaller screen, and modes of film technique were modified.

At the same time, the 1960s saw a significant shift in an understanding of American culture on television when *The Addams Family* (1964–6) and *The Munsters* (1964–6) ushered in one of the first celebrations of popular culture: the monster phenomenon of ghoulish delights that recalled the Universal horror films of the 1930s. The success of *The Munsters* series made it clear that the relationship between film and television could be very close when Herman Munster became a comic reprisal of the role Boris Karloff had played as the Frankenstein monster (1931), and Grandpa, played by Al Lewis, became an over-the-hill but not quite dead Dracula. The fondness for monsters and its syndicated repeats, including two animated series in the 1970s of *The Addams Family*, made the two dysfunctional families one of the most well-known in America.

The TV movie pre-dated the miniseries and had been prompted by the need to replace a diminishing reserve of feature films that had been released to television by Hollywood.[38] Once a week in the schedules each network of the time would present a made-for-TV movie or a theatrical film. However, shifts in the character of the audience caused by the rise of satellite and cable broadcasting caused the three major US networks to turn increasingly to 'event' programming. Television was soon adapting the novels of Stephen King, including the mythical

---

[37] Quoted in Laura Bradley, 'Stranger Things Star David Harbour Explains His "Fiery" SAG Awards Speech', *Vanity Fair*, 30 January 2017. Available at: https://www.vanityfair.com/hollywood/2017/01/stranger-things-david-harbour-sag-awards-speech-winona-ryder

[38] One of the first TV movies was an adaptation of Hemingway's short story, *The Killers* (1964), which because of its inclusion of too much violence was released to the cinema instead.

universe of vampires in *Salem's Lot* (1979), for ABC. Opposed to a clearly defined threat (vampires), David Soul, as the main character of Ben Mears, was deployed within a visual style in which 'themes are generally played out by no more than a handful of protagonists on a very personal level'.[39] Other television horror shows, similarly, adapted a source text as a version of classic narrative cinema that depended on a single originator or could be considered canonical. The telefilm had adapted a cinematic style, but instead of a heightened use of stylization in theatrical horror films, the visual style was unobtrusively subordinated to telling the story, with a reliance on close-ups and medium shots, high-key lighting and continuity editing. For Gary Edgerton, the 'video realism' of the telefilm was suited to stories that concentrated on individual characters.[40] The relatively poor definition of the small screen would have made it a problem depicting special effects and creating a sophisticated visual composition. However, as we have seen, in *Stranger Things*, digital production technologies, particularly nonlinear editing, enable greater depth and more complexity in the construction of character subjectivity and psychical point of view, marrying televisual style to the earlier narrative concerns of the genre (trauma and the monstrous).

In *Stranger Things*, the desire for a feeling of the past suggests a fidelity to the early 1980s. However, the show is a hybrid, combining digital composited elements within discrete props of tape recorders, walkie-talkies and boom boxes that celebrate nostalgia. Moreover, the gap between past and present production values creates a further type of nostalgia. For Svetlana Boym, reflective nostalgia is the practice of exploring the unexplored potentialities in past and ongoing narratives of culture and technology.[41] Reflection, longing and affection go together to start a dialogue with the past. This can include a hybrid indexicality of the material and digitally reimagining, in which the viewer's extra-textural awareness of the digital also plays a role in reflecting on the historicity of pastiche in the show. Production designer Chris Trujillo, cinematographer Chris Ives and special effects coordinator Caius Man collaborated closely to plan the monster and Upside Down world. Their cue was set by the Duffer brothers, who argued:

> It has always been something of a lifelong dream to create a monster and bring it to life on-screen. Not in the computer, but for real. To build it. Like so many filmmakers our age and older, we grew up on genre films that existed before

---

[39] Gary Edgerton, 'The American Made-for-TV Movie', in Brian G. Rose (ed.), *TV Genres* (Westport: Greenwood Press, 1985), 165.
[40] Edgerton, 'The American Made-for-TV Movie', 165.
[41] Svetlana Boym, *The Future of Nostalgia* (New York City: Basic Books, 2001), xvi–xvii.

computer graphics. There was something about the effects being so tangible in those films So from very early on we knew we wanted to build an animatronic monster.⁴²

The monstrous predator of the Demogorgon was designed to be played on set by an actor wearing prosthetic make-up and a foam rubber costume.⁴³ An opposition between animatronics and computer-generated imagery (CGI) can be placed into the wider context of digitally animated bodies becoming common after 2000 in films. Impossible bodies in fantastical situations in productions such as *Hulk* (2003) were produced using a combination of performance capture and digital key frame animation and compositing. However, film reviewers such as Roger Ebert were to criticize these earlier attempts at digital animation.⁴⁴ Ebert accused them of zipping along like perfunctory cartoons, and Mark Kermode, reviewing *Spiderman* (2004), remained 'not entirely convinced by the CGI spidey trespassing into areas of digital animation which seem peculiarly out of place in Raimi's otherwise relentlessly physical universe'.⁴⁵ However, *Lord of the Rings* (2001) was able to render not only physical motion but the CGI character of Gollum, which led Charles Taylor to say, 'There wasn't a moment he [Gollum] was on screen when I felt I could take my eyes off him. He is the most amazing of this installment's wonders.'⁴⁶ The reception of digitally constructed bodies by the critics becomes a binary opposition between digitally replicated figures that replicate cartoons or children's video games and the visual experience of reality. According to Lisa Purse, 'even though the presence of the digital seems to overturn the claim to indexicality more incontrovertibly than ever, what persists is the principle of measuring verisimilitude (believability) in terms of the extent to which the image *looks* as if it has been photographed by a real camera [original italics]'.⁴⁷ For the Duffer brothers, monster movies of the 1970s and 1980s were able to offer an 'elegant simplicity' and the fetishized experience of images that can be trusted or tell the truth. This was made more possible because

---

⁴² Quoted in Amy Rust, 'Analog Nostalgia and the Promise of Props in the Digital Age', *Post45*, 7 April 2019. Available at: http://post45.research.yale.edu/2019/07/analog-nostalgia-and-the-promise-of-props-in-the-digital-age/
⁴³ McIntyre, *Stranger Things*, unpaginated.
⁴⁴ Roger Ebert, *Spider-Man* film review, *Chicago Sun Times*, 3 May 2002. Available at: https://www.rogerebert.com/reviews/spider-man-2002
⁴⁵ Mark Kermode, *Spider-Man* film review, *The Observer*, 18 July 2002. Available at: https://www.theguardian.com/theobserver/2004/jul/18/features.review37
⁴⁶ Charles Taylor, 'The Lord of the Rings: The Two Towers', *Salon*, 19 December 2002. Available at: https://www.salon.com/2002/12/18/two_towers/
⁴⁷ Lisa Purse, *Digital Imaging in Popular Cinema* (Edinburgh: Edinburgh University Press, 2013), 59.

the nostalgia in *Stranger Things* suggests a past that truly existed rather than a fictional world. The photorealism of the Demogorgon is linked back to the mise en scène because it suggests nostalgia is a reliable tool that is able to repeat the past world, as well as the feelings and experience of the historical moment.

Trust in images is how *Stranger Things* captures the viewer's experience of what is imagined to be the 1980s. The monstrous is part of this overall strategy and matches the same meta-text presented by Winona Ryder in her role as Joyce Byers, mother of Will Byers, who has been abducted. In films such as *Beetlejuice* (1988) and *Edward Scissorhands* (1990), she had appeared alongside various monstrous outsiders. The viewer's familiarity with her as a performer reacting to outlandish and absurd situations is a memory that mobilizes a structure of feeling and moment of reflection, which makes the viewer aware of the show's historical constructedness but also the historicity of feelings. The perceptual realism in *Stranger Things* depends on not only cues which display colour, texture and movement of the Demogorgon but how they feed back into the thematic framework of nostalgia in the show.

The team of Trujillo, Ives and Man scoured a range of films, including the early work of body-horror auteur David Cronenberg.[48] To fabricate vines and tendrils belonging to the Upside Down, the special effects team utilized bubble wrap and sheet plastic, which were heated until they melted and then painted. Clear latex was stretched and became the webbing for the alien world. Rather than VFX to create the monster and its colourless underworld overrun by death and decay, according to Man, 'We spent three months fooling around with every chemical and flexible stretchy thing and meltable thing we could lay our hand on.'[49] Upside Down met the requirements of the Duffers to use a minimum of DVFX and instead build a physical, material world. They believed it would add texture and depth that felt real. Yet the props add no more texture than a suitable digital effect. The effort to create a physical alien world can be attributed largely to a need to live up to the affective needs of the viewer than a desire for photorealism. Later, the scenes of Eleven's psychokinetic powers include a stop motion shot of a van flying through the air. In episode seven of the first season, 'The Bathtub', a van is made to soar overhead Mike and Eleven.[50] The effect was accomplished using two nitrogen cannons that physically fired the van. Two images of the van and the children were cropped together to produce the

---

[48] McIntyre, *Stranger Things*, unpaginated.
[49] McIntyre, *Stranger Things*, unpaginated.
[50] Original TX, 15 July 2016.

final image of the vehicle soaring above them. The combination of the sound and image of the van crashing to the ground provides a sense of density and bulk and emphasizes the show's commitment to the physical and tangible. However, by season two, more effects were accomplished using VFX rather than material effects. Nevertheless, a useful narrative about special effects whose nostalgic works had already been established in the show worked well with its audience.

Netflix has a track record of investing in drama that provides nostalgia. *Stranger Things* is a product of this strategy. As we have seen, Netflix had already invested in revivals of shows like *Full House* as *Fuller House* (2016–20) and *Riverdale* and capitalized on the economic success of nostalgia. However, unlike film, the legitimation of television has been less based on a canon but instead on the idea of heritage that suggests a lived experience of culture. In *Stranger Things*, heritage as the embodiment of the memory of television blurs the sense of actual history (the 1980s), as mythologies to do with the telefilm and videotape are celebrated. Such a strategy opens up further questions about recent high-profile drama, whose deployment of nostalgia makes it a site of ongoing industrial and cultural debate about recent textual reconfiguration. In other shows too, the authorial agency of television drama segues with the 'brand-name vision' of its network and becomes a key to its reception, while relying on nostalgia and popular memory.

Boardwalk Empire (2010–14) and *Vinyl* (2016)

Set in New York in 1973, *Vinyl* was produced by Martin Scorsese and Terence Winter, who had also produced and written *The Sopranos* (1999–2007) as well as Scorsese's earlier venture into television, *Boardwalk Empire* (2010–14). Mick Jagger, the lead singer of the Rolling Stones, was also to contribute to the story in the pilot and to become an executive producer. But it was Winter who convinced Scorsese to make *Vinyl* a television series rather than the originally intended film.[51] The publicity from HBO for the show quickly capitalized on Scorsese's reputation as a director whose Academy awards were meant to strengthen the appeal of the forthcoming show.[52] Scorsese had already won an

---

[51] Allison Bowsher, 'Mick Jagger and Martin Scorsese Talk the Making of HBO's Vinyl', *Much*. Available at: https://www.much.com/mick- jagger-martin-scorsese-hbos-vinyl/

[52] Filiipa Jodelka, 'Scratch That: HBO's Vinyl Is a Jagger and Scorsese Stinker', *The Guardian*, 15 February 2016. Available at: https://www.theguardian.com/tv-and-radio/2016/feb/15/vinyl-jagger-scorsese

Emmy for his direction of *Boardwalk* Empire – a drama set in the 1920s about the entanglements of Prohibition. Equally, the prospect of an elite art form had been part of HBO's appeal since, at least, the 1990s. Amanda Lotz explains how 'HBO thrives by defying program standards that appeal to the mass audience, and succeeds by exploiting limited access as the means of acceptance as high (or at least higher) elite art'.[53] Themes about sin and redemption, which have dominated much of Scorsese's canon, would reappear in *Vinyl*. The choice of Scorsese marks the continuing interest by movie directors of reconfiguring a film project into television drama. *Vinyl* would be shot in thirty-five days, and the first episode – the sole episode directed by Scorsese – was shot less like a two-hour pilot but as a film, according to HBO president Michael Lombardo.[54] Additionally, Scorsese was more involved with *Vinyl* than *Boardwalk Empire* because he was able to select the cast and oversee the editing of the nine episodes he did not direct.

Aesthetic excellence was the type of original content that HBO as a premiere US cable channel had already claimed to offer in shows such as Alan Ball's *Six Feet Under* (2001–5) and David Chase's *The Sopranos*. However, with the rise of competition especially from streaming technology, *Boardwalk Empire* was a reaffirmation of HBO's indispensability to producing lavish period detail, as well as a sense of hierarchy between cable and streaming providers. The idea of a canon has been problematic for television, but it has been attractive to channels such as HBO because it concentrates on specific texts as a method of discriminating between types of programmes and cultural meanings. In the case of *Boardwalk Empire*, Terence Winter and Scorsese agreed that despite the lavishness, they would opt for verisimilitude and aim for a shabby elegance. Yet, the show struggled to a degree to assume the status of a 'great text' and one that might seek inclusion in a canon of television classics as critics detected 'something rather lifeless about it'.[55] If the vernacular of New Jersey evokes historical verisimilitude, the attempt at a television saga that disrupts audience expectations due to its lavish eclecticism was, in fact, more of a reminder of *Rome* (2005–7). Like *Rome*, *Boardwalk Empire* would recreate a past place and time, but the aesthetics and style would follow an ambitious trend.

---

[53] Amanda Lotz quoted in Avi Santos, 'Para-Television and Discourses of Distinction', in Marc Leverette et al. (eds), *It's Not TV: Watching HBO in the Post-Television Era* (London: Routledge, 2008), 33.

[54] Tatiana Siegel, 'Personal Best', *Emmy*, 38, no. 2 (2016): 60–5.

[55] John Crace, 'TV Review: Boardwalk Empire', *The Guardian*, 2 February 2011. Available at: https://www.theguardian.com/tv-and- radio/2011/feb/02/tv-review-boardwalk-empire

Variety puts the cost of the eighty-minute pilot of *Boardwalk Empire* at $18 million and the cost of the twelve episodes first season at $65 million.[56] The cost of the pilot included construction of a 300-foot-long boardwalk with period perfect storefronts, including the infamous baby incubator shopfront. A strip of ersatz beach was added by driving in tons of sand. Overall, the effect was to create an impression of 'Times Square on the ocean'. Voluminous research to construct the centre of the saga derived from newspapers of the period, but Winter lists also reading from John Dos Passos's *USA Trilogy*, Herbert Asbury's *An Informal History of Prohibition*, E. L. Doctorow's *Ragtime* and Daniel Okrent's *Last Call: The Rise and Fall of Prohibition*. According to Winter, the in-depth historical research led to the use of arcane detail in the show, including the fact that phone use was still novel and people would answer it with a variety of greetings, such as 'ahoy', 'hail' and 'greetings'.[57] The wardrobe department had the task of clothing a cast of about 150. Production designer Bob Shaw explains, 'We ended up building a lot of [outfits] from pieces of older clothing because the vintage clothing would shred as soon as you put somebody in them.'[58] Costume designer John Dunn would scour the libraries of the Fashion Institute of Technology, the Metropolitan Library of Congress, and Martin Scorsese would compile a film reel of 1920s fashion to take while visiting New York vintage shops and Los Angeles costume warehouses.[59]

Both *Boardwalk Empire* and Scorsese's second venture into television drama, *Vinyl*, have merited the value of a television series by its look. However, as Janet McCabe points out in *Boardwalk Empire*, 'The sepia tone colour palette, chiaroscuro lighting and bravura tracking shots determine the distinctive look of this period piece told in a televisual present tense.'[60] The past is reclaimed through current formal techniques. In other words, there is an imagined past that reflects a particular era's iconography (1920s) but also a meta-textual control of the period as it is depicted on the screen. McCabe adds, 'The Pilot thus puts into discourse the unique response of the series to history, deliberately echoing past visual forms, techniques and genres *in* and *through* how its cinematography,

---

[56] Cynthia Littlemore, 'HBO Lays a Big-Bucks Bet on "Boardwalk"', *Variety*, 7 August 2010. Available at: https://variety.com/2010/tv/features/hbo-lays-a-big-bucks-bet-on-boardwalk-1118022673/
[57] Mike Flaherty, 'Scorsese Takes over from *The Sopranos*', *The Times*, 18 September 2000: 5.
[58] Flaherty, 'Scorsese Takes over from *The Sopranos*'.
[59] Elizabeth Snead, 'Boardwalk Empire' Costume Designer John Dunn Finds the Color', *Deadline*, 19 June 2011. Available at: https://deadline.com/2011/06/emmys-boardwalk-empire-costume-designer-john-dunn-finds-the-color-141327/
[60] Janet McCabe, 'HBO Aesthetics, Quality Television and *Boardwalk Empire*', in Jason Jacobs and Steven Peacock (eds), *Television Aesthetics and Style* (London: Bloomsbury, 2013), 185–97.

aesthetics choices and VFX technologies conserves but reinterprets, to create prestigious television [original italics]'.[61] Ultimately, the artful reworking of the gangster myth in *Boardwalk Empire* relies on the aesthetics and genre forms in the American cultural canon, helping to determine its own value in terms of a period piece within HBO's business model of attracting the affluent and selective cable viewer.

The appeal of *Boardwalk Empire*'s digital aesthetics operates to aggregate eyeballs, and its glamorous aesthetics emphasize its chromatic elements, including dramatic lighting and contrasts. A chromatic remediation exists where digital manipulation attaches a cinematic feel to television images. The use of spectacular lighting creates not a representation of the past but a desire for the show to be felt immediately at a haptic level. Jason Jacobs comments on the exploitation of VFX in *Boardwalk Empire* that its 'vivid colour and dynamic range' creates a spectacle which is 'somewhere between a Magritte and HDR landscape photography'.[62] The high-quality look of *Boardwalk Empire* was achieved by the Süperfad Agency, which was also responsible for the promotional campaign of its release. A special hue was created for what became known as 'Nucky carnation'. The character of Enoch 'Nucky' Thompson (Steve Buscemi), the kingpin of Atlantic county, wears a fresh red carnation on a daily basis. His taste in clothes and colour is bold. The colour of the carnation is obtained in monochrome that involved a process of partial desaturation followed by the emphasis on a single hue. The result was the carnation became a gloomy, dense crimson shade with marked black accents.

The high production values of *Boardwalk Empire* point to how lurid tonalities disengage with historical realism but are commercially valuable. Moreover, Scorsese has argued that colour is 'splashed all over the consciousness of popular culture'.[63] The use of colour interrelates the visual with the tactile, endowing of the image with a felt sensuality. If costumes and props were developed with a goal of historical accuracy, colour grading using state-of-the-art VFX technologies was less about excavating the past. Rather, colour serves to refashion history into a lurid pastiche of saturated reds. The use of the carnation is a recurring cue about moral degeneration and is attached to other moments within the mise en

---

[61] McCabe, 'HBO Aesthetics, Quality Television and *Boardwalk Empire*', 187.
[62] Jason Jacobs, 'Up and Down with Boardwalk Empire', *Critical Studies in Television*, 29 October 2011. Available at: https://cstonline.net/up-and-down-with-boardwalk-empire-by-jason-jacobs/
[63] Mark Kermode, 'Martin Scorsese: '3D Is Liberating. Every Shot Is Rethinking Cinema', *Observer*, 25 January 2012. Available at: www.guardian.co.uk/film/2010/nov/21/martin-scorsese-3d-interview-kermode/print

scène, including a stripper's lipstick and garments. The carnation is also used in contrast to alabaster skin tones, the hue directing attention to the most sensual features of the female characters, such as the shape of lips, breast or hair colour. At other times mute, desaturated hues are used. The opening titles and the vivid cyan, yellow and brown are designed not to recover the past but prove the show's aesthetic virtuosity. Although, the use of muted colour to evoke a sense of decadence exposes the production design as period pieces, inviting a nostalgic reaction to them. Such 'affective mapping' suggests the need to navigate a space whose own visual processes can be understood as the remediation of digital cinematic aesthetics for the television but with some extra attention to film history.

If a strong proponent of shooting on digital video, Scorsese has also been intensely nostalgic for a cinematic past. Films such as *The Aviator* (2004) and *Hugo* (2011), as well as *Boardwalk Empire*, are carefully observed period pieces that negotiate the relationship between past and present cinematic mediation. McCabe mentions how the opening of *Boardwalk Empire* begins with an iris-in on a close-up of a meticulously period pocket watch before the ethereal fog 'conjures ghostly echoes of films like *L'Atlante*' (1934), directed by Jean Virgo.[64] The invocation of French poetic realism and Scorsese's homage of it in *Boardwalk Empire* not only signals his celebration of film history but also (using Dyer's understanding of pastiche) allows audiences to experience film as past audiences would have done. Yet, in the case of digital cinema, John Belton has pointed out that this might lead to an all-fantasy cinema as each film becomes a meditation on a dream or nightmare.[65] Similarly, *Boardwalk Empire*, like Scorsese's recent films, is a show that conflates history with cinematic meditations of the past. Terence Winter has said that 'the best film class you've had is Martin Scorsese sitting with you watching gangster movies'.[66] The films they watched together consisted of *The Public Enemy* (1931), *The Roaring Twenties* (1939) and *Scarface* (1980). In *Boardwalk Empire*, Scorsese's status as a canonical film-maker is embedded as much as the cinematic past to offer an impossibly perfect vision of 1920s New Jersey. Criticisms directed at the series of 'trying too hard to tick all the boxes' may serve to fit the commercial imperatives governing HBO and its notions of exclusivity or 'original content'. However, idealization forbids social reality and complicates an understanding

[64] McCabe, 'HBO Aesthetics, Quality Television and *Boardwalk Empire*', 185.
[65] John Belton, 'Digital Cinema: A False Revolution?', *October*, v100 (Spring 2002): 98–114.
[66] Flaherty, 'Scorsese Takes over from *The Sopranos*', 5.

of the past because it is centred less on an actual time or moment of history and more on film itself. The confusion arises whether a series like *Boardwalk Empire* or *Vinyl* should be understood as historical fidelity rather than digital homage as Scorsese has ventured into television drama after his cinematic achievements.

Despite Belton's observation of the digital becoming all-fantasy cinema – its tricks more a sense of film history rather than actual lived history – *Boardwalk Empire* was able to produce an epic that incorporated ordinary family life. Breakfast in the Darmody household includes shots of the young son stirring his porridge as his father makes plans for the arrival of Prohibition. How the personal is embedded into the gratifications of appreciating the director's cinephilia continues to mark the interplay of style techniques on television and the context of viewing, first remarked on in Chapter 2. In this way, Scorsese's attempts at lavish detail provide mixed textual pleasures that rely on not only the looked at material object of the television text but, in *Vinyl*, more sensual aspects to do with the music and other sense impressions that are evocative of the past.

Vinyl: Musical nostalgia

Vinyl was about the beginnings of punk, hip hop and disco, which were created in near proximity within New York's thriving music scene. The two-hour premiere directed by Scorsese establishes the characters of Richie Finestra, played by Bobby Cannavale, as a record executive trying to resurrect his label, American Century, as well as Zak Yankovich, played by Ray Romano, head of promotions for American Century, and Olivia Wilde as Devon Finestra, Richie's wife, who was once part of Andy Warhol's Factory. Naturally enough, the music plays a significant part in the show's 1970s nostalgia, including Cannavale meeting David Bowie and Led Zeppelin, as well as making visible 1970s props and fashion. As well as the music, the show concentrated on the sleaziness of the 1970s music business and its violence and greed. We first meet Richie buying drugs in the abandoned streets of New York's SoHo before wandering into the Mercer Arts Centre to watch a show by the New York Dolls.

Vinyl draws upon digital cinematic techniques from the Scorsese oeuvre which is not dissimilar to *Boardwalk Empire*, including a clear sense of nostalgia. However, another influence is forms of reflection that explore memory as an understanding of marking the music with the domestic pleasure of sitting down and watching television. The historiographic power of *Vinyl* engages with rock music and includes television within its shaping of cultural memory, unlike other projects by Scorsese. In this way, *Vinyl* can be compared more closely to *Stranger Things*, whose visual style is interplayed with a past that depends more on televisual representation than historical fidelity. Emotions associated with rock music can be argued to occupy a space informed by television programming schedules from the 1960s and 1970s, including when Suzi Quatro would appear on *Happy Days* looking more 1970s than 1950s as the bass player, Leather Tuscadero, on the hit show.

In the early 1970s, rock music was moving towards super groups, preparing the path for punk that sought to rediscover rock's genesis as an unpretentious and accessible cultural form. By 1973, Led Zeppelin was on its ninth North American tour that would see excess celebrated using a series of pyrotechnics and effects and the band dressed in clothes of a flamboyant nature, including Jimmy Page's hummingbird jacket. Meanwhile, the New York Dolls, supported by other groups such as 'Television', wore a concoction of thrift store and Salvation Army clothing. Equally, the music had a pared-down sound. The appearance of bands such as the Dolls highlights how they were evocative of a private relationship with music listened to on Vinyl, as well as on radio and television: the New York Dolls would appear on the BBC's *Old Grey Whistle Test* in November 1973. Live music on TV was important, and shows such as the *Old Grey Whistle Test* formed a synergy between it and the albums' boom of the early 1970s with the rise of high-fidelity equipment in the home. Other rock stars that appear in *Vinyl* were familiar sights on television in the 1970s. Alice Cooper, the godfather of shock rock, came to fame in the early 1970s and appeared in *The Snoop Sisters* (1973–4), airing on NBC. In the episode 'The Devil Made Me Do It', Cooper is involved in a satanic cult as the sisters unravel a mystery murder.[67] The sight of Alice Cooper preparing a prop guillotine with the conjuror the Amazing Randi becomes a shared experience, whose representation in 'Whispering Secrets', episode three of *Vinyl*, marks a historical moment that further relies on popular memory.[68,69]

After one season, HBO in June 2016 chose to cancel the show. In the pilot, Andrea Zito, an image consultant employed to resurrect American Century Records, explains, 'If you wanna change your image, you don't just get a new

[67] Original TX, 5 March 1974.
[68] The Amazing Randi would also appear on *Happy Days* in 1978.
[69] Original TX, 28 February 2016.

shirt, honey. We must be an assault on the past.' *Vinyl* seeks to permit viewers to see and feel what it must have been like in the past using a style that is playfully seeking not an accurate 'truth' but an affective sense of the past. Mimesis is provided by fashions and props, as well as social attitudes, but the eventual failure of *Vinyl* demonstrates how representations of nostalgia adapted to television are not always successful. *Life on Mars* (2008–9) was able to examine changing social attitudes in the main character of Sam Tyler as he travels in time back to 1973. Similarly, authenticity in high-end television drama bands different feelings together as a source of meaning. In *Vinyl*, Zito, Ritchie's former co-worker, is unimpressed with in-house designer Hal Underwood's logo prototypes. For him, the future of the record business is about a rupture from past artists to be replaced by embracing the first signees to the label, the proto-punk Nasty Bits. Yet, as Don Draper in Mad Men reminds us, 'Nostalgia . . . is a twinge in your heart far more powerful than memory alone . . . it takes us to a place where we ache to go again. . . . It's not called the wheel. It's called the carousel.'[70] In the pilot episode of *Vinyl* rather than an assault on the past, the Nasty Bits receive a lesson about the importance of affection for the past.

Vinyl purports an authenticity about the excess in the music industry using the cachet of Scorsese and Jagger, but the production design and props fetishize the past beginning with obvious codes about a rock show reflected in Ritchie's aviator sunglasses. Similarly, we have scuffed-up lettering of the logo that suggests not so much a historical moment but the exercise of nostalgia. If like *Stranger Things*, the set design and costuming was aesthetically perfect, it was like its predecessor, a hyper-reality using high-end image-making techniques. For example, close-up shots linger over analogue media, including the office reel-to-reel tape in Ritchie's office, the chunky AM radio in his limo as well as numerous record players. The effect is to re-negotiate the value of a high-end series in terms of an exalted cultural form. The music from the series was released two days before the series was broadcast by Atlantic and Warner Brothers Records, and the music budget for each episode was reported to be six figures and featuring up to thirty songs.[71] Randall Poster and Meghan Currier, the music supervisors, paid close attention to the instruments and studio equipment to ensure they were of the period. However, the music was to sell the current show rather than

---

[70] Quoted in season 1, episode 13, 'The Wheel', original TX, 18 October 2007.
[71] Melinda Newman, 'HBO's Vinyl Series Soundtrack to Feature Otis Redding, Sturgill Simpson, David Johansen', *Billboard*, 15 January 2016. Available at: https://www.billboard.com/articles/news/6843767/hbo-vinyl-soundtrack-exclusive

serve the telling of the story. The retro aesthetics of the music and other elements demonstrate in *Vinyl* the limits of memories of material cultures from the past and the construction of a high-end television based on hierarchies of value and a canon of music and styles.

Conclusion

If nostalgia has become important in both film and television, in the case of the latter, it is as much about how it has framed an understanding of the past to do with an imaginary that can be labelled 'televisionland'. The economic value of *Stranger Things* can be ascribed to digital aesthetics and its remediation from the cinema to television. Moreover, high-end image-producing techniques point to a continuing canon amid cultural and technological changes. However, *Stranger Things* and, to a degree, *Vinyl* rely on an understanding of how the intimacy of engaging with television (including films watched on domestic video) is reflective of a shared experience of viewing. Formal possibilities can therefore be understood by its interpellation with television consumption.

In the case of *Stranger Things*, such engagement can be linked back to the Duffer brothers growing up in front of the television, watching favourite films at home on video. Other cultural references, including the game of Dungeons and Dragons, are generationally specific to appeal to anyone who grew up in that time. Yet the idea behind 'televisionland' suggests a constant circulation of culture which is cross-generational and a constantly evolving television heritage, allowing for the interplay between old and new. Examples of US television drama have reorganized the act of viewing into discourses about memory and nostalgia. Such feelings about the past suggest another interpretative purpose of the shows looked at in this chapter. A larger meta-textual aesthetic has been created. If the Duffer brothers have in *Stranger Things* sought to use latex visual effects and a 'stunt guy in a suit' for the Demogorgon, the issue is not how close to physical realism the show has become. Rather, the use of retro technology or the setting of Hawkins, Indiana, asks how such shows have added cultural and economic purpose.

In the shows looked at in this chapter, the iconography of nostalgia exists, but we are made aware of the repackaging of nostalgia into its 'retro-feel' – an ersatz past whose highly stylized look serves either Netflix or HBO economically.

Equally, the deployment of style, including music, makes the shows more accessible and creates a tension between its digital cinematography and a sense of personal anecdote and reminiscence. The personal experience of the Duffer brothers or listening to album music guarantees the mythologies in shows about the 1980s or 1970s, which, in turn, raises questions about how style has become a desire to see the past through contemporary eyes and its link to television history.

6

Performance modes in collision

The Leftovers

A key methodology of this book is the close study of style, in order to expand the understanding of Televisuality in recent high-end TV drama. A close reading of performance in *The Leftovers* (HBO, 2013–17) demonstrates not only the nuance of tormented souls but also the diverse portrayal of a range of characters. An interest in the work of actors and their presentation on screen is not to separate performance from the many other elements of style that support the viewer's reading of a televisual text. Instead, it is to highlight the development of new sensibilities and performance modes in one example of high-end drama. A discussion of recent acting modes has gathered pace in television studies,[1] although leading theorists have noted that, in comparison with the specific traditions seen in other media, 'the same tradition of actor-focused research does not currently exist in relation to television drama'.[2]

Nevertheless, it should be noted that within the analysis of 'high-end' television, Christine Cornea views the study of performance as increasingly significant in developing the characteristics of contemporary American drama:

> The arrival of what is commonly called 'quality' television has also increased the relevance of performance as central to the meaning and success of a genre series: if film genres were often criticised for their one-dimensional characters, then recent television drama series seem to have taken those characters and added a depth, complexity and degree of reflexivity that foregrounds the work of the performer.[3]

---

[1] For example, Christine Cornea (ed.), *Genre and Performance: Film and Television* (Manchester: Manchester University Press, 2010); Tom Cantrell and Christopher Hogg, *Acting in British Television* (Basingstoke: Palgrave Macmillan, 2016); 'Acting on Television: Analytical Methods and Approaches', themed edition of *Critical Studies in Television*, 13, no. 3 (September 2018).

[2] Tom Cantrell and Christopher Hogg, 'Returning to an Old Question: What Do Television Actors Do When They're Acting?' *Critical Studies in Television*, 1, no. 3 (September 2016): 284.

[3] Cornea, *Genre and Performance*, 10–11.

Cornea's analysis refers more specifically to performance in television drama of the 1980s and 1990s, and she is making a broad point about acting within generic products. However, the highlighting of television drama's ability to add depth to performance contributes to the debate about contemporary high-end drama. In this chapter, the development of the work of the actor in *The Leftovers* is linked to what Jason Mittell describes as 'a new model of storytelling [. . .] narrative complexity'.[4]

The analysis of television performance carries inherent methodological problems. The raw data for any discussion is the final recording of actors in the completed television show. Yet, there are multiple processes that generate screen performance – a sequence of collaborations between the actor and other creative personnel that culminates in the final work on screen. However, a style-based analysis of performance is concerned with the text itself, an exploration of the TV show that is fixed. The highly personal nature of performance also involves a range of other intellectual obstacles. Any description of performance is by its nature subjective, based on selectivity and prioritizing elements of performance for critical attention. This is perhaps why some scholars have been reluctant to engage wholeheartedly in it. As Cantrell and Hogg note, 'existing academic considerations of television acting collectively evidence ambiguity and discord in precisely delineating their object of study.'[5] Such unsolid ground of describing and analysing screen performance may be the intellectual basis for the decision to focus attention on the industrial context of television performance and the process of actors' preparation based on an understanding of professionalism.[6] However, authors, including Simone Knox and Gary Cassidy, have developed a methodology that offers a close textual approach to television acting.[7] This chapter seeks to build on this approach to offer an understanding of the choices shaping performance as an example of 'original content' in high-end drama.

[4] Jason Mittell, *Complex TV: The Poetics of Contemporary Television Storytelling* (New York: New York University Press, 2015), 17.Original emphasis.
[5] Cantrell and Hogg, 'Returning to an Old Question: What Do Television Actors Do When They're Acting?', 285.
[6] Douglas McNaughton, 'Performance, Place and Screen: "Visible" and "invisible" Performance in Outside Broadcast Television Drama', *Critical Studies in Television*, 13, no. 3 (September 2018): 280–96.
[7] Simone Knox and Gary Cassidy, 'Game of Thrones: Investigating British Acting', in M. Hills, M. Hilmes and R. Pearson (eds), *Transatlantic Television Drama: Industries, Programs and Fans* (Oxford: Oxford University Press, 2019), 181–202.

The Leftovers: Production context

The Leftovers is a series that re-imagines American society three years after a calamitous world event, the Sudden Departure, in which 2 per cent of the population has instantly and inexplicably disappeared. The pilot begins with a flashback to the moment this occurs: a young mother secures her baby into his car seat, but before she can drive away, he is gone. Meanwhile, a laden supermarket trolley rolls across a parking lot with no one pushing, the child walking beside it cries for his lost parent, while a driverless car collides into another. Throughout the world, 140 million people have disappeared. Since the Sudden Departure, some have interpreted this global phenomenon as the Rapture, as predicted in Christian texts: those who have departed are in heaven, and those left behind are sinners who will not be saved. But there is no definitive explanation, and others see the event as devoid of any teleological meaning. The drama follows the survivors to see how they respond to their collective trauma. Community bonds break down, families are fractured and mental health problems are expressed in bizarre and unpredictable ways. Finally, religious faith intensifies for some and diminishes for others.

Based on the 2011 novel by Tom Perrotta, its adaptation to television was led by star television showrunner Damon Lindelof, who had previously created *Lost* (ABC, 2004–10). *The Leftovers* represented a key moment in the business development of HBO and the company's struggle to retain its market-leading reputation for high-end drama. The business model of Netflix, already mentioned in Chapter 2, threatened to eclipse the power of HBO. In response, the company developed a policy of investment, which, Lesley Goldberg noted in *The Hollywood Reporter*, for the first time sought to expand its offering with co-productions:

> *The Leftovers* marks the first of what is likely to be a new stream of outside studio buys for HBO ... programming chief Michael Lombardo acknowledged that his network has loosened up with its long-held philosophy about the importance of owning its own programming.[8]

The change in policy meant that HBO could share costs of big-budget television series with partners, in this case Warner Brothers Television, allowing the

---

[8] Lesley Goldberg, 'Damon Lindelof's "The Leftovers" Ordered to Series at HBO', *The Hollywood Reporter*, 16 September 2013. Available at: https://www.hollywoodreporter.com/live-feed/damon-lindelofs-leftovers-ordered-series-628497#

channel to entice its viewers with ever more ambitiously expensive high-end shows (*Game of Thrones* was entering its third season at this time). *The Leftovers* also joined a surge in bleak, dystopian dramas that were significant in the second decade of the twenty-first century. These included *The Handmaid's Tale* (MGM, 2017–20) and *Westworld* (HBO, 2016–20). The shows were also produced against a background of highly successful genre dramas that appealed to the audience's taste for post-apocalyptic narratives (*The Walking Dead*, AMC, 2010–22).

Casting: Initiating screen performance

A television text presents a cast of actors whose affective impact on the audience will be one of the show's central pleasures. The choice of the cast as stars is subject to accommodations to the market but, as actors, confirms their expressive individualism. The ability of the showrunner to appoint their chosen cast is central to the concept of authorial influence over the show. If Damon Lindelof's role is only part of a congruence of influence that shaped the decision making in building the show's cast, it is clear that his interest in risk-taking in casting impacted the show.

Choices in television casting are made on the basis of a number of factors:

- the professional quality of the actor,
- how well an actor fits within the ensemble,
- believability within the fictitious family and community groupings of the narrative and
- the star power of the actor and how this profile fits the commercial intentions of the show.

Many casting decisions in television rest on the look of an individual actor. Their physiognomy, physical stature and ethnicity become central to the viewer's reading of their performance.

At the point of casting, a show's characters exist only on the script page. The decisions over which actors will play the scripted roles profoundly impacts the characteristics and tone of performances in the final television text. In 2013, HBO gave Lindelof the task of matching characters he had written with his own awareness of the depth as well as range he wished to bring to the series. In making choices, he was supported by two professional casting directors (Ellen

Lewis and Meghan Rafferty), and the pilot episode director, Peter Berg. But the final casting decision remained with Lindelof, suggesting his primary role.

The cast for season one – a roster of fourteen actors – revealed that Lindelof favoured novelty over stability in the choice of performers for the ensemble of the show. At the same time, a major HBO/Warner project would always require a cast with names that are familiar with the target audience and convey a sense of quality: factors that play into the marketing opportunities for a high-profile show. An examination of the key players in *The Leftovers* demonstrates how Damon Lindelof provided HBO with the minimum of safe casting for the new show but used his industry weight to push through a sequence of unusual decisions that would shape the balance of performance in his new drama. Of the fourteen cast names in the first season, just two were actors with established careers in television acting as well as having cultural recognition that would be beneficial to the production.

Justin Theroux

As the star of *The Leftovers*, in the role of Police Chief Kevin Garvey, Justin Theroux was a choice that delivered solid recognizability from popular television and film. Theroux had acted as Nick Pierce in twenty-seven episodes of Washington, DC, law enforcement drama *The District* (2000–1); for HBO, he had appeared in eight episodes of *Six Feet Under* (2003–4) and as John Hancock in the miniseries *John Adams* (2008). He had also played in NBC's political satire, *Parks and Recreation* (four episodes, 2010). Justin Theroux's film career had been equally prominent. He first came to wide recognition in *Mulholland Drive* (David Lynch, 2001).

Amy Brenneman

Playing Laurie Garvey, Kevin's estranged wife, Amy Brenneman brought a high profile and depth of experience to *The Leftovers*. From the early 1990s, Brenneman had been associated with quality TV drama, playing Janice Licalsi in the first season of *NYPD Blue*, followed by a recurring role in NBC's *Frasier* and then creating and starring in the long-running *Judging Amy* (1999–2005) for CBS. Immediately before being cast in *The Leftovers*, Brenneman had played Dr Violet Turner in *Private Practice* (2007–13), alongside roles for independent film-makers.

The remaining cast names that appear in season one continue to point to casting decisions that favour novelty in the formation of the ensemble. Many of the other members of the main cast are from outside mainstream American television, and this indicates a willingness on the part of Lindelof to include diverse performances in the show. Four of these deserve attention.

Liv Tyler

Before accepting her role in *The Leftovers* in 2013, Liv Tyler had never worked in television. Her particular appetite for unusual roles attracted Tyler to the part of Meg Abbott for her TV debut: 'I read the script and absolutely loved everything about it; I thought it was intelligent, emotional and weird – all the things I find interesting in a project.'[9] Tyler's status in cinema had developed from her early work with Bernardo Bertolucci (*Stealing Beauty*, 1996) to her major roles in high-profile studio films (*The Lord of the Rings* trilogy, Peter Jackson, 2001–3) and *The Incredible Hulk* (Louis Leterrier, 2008). Unlike Christopher Eccleston, her commercial profile links *The Leftovers* with other high-end shows that have attracted major actors from the cinema (Jude Law in *The Young Pope*, Billy Bob Thornton in *Fargo*), reinforcing the clear desire for economic, as well as critical, success.

Christopher Eccleston

The choice of Eccleston to play Reverend Matt Jamison, the preacher who is certain that the Sudden Departure was *not* The Rapture, shows the willingness of Lindelof to draw a British actor into high-end American drama. Since the 1990s, Eccleston had worked with major figures such as Danny Boyle, but his profile with the US television audience was weak. His single series as *Doctor Who* (BBC, 2005) had begun to internationalize his reputation, but Eccleston had tested himself in only one major studio production, *Thor: the Dark World* (Alan Taylor, 2013), in which he followed in the footsteps of so many British actors who have been invited to Hollywood to play villains. Eccleston's style of acting is highly expressive and less of a logical accommodation with economic

---

[9] Ashley Morton, 'Liv Tyler Falling in Love with Meg and Embracing Impulsiveness', *Watching* The Leftovers, HBO Online, 31 May 2017. Available at: http://www.watchingtheleftovers.com/blog/liv-tyler-on-falling-in-love-with-meg-and-embracing- impulsiveness?rq=Liv%20Tyler

or popular success by guaranteeing a radically different tone of performance from other members of the cast in *The Leftovers*.

Carrie Coon

Carrie Coon was one of the most ambitious casting decisions in the formation of the main cast of *The Leftovers*. The role of Nora Durst puts her at the centre of the drama, and the romantic relationship with Kevin Garvey is key to the character development of the protagonist. Nora is the primary representative of tragedy in the Sudden Departure, having lost her husband and both her children. Casting Carrie Coon in such a major role in a production of this scale was highly unusual; she had only appeared in a handful of single-episode guest roles in television drama. Coon's reputation came from her work on stage, although these appearances were increasingly high profile, with groups such as the American Players Theatre and Steppenwolf Theatre Company. Lindelof could be assured of Coon's quality as an actor, but there was no guarantee of her success with a large television audience.

Margaret Qualley

The casting of the two children of the Garvey family reflects the balance between stability and novelty in the choice of actors for *The Leftovers*. Chris Zylka, as Tom Garvey, was an actor who had enjoyed a prolific career, appearing in young adult TV dramas, such as the fantasy drama *The Secret Circle* (CBS, 2010–11) and *10 Things I Hate About You* (ABC, 2009–10). In contrast to this safe casting choice, Damon Lindelof chose the unknown actor Margaret Qualley to play Jill Garvey. Qualley had almost no professional acting experience – a single minor role in a very small feature, *Palo Alto* (Gia Coppola, 2013) – having previously trained as a dancer. As Jill Garvey, Qualley would play a major supporting role from the start of the first season of *The Leftovers* as the daughter to the single-parent protagonist, Kevin Garvey, since his wife's decision to abandon the family and join the cult group, the Guilty Remnant.

Casting in *The Leftovers* establishes how the centrality of market pressures affects economic values linked to performance but also how the criteria for 'acting accomplishment' in high-end drama offer further insight into the range and depth of performances.

Agency of the performer

Variations in the tone of screen performance have usefully been described as variations in the level of expressiveness of the actor. This may be guided by the director during the shoot, as Sharon Marie Carnicke observes: 'Many actors see their ability to adapt to narrative and directorial demands as the special expertise for which they are hired.'[10] She goes on to offer examples from the work of film actors: 'Jack Nicholson[. . .] notes that his truncated performance in *The Passenger* (1975) is exactly what [Antonioni] wanted, and that his exaggerated performance in *The Shining* was just what Kubrick wanted.'[11] Nicholson's expressive range, and ability to deliver to his directors the tone of performance that fitted with their creative vision, constituted an important part of his professional pride as an actor.

In television drama, the prime agency of authorship over the actor – the director – becomes more complicated. In season one of *The Leftovers*, there were seven directors working across ten episodes. If continuity of performance style for each character was essential to the viewer's understanding of the drama, the individual director would take less of a role in shaping the expressiveness of an actor's performance which had been established in the pilot episode. In the context of a series of high-end drama seeking edgy, adult programming, the creative agency of the actor becomes heightened due to this decentralizing aspect. An actor in a main role is able to bring their personal interpretation of a character, along with the tone that they feel is appropriate to their performance. This suggests a variable authorial approach to high-end television, complicating notions of directorial control.

Pilot episode: Framing the performance

The pilot episode of *The Leftovers* shows us the minutes before the Sudden Departure in Mapleton, New York, through the quotidian actions of a young mother (Natalie Gold). Struggling at a laundrette with her infant son, Sam, sitting beside her in his babyseat and crying, she handles cell phone calls and

---

[10] Sharon Marie Carnicke, 'Screen Performance and Directors' Visions', in Cynthia Baron, Diane Carson and Frank P. Tomasulo (eds), *More Than a Method: Trends and Traditions in Contemporary Film Performance* (Detroit: Wayne University Press, 2004), 47.
[11] Carnicke, 'Screen Performance and Directors' Visions'.

does daily chores, before finally returning to her parking place and strapping the babyseat into the back of the car. The Sudden Departure occurs as she continues her phone conversation. It is a fleeting and imperceptible moment: Sam's crying stops, she looks behind her and the baby is gone.

Natalie Gold's performance shifts across three acting registers. In a fast succession of narrative beats in the laundrette sequence, she provides a naturalistic portrayal of an ordinary Mom, dealing with banal phone calls while multitasking roles as housewife and carer for her tiny son. Gold delivers the cell phone dialogue rapidly and gives a very physical performance, in which her work – loading laundry into the machine, finding coins to operate it, lugging the awkward babyseat under her arm – is a demonstration of the fatiguing experience of life as a young parent, as well as her overburdened psychological state. Gold's second register is the stillness of shock and stunned bewilderment: How can a baby, seat-belted into his car seat, disappear? The only possible explanation is that a kidnapper has taken the baby while she was distracted, but there is no sound of running feet of a criminal, nor screeching tyres. Gold's final performance register is an outpouring of panic and desperation (Figure 8). She is surrounded by other signs of the Sudden Departure: a car, now driverless, collides into another, and an abandoned child cries.

Gold's screams of Sam's name at the end of the scene seem to stem from a presentiment that she will never see her son again. In the show's pilot episode, enormous care is taken to carefully calibrate the cast's performances: the

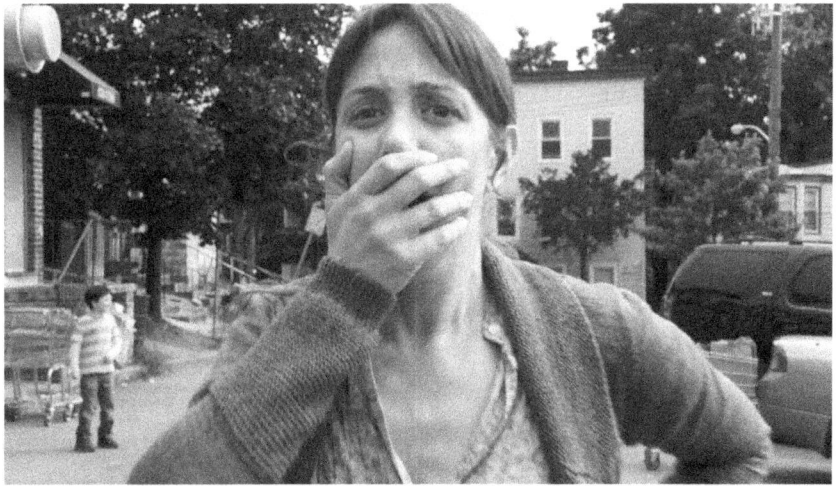

Figure 8 Sudden Departure.

exaggerated quality of Gold's acting is a deliberate creative choice by both Natalie Gold and episode director Peter Berg. Her over-heightened performance emphasizes the calamity that has just struck the world's population. Following this, the storyline takes us to 'Three Years Later'. In the portrayal of communities now recovering from the Sudden Departure, almost all the performances are subdued. The core creative decision is based on the sense of repression: these are characters struggling stoically to handle the scale of their loss, in the face of no clear explanation as to what happened in the Sudden Departure. The cast of *The Leftovers* express a further understanding of the status of those remaining after the Departure:

> Laurie knew. Deep in her heart, as soon as it happened, she *knew*. She'd been left behind. They all had. [...] And yet she chose to ignore this knowledge, to banish it to some murky recess of her mind – the basement storage area for things you couldn't bear to think about.[12]

The strength of Lindelof's adaptation of the novel is based on this residing tension within its characters and expressed through performances that signify unpredictable and extreme behaviours. However, key characters in the show behave quite differently, and this creates a clash of performance tones. This uneven range of performance in *The Leftovers* is already demonstrated with Natalie Gold's character; when we see her again at the end of the pilot episode – a chance meeting with Kevin Garvey in a bar – she is a subdued single woman, harbouring the grief of the loss of her child three years ago, unable to voice her burden aloud. More widely, Gold's performance focuses on the fragility and ambiguity of human relationships, transcending a naturalistic discourse rooted in the familiarity of the everyday.

Extreme performance modes: 'The Guilty Remnant'

In the storyworld of *The Leftovers*, the most extreme reaction to the Sudden Departure comes from a cult called the Guilty Remnant. These are people who believe that the event renders normal life irrelevant, and their role is to be a constant reminder to the rest of the population that they have been 'left behind'. Those who join the group are required to separate themselves from their

---

[12] Tom Perrotta, *The Leftovers*, 3rd edn (London: 4th Estate, 2014), 3.

families; they may never speak, they wear only white clothing, they forsake the comforts of modern life and they chain-smoke cigarettes. The belief system of the Guilty Remnant is obscure: their one certain insight is society's attempt to return to normal after the Sudden Departure is hopeless. This clarity gives the sect a pessimistic charisma that becomes a desperate remedy for those willing to join it.

Members of the Guilty Remnant (GR) play the self-appointed role of 'Watchers', working in pairs to stalk chosen targets among the townsfolk. These targets are often people who are insecure about the Departure and find it difficult to accept the return to normality. The Watchers stand like ghosts outside their target houses, or on the street, staring at an individual while smoking their cigarettes. The 'GR' is reviled by the population and are frequently attacked, but they remain impassive at all times, refusing to respond in kind.

One precedent that could be linked to the performance of the GR is mime, a theatrical tradition which shares the concept of wordless characters but uses excessive facial expression as a compensatory strategy to convey meaning. Interestingly, some of the most famed mime artists, including Marcel Marceau, favoured white costumes, a tradition which the creators of *The Leftovers* follow. In this tradition of speechless performance, the response to the restriction in verbal communication is to use highly expressive acting, both facially and in terms of the actor's body. In *The Leftovers*, however, the acting style of the main cast and extras playing members of the GR is restrained, with a minimal level of expressiveness. Consistently throughout the show, these characters' interactions with ordinary citizens betray no emotion whatsoever; their behaviour is impassive, giving the GR psychological strength in comparison to the damaged and struggling people of Mapleton.

The sect's voluntary speechlessness imposes problems on its members that mirror the restrictions on actors in early cinema. Silent film might appear to be a precedent for the performance mode of the GR; however, acting styles in the silent era can only partly be linked to *The Leftovers*. Frequently in silent movies, we see actors mouthing lines that we cannot hear, but these are performances with unrecorded dialogue, not the wordless performance that we see in *The Leftovers*. However, there is one striking link to silent film. The GR allows its people to use the written word. They carry marker pens and pads and write short messages to each other to overcome difficulties in communication. In one sense, the GR are providing their own intertitle cards.

The link between *The Leftovers* and a possible silent cinema performance mode was addressed directly by Liv Tyler in an interview that she gave while shooting the series. In playing Meg Abbott, a member of the GR, she was very deliberate in drawing on her extensive experience as a film actor:

> It's interesting, the whole silent thing. As an actress, I tend to trim my dialogue back and feel I can convey certain things through emotions or feelings or looks. Sometimes my costars laugh and say that I should be a silent film star and that I was born in the wrong era. But it's very tricky. It took us a minute. We had one scene, it was three pages long. No one was talking, and we're writing and emoting and frustrated. It's being comfortable being uncomfortable.[13]

The creators of the show would have been aware of Tyler's past career attainments as an actor, with her preference for a cinematic performance mode that minimizes dialogue.

Yet, there is a noticeable difference within a close reading of Tyler's acting in *The Leftovers* and others such as Eccleston, which develops an analysis of the competing modes of performance in the show. Meg Abbott's character journey is one of the strongest illustrations of the central theme of *The Leftovers*. In the pilot episode, Meg is one of many characters struggling with the normalization of life after the Sudden Departure. Her storyline begins with her fiancé: they are planning their forthcoming wedding. The banality of this process is unbearable to Meg in the context of the Sudden Departure. She comes to conclude that the GR represents the only honest reaction to the Sudden Departure, with their sullen but provocative campaign to prevent the world from returning to normality. She next joins the sect, and by the second season of *The Leftovers*, Meg Abbott is the leader of an extremist, breakaway branch of the GR.

Tyler constructs her performance across the show as a transition between acting modes. In her early scenes, she plays Meg in an upbeat, fully expressive mode; the character is integrated into the behavioural patterns of normal middle-class life in small-town America (Figure 9).

In parallel with this mode, Liv Tyler hints at the internal struggles of her character, but the insights into this darker tone are carefully subsumed within a dominant naturalism. In two key moments, the repressed internal psychological state of Meg Abbott is allowed to break through her controlled behaviour. The first is a confrontation with two 'Watchers' from the GR, who have selected

---

[13] Anon, 'Liv Tyler Fell in Love with Meg Instantly', 6 July 2014. Available at: http://www.watchingtheleftovers.com/blog/2014/7/6/liv-tyler-fell-in-love-with-meg-instantly

Figure 9 Meg Abbott (Liv Tyler) in the pilot episode.

Meg as a target for their silent vigil. Meg's fury reveals a lurking violence in her character, a feature that Liv Tyler redoubles in a scene when her character becomes a trainee with the GR. Her trainer takes her to a wood and indicates for her to cut down a tree. Meg is at first confused and ineffectual, but later her anger takes hold, unleashing a delirious outburst of violence. The qualities of this performance conform with features of melodrama. Jonathan Bignell describes how features of style, including performance, are heightened in this dramatic mode:

> The mode of melodrama heightens moral conflict and pushes narrative and style towards excess, thus provoking the revelation of an otherwise buried realm of moral and social values. Violent emotions and physical action emerge. [...] Film and television melodramas have developed these schemas to focus primarily on relationships within the family, and between familial groups and a broader society.[14]

The 'buried realm' is a fitting description of the internal world of Meg Abbott; it is here that the character wrestles with the contradictions about family, showing her relationship to her husband as fissile rather than harmonious. Her violent response which undermines models of family life later forms a variant of the

---

[14] Jonathan Bignell, 'Docudrama Performance: Realism, Recognition and Representation', in Christine Cornea (ed.), *Genre and Performance: Film and Television* (Manchester: Manchester University Press, 2010), 70.

melodramatic mode. Once Meg Abbott has made her violent rejection of her marriage, she enters the GR, where all emotions are repressed. For a screen performer such as Tyler, this allows her to return to the mode of performance that she most favours: a wordless, internalized style she describes as her natural mode of acting.

Close reading of performance: Liv Tyler as Meg Abbott

To explore in more detail the performance style of Liv Tyler, this section looks at an extended sequence in the third episode of season two, *Off Ramp*, in which Tyler/Meg is on screen for four and a half minutes.[15] The scene is particularly interesting because she has no dialogue at all until its final moments. This is not because her character conforms to the vow of silence from the GR; we have already been made aware that she is a rebellious spirit within the cult, who refuses to fully conform to their requirement. Rather, the episode screenwriters, Damon Lindelof and Patrick Somerville, along with director Carl Franklin, use the silence of Meg Abbott in the scene as an opportunity to deploy the particular skills of Liv Tyler as a screen performer.

The nature of the GR allows actors to develop varied approaches of minimal screen performance. Tyler's decision to play Meg Abbott as cold, devoid of emotion and humanity, creates a frightening figure. The central storyline of *Off Ramp* sees Tom Garvey working with his mother, Laurie, who has now left the GR and is pursuing a personal mission to help other cult members leave. Laurie establishes a centre where ex-GR members can be counselled to find mutual support as they transition back into society. Tom's role is to work undercover within the GR, spotting members who may have doubts and offering them support as a way out through his mother's rehabilitation organization. In the first act of the episode, he successfully helps a middle-aged woman. Returning undercover, Tom makes a secret appeal to a second GR member, but she blows a warning whistle, and Tom is violently attacked and overwhelmed.

The scene used for this close reading narrates Tom's punishment for betraying the GR.[16] He is first raped by Meg Abbott and then doused in petrol, threatened with immolation, before being abandoned, terrified, on a dirt road. The sequence

---

[15] Original TX, 18 October 2015.
[16] Start time at 29'28".

opens with a shot of Tom's hands, cuffed above him. He is locked in the back of a GR laundry van, alone, drenched in sweat, strung up like an animal in a butcher's fridge. Bright daylight through the windows of the rear door illuminates him. The van comes to a halt, and Tom struggles to fight to release his hands; the sound of his chains rattling reinforces the sense of a prison cell. The rear doors open quietly, harsh light pouring into the van. Tom looks to see who has opened the doors, but due to the intensity of the light, he can see nothing.

Using an out-of-focus and overexposed shot conveys Tom's point of view as a black saloon car parks nearby on the wide dirt track. A figure gets out and walks towards Tom. We soon recognize it as Meg Abbott. She is wearing a loose cotton summer dress. The musical score develops a sense of dread with a simple piano motif, a rising semitone (A-sharp, B), in slow repetition against a bed of electronic strings, restrained and discordant. Meg stops at the open doors of the van and looks at Tom. In a medium over-the-shoulder shot (OTS), barely in focus, Meg shows no emotional engagement: no anger, not even curiosity. Tom looks at her, a side angle close-up. His features show fear, emphasizing the forthcoming clash. Meg, impassive, lifts the skirts of her dress and steps up into the van. She approaches Tom as the doors are closed by GR guards behind her. They are alone together in the half-light.

Chris Zylka plays the scene with extreme emotion: in medium close-up, his face is framed by his muscular arms, held by the chain above him. There is desperation and pleading in his eyes; make-up (glistening sweat, morsels of blood on his white T-shirt, a dark line of scabbed blood on his split upper lip) supports the expressiveness of Zylka's performance. Tom writhes and his chains clink as he tries to lift himself from the bench: he murmurs, pleadingly, 'You don't have to . . . I didn't do anything.' There is a cut to the first close-up of Meg: a two-third's profile. This shot, lasting less than three seconds, plays an important moment in the scene because it drives a major narrative shift. The editor, David Eisenberg, uses the shot size to rebalance the storytelling of the scene. Henceforth, it is not just about Tom as the victim. We are also drawn into the thought processes of Meg, the abuser. The shot provides a narrative beat that offers to the spectator new insight into the character journey of Meg Abbott.

In her use of eye movements, Tyler very carefully leads the audience through the sequence of ideas within her character's mind. At the entry cutting point, her eyeline is to Zylka, blankly considering his line, 'I didn't do anything'. It next sharply tilts upwards to the point where Tyler is looking straight ahead of her. Out-of-vision, we know that she must see the manacles that hold Tom's wrists, but there is an internal thought process behind Meg's eyes. Although we are aware that Meg is here for retribution against Tom, it is only at this moment that she is deciding what she will do to him. Tyler's eyes flick to camera right, a further beat in which she confirms to herself the decision she must take. Their next movement abruptly brings her eyeline down again to Tom. David Eisenberg takes the directorial decision to cut hard on this look, back to the close-up of Tom, who registers immediately that she has chosen his punishment.

The next shot in the sequence is from a completely new camera angle. Meg is in medium close-up from behind Tom, his head, shoulder and raised arm darkly framing her. The use of shadow in the composition accomplishes two key meanings: first, the out-of-focus shape of Tom edges almost the entire frame. Second, an inner circle of darkness – Tyler's black hair – surrounds her white face. Meg's wide blue eyes regard her victim and demonstrate her hatred of Tom (Plate 15). She bends down to disappear out of frame, constructing a moment of anticipation.

Director Carl Franklin shoots the rape itself in three standard tight angles: an equal profile two-shot in medium close-up size, and OTS close-up of each of the characters.

In the second and third cuts to Tom/Meg's close-ups, Tyler registers a shift from the malice of the torturer to restrained physical pleasure. This carefully played change adds a complexity to Meg Abbott, a moment of simple human desire that hints at her former life before she joined the austere cult. As the rape ends, Eisenberg cuts to a profile two-shot and here he captures a remarkable moment of screen performance. Although this framing emphasizes equality between the characters, Tyler achieves complete dominance: she holds herself slightly higher in the frame than Zylka and again uses eye movement to establish her supremacy. Her eyes roam over his face, hinting at her desire for him, but then a tiny pursing of Tyler's lips delineates the moment when Meg re-establishes control of her desires. Finally, she gets up, pushes open the doors to allow burning sunlight back into the van and walks away nonchalantly, without looking back. The two GR guards know their next move: they grab Tom and violently pull him out, throwing him onto the dry dirt road and drenching him with gasoline. Handcuffed and in a foetal position, Tom lies helpless in the dust. Meg walks back to him: she is framed in a very low-angle medium shot, and we watch her from Tom Garvey's perspective as she pulls out a zippo lighter. Tyler again plays her character with complete coldness as she bends down into a close-up. She strikes the lighter, terrifying Tom, before calmly using it to light a cigarette. Now in a loosely framed OTS medium shot, Tyler delivers her only line of the sequence: 'Tell your Mom, Meg says hello.'

Throughout this sequence, the hallmark of Tyler's performance is an economy of expression. Yet within this minimalist style of acting, Tyler conveys a detailed and complex sequence of her character's thoughts with complete clarity. Her careful emphases of the internal workings of Meg Abbott's mind, through the minutiae of acting technique, contrast with the 'blank' mode of performance seen earlier. The cult members in the show can also be divided into the majority who maintain a consistently impassive mode and its leading figures – Ann Dowd/Patti, Amy Brenneman/Laurie (in season one), Liv Tyler/Meg – whose performances as more powerful members offer a greater range of expression. This is, in part, a strategy in *The Leftovers* that uses acting to differentiate supporting artists (extras) in the GR from leading actors or stars. However, in the case of Liv Tyler's performance, a powerful hybrid is achieved. Unlike Dowd and Brenneman, Tyler's acting is so minimalist that it feels rooted in the impassive GR players who surround her, yet it also conforms to a thematic range of emotional engagement expected from her in the show.

Close reading of performance: Christopher Eccleston as Matt Jamison

The casting of the highly experienced British television and film actor Christopher Eccleston as Matt Jamison in *The Leftovers* represented a willingness to mingle extremely varied acting styles in the show. In complete contrast to Liv Tyler, Eccleston adopts a heightened expressiveness in his portrayal of the preacher, who is the brother-in-law to the show's main protagonist, Kevin Garvey (Justin Theroux).

A close reading of a scene from the fifth episode of season three, *It's a Matt, Matt, Matt, Matt World*, will be used to develop an analysis of the qualities of performance style that Eccleston brings to the ensemble.[17] This episode's storyline is characterized by the extreme, unhinged quality that is a hallmark of how Damon Lindelof writes the later episodes of his TV dramas. Scripted together with Lila Byock, who also acted as story editor for the whole of season three, the action takes place on a passenger ferry between Tasmania and Melbourne: Matt is trying to reach Kevin Garvey, who he believes is the Messiah. Kevin has travelled to join his dad in Australia, and Matt is determined to bring him home

---

[17] Original TX, 14 May 2017.

for the auspicious seventh anniversary of the Sudden Departure. Bizarrely, the night ferry has been taken over by a lion-worshipping sex cult, who conduct a costumed orgy during the journey.

In a key sequence in the later part of the episode, starting at 41' 08", Matt witnesses a passenger being thrown overboard by a strange, illusive man who has nothing to do with the orgiastic party on board. The ferry's captain identifies the perpetrator as his personal friend, David Burton, a man who had a miraculous return from death and believes himself to be God. Neither the captain nor the other passengers have any concern about Burton's crime. Matt is righteously furious; he finds Burton and ties him to a wheelchair, taking him to a deserted part of the ship. Nearby is the lion cage: the animal sits, observing, with occasional growls. The close reading of performance style will focus on the ensuing two-hander scene between Matt and David.

Matt's intention in the scene is to unmask the false idol. He believes that David Burton is a fake, and for Matt, the existence of a man pretending to be God is an affront to his absolutist beliefs. But his challenge to Burton is slowly reversed, Matt finding himself explaining the many sacrifices – including leaving his wife and son – that he has made for his faith. 'Why?' Burton asks, repeatedly. Finally, Matt shouts, 'For You!' Matt loses control in this outburst (accompanied by a growl from the lion), as he unexpectedly finds himself to be a believer in the false idol. Matt kneels before Burton, untying the ropes that bind him to the wheelchair, and he looks up, adoringly. Burton slowly reaches a hand out to his new disciple but then breaks the spell with a click of his fingers. 'Ta Da!' he says, ironically, 'You're saved'. Matt ends the scene humiliated by his own gullibility and with a new insight into the frailty of his own faith.

In this scene, Eccleston plays opposite Bill Camp as David Burton. The remarkably extended scene (more than seven minutes out of the episode running time of 52'42") is of particular relevance to the discussion of performance style in *The Leftovers* due to the clash between acting styles of the two players. Bill Camp adopts a minimalist style, restricting the range of his expression in a manner that reminds us of Liv Tyler, while Christopher Eccleston develops the highly expressive performance mode that he chose for Matt Jamison throughout the show's three seasons.

In discussing the extremities of Christopher Eccleston's performance, it must be understood that his creative decisions were not simply individual choices but came from the production structures around him. He had discussed the character of Matt Jamison with Damon Lindelof early in the show's development and claims credit for having encouraged the inclusion of Matt in the show.[18] Furthermore, in the scene that we will examine, director Nicole Kassell chose to place a caged lion just a few metres from the actors throughout the shoot, a decision that was certain to heighten performances. Eccleston describes how the lion's presence created a tangible fear: 'He scared the shit out of me during one take! Suddenly, during one take, I think he decided that I was edible. He let out this snarl and I jumped about six foot in the air!'[19] This moment is captured in the edit, Kassell next cutting to a close-up of the roaring lion baring his teeth.[20]

Kassell, who had also worked for Damon Lindelof in the second season, shoots the scene with remarkably tight angles; after establishing the deserted space of the ferry deck and the lion's cage, she concentrates on medium close-ups and close-ups, a framing strategy that emphasizes performance over other narrative signals in the scene. The choice of shot size underlines how Eccleston's performance is a concentration on facial and vocal expressiveness.

Matt Jamison's opening attack on David Burton uses sarcasm to undermine the credibility of the man who believes himself to be God. The nature of sarcasm involves a form of performed exaggeration, and Eccleston's voice assumes an over-emphatic tone:

DAVID: You're being sarcastic.
MATT: No, I'm just wondering why I haven't been struck down by lightning yet. Why don't you transform those ropes into serpents and free yourself?

Eccleston steadily develops the theatricality of his vocal performance, incorporating abrupt tonal shifts and sudden changes of pitch. These steep inclines between pitches, from higher to lower, take the quality of Eccleston's acting further and further away from the flat, inexpressive tone of Bill Camp as David Burton. The vocal technique reaches an early climax when Matt insists that David confess to the murder of the man-overboard: 'Admit what you did!' Here, Eccleston deliberately enunciates, invoking an emphasis that, if motivated by the script, is highly theatrical.

Within a scene of such length, Eccleston's control of the changing rhythms and tones of his voice contributes to a highly crafted performance that permits

---

[18] Morgan Jeffery, 'Christopher Eccleston Reflects on *The Leftovers*: I Convinced Damon Lindelof to Make Matt Part of the Series', *Digital Spy*, 7 November 2017. Available at: https://www.digitalspy.com/tv/ustv/a832798/christopher-eccleston-the- leftovers/
[19] Jeffery, 'Christopher Eccleston Reflects on *The Leftovers*: I Convinced Damon Lindelof to Make Matt Part of the Series'.
[20] At 42'49".

the nuance of the script's ideas to encourage further interpretation by the viewer. But the modulations that he adopts also have the pitch of political oratory. Matt is flabbergasted by David Burton's admission of having created the Sudden Departure. Eccleston reduces the power and volume of his voice to a minimum and then slowly builds it up again in a crescendo: the same technique of a speaker constructing rhetoric for a rapt audience. He also includes a vocal quality that we have not heard so far, a breathiness that indicates his passionate involvement in what he is saying. This is a deliberate contrast with the sarcasm of the early section of the scene, when Eccleston used a staccato delivery of his consonants to produce the sense of Matt's antagonism towards David. The climax of the crescendo is the shout, 'For You!' The next beat of the scene is wordless: it is an exchange between the two men in which Matt realizes his sudden faith in David-as-God. When Eccleston begins his next line of dialogue, his voice is utterly transformed: it is child-like, diminished like his status in the scene. The childish vocal tone adds to the already extreme range of Eccleston's acting. Crucially, this performance decision adds to the success of the next narrative beat. Eccleston's voice characterizes Matt as utterly powerless. It is inevitable that he will untie David Burton's hands as instructed.

Christopher Eccleston's techniques of facial performance contribute to the expressive range in his portrayal of Matt Jamison. There is a theatricality about the use of his face and his head movements from the beginning of the scene. Eccleston uses elements of his physiognomy. His eyes are first narrowed and hooded by his brow; midway through the scene, when David-as-God says that Jesus was not his son, Eccleston's eyes widen as he delivers his aghast line, 'You're denying paternity!' By the end of the scene, Eccleston's eyes are still, with the eyeballs so intensely focused on David that they seem to protrude from their sockets as he says, 'When I was a boy, I was sick, and I prayed to you to save me. And you did.'[21] The status of the eyes reflects the progression of Matt's emotions in the scene, from sarcastic hostility, to righteous anger, to devotion. Eccleston's facial technique is showing us that Matt is a character who hides nothing.

Head movements are another highly expressive technique in the performance. While Bill Camp, seated in the wheelchair, holds his head almost static throughout the scene, Eccleston uses extremes; in some moments, his stillness emphasizes determination. In others, his jabbing head movements support the staccato aggression of his vocal delivery. A frequent performance idea that Eccleston uses is a disbelieving throwing-back of his head, theatricalizing his sarcasm.

[21] At 46'32".

Nicole Kassell's three-quarters profile close-up of Eccleston accentuates the head movements, his face plunging to the edges of the frame. When Matt traduces David Bruton for his fake story of returning from the dead, this becomes so extreme that it forces editor Henk Van Eeghen to cut to an OTS medium shot, which frames Eccleston's rapid movements.[22]

A clear example of Eccleston's combined facial performance comes at the point when David takes responsibility for the Sudden Departure. Matt has been challenging him:

> **Matt:** Then what do you take responsibility for? Dinosaurs? The Black Plague? Mount Everest, the Mona Lisa, the Sudden Departure?
> **David:** Yeah, that was me.

At this point (44'56"), Van Eeghen cuts to an OTS close-up of Matt, who is stunned into silence. Eccleston emits a tiny vocal sound as if his throat is blocked by his astonishment; there is a tiny twitch of his nose, and he throws his head back to look into the distance, gathering his thoughts. Next, Eccleston swings his head abruptly back to Bill Camp, his chin low so that his eyes are hooded by his eyebrows, like a bull preparing to charge. Each of these performance details is highly emphatic; in combination, they mark the range of Eccleston's heightened performance. Within the ensemble of actors cast for *The Leftovers*, Eccleston's mode of performance adds to the styles, offering an unusually wide range of emotional expressiveness.

Conclusion

Within the stylistic features of *The Leftovers*, we can identify dramatic clashes of performance technique and tone. However, such close analysis does not, of course, propose a generalization about the range of acting styles in all high-end drama within contemporary US television. Each high-end project undertaken will have its own unique characteristics, which will lead to specific casting decisions and strategies of directing performance. At the same time, looking at the performances in *The Leftovers*, it can be argued that a model of high particularity that is distinct to the show is visible. The characters of Meg Abbott and Matt Jamison warrant the accentuated differences in acting styles from Liv Tyler and Christopher Eccleston.

---

[22] At 43'57".

Many commentators have noted the influx of talent from cinema into high-end TV drama in the first decades of the twenty-first century. This chapter has looked in detail at the qualities of Liv Tyler's acting in her first television role in *The Leftovers*. As an actor, Tyler has used a particular mode of cinematic performance developed through her extensive career at the top end of international film. The fact that high-end drama, unlike earlier US television drama, no longer looks for its acting talent from established television stars but recruits its talent from cinema allowed Damon Lindelof to draw Tyler into his project and broaden its range of performance styles. However, the acting styles of two major screen actors, Tyler and Eccleston, are not only a claim about cinema and television's convergence. In *The Leftovers*, a close analysis of the performance styles of the actors reveals how high-end drama appropriates styles from theatre, as well as film. Importantly, contemporary showrunners, such as Damon Lindelof, are willing to cast actors drawn from several media to expand the possible range on television.

An analysis of diverse performance styles feeds into a broader understanding of high-end television authorship as a site of high particularity, while seeking to accommodate variability. The thematic range of *The Leftovers* and treatment of emotional states such as grief, trauma, depression and rage marked the preference to cast ambitiously. But, although authorship is usually attributed to the showrunner in the high-end series, the greater agency given to the performer by Lindelof in *The Leftovers* derives from both a cultural desire and economic need for distinctive drama.

7

Televisual spectacle

Mars

If immersion in the story is often the goal in high-end drama, a high degree of experiential viewing in high-definition television emphasizes several tendencies. The first is television's continuing unprecedented visibility forming its cultural logic of being able to survey places beyond the Earth, including the spectacle of an expedition landing on Mars. The second tendency is the embodied experience recalling earlier descriptions of television's electronic textuality that crafts an impression of immediacy and intimacy.[1] In *Mars*, there is the mapping of terrain and an unsurpassed mobility as astronauts survey the Red Planet. The widening of the physical terrain and the use of epic scale mark the centrality of the display of visual style in high-end television. However, if a more complex image about place encourages a greater monitoring of the location, it may also encourage haptic sensations about the visited landscape. In this way, with the inclusion of new production technologies, including the advanced precision use of colour grading, the interplay between spectacle and the process of creating new experiences on television is the subject of this final chapter.

Mars (2016–18)

In November 2016, National Geographic Channel was rebranded, dropping 'Channel' from its name. Tracing its roots from Alexander Graham Bell, inventor of the telephone, National Geographic had been launched as a television channel in 2001, producing shows such as *Doomsday Preppers* (2011–14), a reality show about survivalists, which, in some ways, prepared the ground for the challenge

---

[1] See Glen Creeber, *Small Screen Aesthetics: From TV to the Internet* (Basingstoke: Palgrave Macmillan, 2013), 11–14.

of surviving on the barren and hostile Martian terrain. In 2014, the arrival of Courteney Monroe, a marketing executive from HBO, to become the channel's chief executive raised the possibility of the HBO version of National Geographic. A shift in programming marked the premiere of *Mars*, a six-part series. For Monroe, rebranding National Geographic would move it from reality TV shows to more scripted drama – another break with the past. For example, Carolyn Bernstein became head of scripted development and production that would also lead to the anthology series, *Genius* (2017–20). At the same time, National Geographic would maintain its commitment to documentary production, including committing to 100 weeks of production for *One Strange Rock* (2018–19). Finally, much of Monroe's ability to attract big-name talent, as well as increased production budgets, was due to National Geographic being fully owned by Fox and funding arriving from 21st Century Fox.[2]

A similar aspiration for 'elite art' as already seen at HBO and an increase in the value of National Geographic's programmes would lead to the possibility of named directors from film producing its shows. Darren Aronofsky, the director of films such as *Pi* (1997), co-produced with Nutopia[3] *One Strange Rock*, which views the history of life on Earth from the point of view of several astronauts. Meanwhile, competition from the BBC's *The Frozen Planet* (2011) or Netflix's *Our Planet* (2019) has, subsequently, confirmed the appeal of television documentary content relying on spectacle as a method of celebrating the Earthly environment, as well as a sense of adventure. *Mars* combines scripted drama with special effects and documentary segments and was one of the earlier pioneers of this form of content that can compete with Netflix and the BBC, despite the financial cost of doing so. Other shows, such as the eleven episodes of *Planet Earth* (2005), were the result of a complicated co-production by the BBC, Canadian Broadcasting Corporation and Discovery.[4] *Mars* added the cachet of having Ron Howard as its executive producer. Besides being an Oscar-winning director, Howard is co-chairman with Brian Grazer of Imagine Entertainment. The first season of *Mars* would be filmed in forty days over the course of three months and eventually drew a global audience of thirty-six million viewers, thus becoming National Geographic's most recorded series.[5]

[2] Christine Champagne, 'To Space and Beyond', *Emmy*, 39, no. 1 (2017): 16.
[3] A British independent television production company, owned by Jane Root, former president of the Discovery Channel.
[4] Martin Curtin and Jane Shattuc, *The American Television Industry* (Basingstoke: Palgrave Macmillan, 2009), 129.
[5] Libby Slate, 'Making Morocco into Mars', *Emmy*, 39, no. 6 (2017): 122–8.

If Ron Howard was able to provide the cachet, the history of travel to Mars and space exploration generally has been a vital appeal of much of television since before the Space Race of the 1960s. Disney was to combine entertainment and education in the mid-1950s, when the studio agreed to produce the TV show *Disneyland* (1954–8) for ABC. Its Tomorrowland-themed series about space travel included *Man in Space* (9 March 1955), *Man on the Moon* (28 December 1955) and *Man and Beyond* (4 December 1957), the latter being an exploration of the planet Mars. The show pioneered a similar technique to *Mars* of combining the personae of various experts and archive documentary footage with animation planned to look like science fact rather than fiction. The effect is of the programme transmitting to the living room the direct experience of the experts in their offices, as the Space Race unfolds before our eyes.

Perhaps the most important moment in television history for exploring the universe has been *Star Trek: The Original Series* (*TOS*; 1966–9). *TOS* presented a future world when humans had colonized space and hundreds of worlds but *Mars* was to dramatize the first instance of colonizing space. In more than thirty years of voyaging space, *Star Trek* created a compellingly real world, with its own history, rules and fascination for futuristic technology. Its ability to create greater verisimilitude as the show mapped alien territories was despite the fact *TOS* had deployed unconvincingly cardboard sets. Although, according to Catherine Johnson,[6] the sets of alien worlds may have seemed futuristic on its first showing, these became more outdated as the show was endlessly repeated throughout the 1970s and 1980s. Nevertheless, if not entirely plausible, papier-mâché rocks and a style of mannered acting shot on a Paramount soundstage in the 1960s opened the possibility of exploring not only the quotidian but also the exotic on television. The textural universe of *Star Trek* accrued a visible reality because of its ability to create a spatiality populated by various alien races, as well as planetary environments. In *Mars*, the spatial arrangement would be limited to events on Earth and on Mars, casting the Red Planet as a foreign land and different from Earth if not, in fact, exotic. The space within the spaceship – Daedalus – taking the six astronauts to Mars and later to the base on the Red Planet was a state-of-the-art laboratory (Olympus Town), following conventions set by earlier shows such as *TOS* of futuristic electronics and life-support systems.

Based on the book *How We'll Live on Mars* (2015), the initial series on National Geographic was set between 2033 and 2037 about the first manned expedition

---

[6] Catherine Johnson, *Telefantasy* (London: British Film Institute, 2005), 86.

to the Red Planet. *Mars* combines documentary and drama to tell parallel stories of two groups of people: the fictional future explorers who will make that first journey and the pioneers of today – scientists, astronauts and strategists – who are blazing the trail. The 'science future' of *Mars* was first planned as a feature-length documentary before becoming a series using a hybrid of drama and documentary. The combination of scripted drama and true-life interviews was to make the engineering and science as factual as possible, exemplifying the imagery of space travel as scientific experiments and advancing technology. Every piece of tech in the show was designed to accurately reflect the current scientific vision of how to get to Mars and avoid the errors of recent films which have invited criticism from astrophysicist/space ombudsman Neil deGrasse Tyson, who appears in *Mars*.[7] As executive producer Ron Howard puts it, 'It's not sci-fi!', and indeed, President Obama was to outline a vision to send humans into Mars' orbit by the mid-2030s.[8] 'This is technology that will probably be tested in the next five years,' explains the show's executive producer Justin Wilkes.[9] For example, the spacecraft is heavily inspired by Elon Musk's SpaceX, but it also borrows design elements from NASA, Boeing and even the Russian space program.

Beyond the science, for Ron Howard, the appeal of *Mars* was because the programme could celebrate exploration viscerally. Echoing this sentiment, the project's director, Everardo Gout, explained how time in confined quarters on Mars is 'a very visceral experience. . . . Think a little of *Das Boot*, but in space where you're there with the characters and you're feeling with them and it's all about sweat and blood and everything you would experience if you were the seventh passenger with them.'[10] *Mars* is inflected with a sense of 'being-there' due to the work of the director as well as the production designer, Sophie Becher. Immersed in the project with Becher was the DoP, Damian Garcia, and the visual effects supervisor, Russell Dodgson, who themselves 'felt like astronauts

---

[7] Katrina Tulloch, 'Neil deGrasse Tyson Unpacks, Debunks 11 Sci-fi Movie Moments', 20 April 2017. Available at: https://www.syracuse.com/entertainment/2017/04/neil_degrasse_tyson_unpacks_11_sci-fi_movie_moments.html

[8] Anon, 'Barack Obama Revives Call to Put Humans on Mars by the 2030s', *The Guardian*, 11 October 2016. Available at: https://www.theguardian.com/science/2016/oct/11/obama-mars-mission-nasa-habitats-space-travel-2030

[9] Logan Hill, 'Inside Nat Geo's Incredible Documentary Mission to Mars', *Wired*, 17 October 2016. Available at: https://www.wired.com/2016/10/how-we-will-get-to-mars/

[10] Michael Idato, 'Everything Is Real: Nat Geo launches Mars Drama into Dramatic Orbit', *Stuff*, 7 November 2016. Available at: https://www.stuff.co.nz/entertainment/tv-radio/86182126/everything-is-real-nat-geo-launches-new-mars-drama-into-dramatic-orbit

in training'.[11] Becher was tasked with creating an array of locations, from the headquarters of the International Mars Science Foundation to the interior of the Daedalus and the habitat on Mars. Importantly, she approached the projects from the characters' point of view, offering a strong sense of embodied vision, especially when designing the extraterrestrial environments.

The series is about an international crew of astronauts on the first manned mission to *Mars* aboard the Daedalus, living on the ship during a two-year journey in space before landing and exploring the planet. Film locations included the deserts of Morocco, as well as various interiors built in Budapest during the second series shot in 2017, doubling for mission-related headquarters in London and Vienna. The crew is made up of the mission commander, American Ben Sawyer, played by Ben Cotton, who leads three woman and three men representing diverse countries, including Korea, Spain, France, Nigeria and Russia, who grapple with the technological and psychological complications of exploring Mars. The exploration of an unknown territory becomes a method of exploring the various sensations of the astronauts as they become displaced from their home environments on Earth. A crushing homesickness is made worse by the frustration of technological failures, opening multiple experiences while mapping the terrain of Mars.

The cinematography of the Martian desert points not only to the increased popularity of spectacle on television but also to how it is used to open the narrative. An increased spectacle permits a documentary use of the camera at particular moments to allow the recording of a new planet. However, *Mars* allows other spaces: the day-to-day existence aboard Daedalus followed by the base camps on the planet. The feeling offered by the visual design of claustrophobia in these small spaces and other psychological stresses of the mission is contrasted to the spectacular. The director, Gout, wanted to concentrate on the humanity of the people in the mission and not the ship. For him, it had to be not only a visual journey but an 'organic' experience. 'Ultimately it's about building life on Mars,' he explains.[12] *Mars* was able to explore the various types of spaces to form distinct or proximate worlds. For example, with much of the action taking place within a space capsule or Mars transporter rather than on the surface of the planet itself, the interiors had to be crafted in detail. Despite the budget, every square foot counted, including raising the Steadicam to a level to offer more

---

[11] Slate, 'Making Morocco into Mars', 125.
[12] Slate, 'Making Morocco into Mars', 126.

scope and scale. At the same time, long sightlines offering an unobstructed view make the interior sites, such as the permanent base, feel as real as possible to give the scenes the necessary space and range to feel dynamic.

Temporal realism and the epistemic

'Everything that you're seeing is real,' explained the show's executive producer Justin Wilkes.[13] One problem the director, Everardo Gout, faced was how scientific fact lent itself to exciting visuals. The first space to be designed was aboard the Daedalus. Becher, the production designer, would study images from NASA and Elon Musk's company, SpaceX, to imagine space as a premium without clutter. With cinematographer Damian Garcia, she would also imagine being an astronaut and design the tiny spaces before Garcia would plan how to position the camera and light the small sets. As well as planning for small spaces, Becher noticed that astronauts preferred control buttons on instrument panels rather than touch screens. Her series adviser and former NASA astronaut, Mae Jemison, explained that astronauts preferred the tactile quality of buttons and throttles: a haptic feedback and a sense of connection to the physical, material world. Unlike older shows set in space, Becher asked, 'How's this going to function? Where are they going to use the bathroom?'[14] Design questions were dealt with using real engineering: 'How big does the environmental control and life support system need to be for x number of astronauts for y number of days? How much recycling of water and oxygen can these systems handle before they have reliability issues?'[15] Similarly, the walls of the domes were padded to simulate the cold climate of Mars outside. Becher also personalized the spaces for the individual characters. 'I thought that people could choose the colors that they'd like in advance from within a certain palette – like in your own home when you choose the color of the walls,' she explained. 'I also decided that in some of the domes there'd be a window that the characters could choose an image for. It's the image they've taken with them to ground them and make them

---

[13] Idato, 'Everything Is Real: Nat Geo Launches Mars Drama into Dramatic Orbit'.
[14] Logan Hill, 'Inside Nat Geo's Incredible Documentary Mission to Mars', *Wired*, 17 October 2016. Available at: https://www.wired.com/2016/10/how-we-will-get-to-mars/
[15] Hill, 'Inside Nat Geo's Incredible Documentary Mission to Mars'.

feel calm.'[16] An example would be the association of green fields with botanist Peter Richardson, which is discussed later.

The confinement of the spaceship and Olympian Town settlement was counterpointed with the spectacular terrain of Mars. The shift from claustrophobic to expansive vistas would mean Garcia would deploy wide shots to fully convey the sense of scale outside the ship and base camp. At this point, the camera remains mostly stationary until it moves to follow the action of the astronauts. The footage was shot with an ARRI Alexa, and due to its dynamic range, it was possible to shoot a Martian sunrise to not silhouette the actors' faces but observe them at the same time. Equally, further digital affordances shape *Mars* as an example of 'science fact' as the show's exploitation of DVFX provides a greater degree of immersion due to its enhanced visual realism. The resulting phenomenological quality of its televisual style and the transformation by digital effects fostered in *Mars* allow for the emergence of spectacular images that are determined by supposed indexical evidence.

Visual effects in *Mars* were completed by Framestore: a London-based company that had previously won an Oscar for the 2013 film *Gravity* and been nominated for *The Martian* (2015). The visual effects supervisor on *Mars*, Russell Dodgson, was able to devise 960 shots plus those for the title sequence: an eighty-second spot that used striking aerial views of Mars.[17] The purpose of the opening credits was to provide cryptic clues of what the series was about. For Dodgson, high-resolution satellite images were able to be used to show how the topology of Mars is similar to Earth, creating a sense of familiarity, as well as draw in the spectator's extra-textural knowledge of Mars from images collected by the Mars Rover. Dodgson was to use some of the topography images to build horizons on which the rest of the landscape could be filled in. Every shot, he explains, 'involved some 3-D work and digital background extensions. Effects included a dust storm. The soil on Mars is incredibly fine; we had a huge wave of dust lifted off the ground . . . and an unusually dark atmosphere when crew members lower themselves into a cavern to look for ice to melt for water.'[18] Moreover, a glittering night sky shifts in the background as the camera traces a curved path around the camp in an extended take. This digital shot exposes the camp's vulnerability against the bleakly, wondrous Martian landscape. Equally importantly, Framestore designed monitors and other elements in Daedalus and

[16] Hill, 'Inside Nat Geo's Incredible Documentary Mission to Mars'.
[17] Slate, 'Making Morocco into Mars', 128.
[18] Slate, 'Making Morocco into Mars', 128.

Mission Control in London or Vienna, customizing screen content. At the same time, Dodgson acknowledges that if digital effects at the movies are about the power of spectacle, Framestore also chose to be judicious and not overreach themselves within the production of Mars.

Yet, this is the opposite to a style whose use of the digital at the cinema has privileged spectacle over the limitations of the indexical trace. VFX technology has provided film producers an enhanced ability to construct an image like a painting (one of the earliest software packages for digitally manipulating the image was the Quantel Paintbox).[19] For Lev Manovich, digitalizing the image in film has meant that

> If live-action footage was left in traditional film-making, now it functions as raw material for further compositing, animating and morphing. . . . To use the suggestive title of a popular morphing software, digital film-makers work with 'elastic reality'. For example, the opening shot of *Forrest Gump* (Robert Zemeckis, Paramount Pictures, 1994; special effects by Industrial Light and Magic) tracks an unusually long and intricate flight of a feather. To create the shot, the real feather was filmed against a blue background in different positions; this material was then animated and composited against shots of a landscape. The result: a new kind of realism, which can be described as 'something which looks exactly as if it could have happened, although it really could not'.[20]

Although 'elastic realism' exists in televisual examples such as *Pushing Daisies* (2007–9), such realism does not exist in *Mars*. We have already seen in Chapter 4 how digital imaging has been avoided by many makers of television drama. Indexicality in *Stranger Things* favours a greater 'reality effect' by filming an actual physical event such as a van made to soar over the children. Such special effects invoke the idea of the moving image as a document based on its indexical connection to the place or event being recorded.

Television science fiction such as *Battlestar Galactica* (2004–9) or *Doctor Who* (1963–2020) has always visualized advanced technologies and futuristic machines to signify strange new worlds and evoke alien landscapes. However, unlike its cinematic counterpart, television has sought to be more perceptual but, at the same time, seek a greater sense of presence that, by documenting

---

[19] David Hockney, the artist, was one of the first to celebrate the new techniques made possible using Paintbox. See Henry Fenwick, 'Paint Box of Tricks', *Radio Times*, 3 May 1987: 83–5. Although initially developed for broadcast graphics, directors such as Peter Greenway were making use of Paintbox by the 1990s.
[20] Lev Manovich, *The Language of New Media* (London: MIT Press, 2001), 301.

the real world, encourages emotional involvement. On television, the electronic image possesses similar qualities to photorealism but relies on another technological aspect and the cultural history of being broadcast live. The experience of liveness continues to be most acute in broadcasts of information such as news or documentary. In *Mars*, the illusion of the omnipresent and live electronic eye is that it is surveying events as they unfold, maintaining a sense of shared intimacy and empathy as National Geographic offers a near future in the year 2033. Inscribed into this process is the creation of a historiography which is narrated as if the landing of Mars is being recounted as a 'happening'. The production design of claustrophobic spaces on *Mars* and the use of digitally manipulated images are modified for the temporal nature of television and made to be distinct from the cinema.

The encroachment of digital images within television raises the difficulty of maintaining the status of *Mars* as epistemically accurate without offering an intensely stylized view of *Mars* that has been altered in post-production. Science-fiction film often celebrates special effects technology to create a sense of spectacle or, more recently, an elastic realism incorporating other-worldliness or the *simulations* of what is technologically impossible rather than *representations* of what is technologically possible. The value set on a high-end television show such as *Mars* might be expected to hinge on its ability to operate as a commodity which benefits from sophisticated sound systems and state-of-the-art camera technologies. In high-end drama, these have most recently utilized a visual high dynamic range (HDR), which can be manipulated using recording formats such as OpenEXR, an open source HDR format originally developed by Industrial Light and Magic. *Mars* does rely on digital technologies appearing within high-end television drama to create a fictional world which is more comprehensive through its vivid visibility. However, the success of *Mars* depends as much on the conjunction of immediacy, actuality and intimacy in a complex temporal framework, which is worked into the rhetorical fabric of the programme.

Dee Johnson, an executive producer for the show, explained that she believes the format of documentary and fiction could be replicated for other genres, such as historical dramas, to offer an interesting prospect for the future of television.[21] *Mars* was assembled using more than 100 hours of documentary footage, while

---

[21] Sophia Moir, 'Mars Series 2: Why the National Geographic Hybrid Docudrama Is Like Nothing Else on TV Right Now', 6 November 2018. Available at: http://tv.bt.com/tv/tv-from-bt/mars-series-2-why-the-hybrid-documentary-drama-on-national-geographic-is-like-nothing-else-on-tv-right-now-11364306572152

the scripted drama is a presentation of history-future, acting as a reminder of the link between television as a viewing event and its documentation of the real world. The collapse between the distinction between factual and fictional programming on television is part of the dynamic appeal of the relationship between the audience and the astronauts. The temporalities of the real in *Mars* as an experience are reinforced by the earlier documentary footage from the Apollo missions, whose landing on the moon became a global televised event, with audiences of an estimated 650 million people.[22] In episode one of *Mars*, *Novo Mundo*, within the viewing event of the launch into space, the audience is also able to enjoy the unpredictability of events.[23] The danger of space travel is reiterated as past astronauts describe the loss of the Space Shuttle in 1986, as well as the near disaster of the Apollo 13 mission.

If a blurring of the distinction between the documentary interviews and scripted drama exists in the launching to Mars, they equally point to an immediacy of the Martian landing that re-emphasizes the show's complex temporal framework. Although the interviews are recorded in the present of 2016, they represent the past to the astronauts landing in 2033. On the one hand, the structure of the documentary interviews acts as a news broadcast that is able to comment on the events unfolding in *Mars*. However, this further complicates the status of the footage: Is it to be understood as the live transmission of an actual landing, or are we viewing past recollections of the landing on Mars? Despite the comment by Dee Johnson about the use of the hybrid format as an interesting possibility for future television, such a temporal structure is not entirely original. The ability to blur the distinction between factual and fictional programming had precedents in shows such as *You Are There* (1953–72) on CBS. In *You Are There*, a desk anchor might comment on simulated historical events like the execution of Joan of Arc or Cortez's conquest of Mexico. In the show, a method of anachrony reinforced the belief that history was unfolding in a live event as the show strove for accuracy within the limits of historical knowledge and pedagogy.

In *Novo Mundo*, segments of *Mars* include archival film footage and photographs of the Apollo missions as a reminder of the tradition of space exploration and a journey to Mars as part of a broader trajectory of grappling with risk and danger. The bringing to life of scientific innovations to optimize

[22] NASA, Apollo 11 Mission Overview. Available at: https://www.nasa.gov/mission_pages/apollo/missions/apollo11.html
[23] Original TX, 14 November 2016.

human existence is primarily formulated as a problem to be solved. A voice-over informs the audience:

> We dream. It's who we are. Down to our bones, our cells. That instinct to build. That drive to seek beyond what we know. It's in our DNA. We crossed the oceans, we conquered the skies. And when there were no more frontiers on Earth we launched ourselves among the stars. The heavens beckoned a new generation of innovators and explorers, seeking to take human kind even further.

In *Mars*, the desire for witnessing a viewing event becomes another temporal shift to the near future, although, crucially, still through contemporary eyes. The assurance from the experts in 2016 is the expedition to Mars is happening now as though the present can determine the future. The digital production of images of the Martin landscape serves to confirm the claims by the experts as they discuss the technology of long-term space colonization. Yet the difficulty of the landing on Mars, accompanied by dramatic footage of the 'actual' descent onto the planet and the problems of surviving on Mars, suggests a less certain future. The virtualities of exploring Mars using digital imagery to foster the illusion of access to an indexical reality remains televisual rather than cinematic due to the sense of a live event. The concomitance of the present with the near future suggests a temporal contiguity, as well as proximity to the subjects, as we experience the material reality of exploring Mars.

Greater knowledge will resolve the challenge of visiting Mars. The archival material using the picture and video library held by National Geographic begins to suggest the tremendous resources available both inside and outside the drama. The budget for Mars was $20 million – the network's most expensive TV project ever – and represents the promise of compelling visuals.[24] However, these are planned to serve the purpose of public enlightenment, developing a process of adding documentary-style work to drama. Interviews of contemporary scientists included Jennifer Trosper (project systems engineer, Jet Propulsion Laboratory), as well as authors Andrew Weir (*The Martian*, 2011) and Stephen Petranek (*How We'll Live on Mars*, 2015), former astronauts John Grunsfield and James A. Lovell, several employees of SpaceX, including CEO and Lead Designer Elon Musk, and Shana Diez, director of Build Reliability. The reassurance is that images of Mars are based on fact and pedagogy. Multiple perspectives offered by

---

[24] John Jurgensen, 'Mars and the Rise of Premium Nonfiction TV', *The Wall Street Journal*, 14 November 2016. Available at: https://www.wsj.com/articles/mars-and-the-rise-of-premium-nonfiction-tv-1478952003

the interviewees function as analysis, offering a presentation of the facts that can be built into a form of 'living futurism': the spectator learns new ways to navigate into the future.

However, the presumed omnipotence of the viewer is also limited by the show's temporal structure. Unlike other shows about an anticipated future such as documentaries like *Life Without People* (History Channel, 2008–10), images in *Mars* do not have an 'excess of designation'. *Life Without People* was a series in which scientists and engineers speculate about the fate of the Earth if human beings disappeared. The series began with the intriguing premise of 'What would happen if every human on Earth disappeared? This isn't the story of how we might vanish . . . it's the story of what will happen to the world we leave behind.' The series fascinated the viewer with examples of urban decay as well-known buildings come crashing down after the passage of possible millennia. But if *Life Without People* was able to suggest 'future time', the VFX was plausible without being convincing because the audience is aware that these images are virtual. One reviewer was to comment about the show:

> I'm not even that impressed with the computer-generated imagery, which is at the heart of this show, if indeed it has a heart. I don't know how many monkeys with Macs it took, but it still doesn't look real, especially when it starts moving. Someone's pleased with it though, so much so that everything needs multiple showings. Tower Bridge – down it comes, again and again. And the Seattle Space Needle – crash, crash, crash (from a slightly different angle). Stop it![25]

In *Life After People* and similar documentaries, the thrill that a sense of liveness delivers on the promise of its moment-by-moment unfolding is absent. In fact, what is being shown is not so much 'real' but 'virtual futurism' that ignores a sense of the immediacy of events and their contingent aspect. In *Mars*, using a concomitance between present and near future, a sense of contingency unsettles reality as events unfold. A reminder of the perils faced by the astronauts is structured into contingencies of actual places denoted by their physical presence that can be engaged with epistemically. The combination of a strong sense of place and television aesthetics creates an accessible, knowable place that is able to immerse audiences into an accumulation of memories of characters and places. In this way, set design and the limited digital effects lend to the hybrid

---

[25] Sam Wollaston, 'What Would the World Look Without Us? *Life After People* Showed Us – Again and Again', *The Guardian*, 26 May 2008. Available at: http://www.guardian.co.uk/media/2008/may/26/television1

storytelling technique of mixing drama with true-life interviews as an actual viewing event.

Beautiful TV

The landscape of Mars has been an object of fantastic speculations, including the mythical planet of Barsoom from the pen of Edgar Rice Burroughs.[26] Later, Ray Bradbury wrote his *Martian Chronicles* (1950), which in 1980 was adapted as a television miniseries.[27] That series began with a discussion of whether Maris is inhabited. In the show, the original Viking probe to Mars in 1976 lands in an empty corner of the planet, but further afield is a landscape of water-filled canals and desert vegetation, recalling Barsoom. The expectation of humankind arriving on Mars recalls similar Moon landings and memorable lines such as 'one small step for man, one giant leap for Mankind'. The flag planting on the Moon articulates a memory from the compendium of television, including the flag planting transferred to MTV and its guitar riff.

However, unlike the use of earlier fantastical representations of Mars, Everardo Gout chose to mainly ignore the possibility of digital enhancement conferring a wealth of detail that aids the navigation of alien landscapes. Instead, the seven-month space flight and landing are almost startling by the lack of fanfare. In fact, there is very little time to enjoy the beauty of the Martin landscape. Part of the reason for this foregoing of wonder was probably because the mythical Mars had already been consigned to oblivion after earlier probe landings on the planet, severing the thin thread of hopeful possibility of extraterrestrial life. Yet the theme of an ancient, exhausted planet in Burroughs and Bradbury continues to echo: life ebbing away as the mission commander, Ben Sawyer, sacrifices his life to save the other astronauts amid spectacular but hostile Martian terrain under a pinkish-red sky. At this point, a parallel exists between footage of Ben on Earth exploring the desert with his father and travelling over similar terrain on Mars. Ben's flashbacks to his time with his father become a mode of remembering that suggests another aesthetic approach to the images. The footage of Ben on Earth includes several shots of the pair walking in the desert, which is followed by the astronauts forced to abandon their transporter and going on foot across

---

[26] See Richard A. Lupoff, *The Worlds of Edgar Rice Burroughs* (Lincoln: University of Nebraska, 2005).
[27] Original TX, 27–29 January 1980, on NBC.

the sandy dunes of Mars. The fact that the desert scenes on Earth are from the perspective of a dying man creates a sense of time that is distorted or out of joint. The boundaries between Earth and Mars overflow into one another as we easily shift between them. To fully capture this effect, Gout uses lighting and an oversaturated colour scheme to create a liminal spatiality between the terrestrial and Martian deserts. In this way, the viewer shifts between a gaze of the terrain and narrative involvement as wide-angle shots connote the sterile emptiness of the landscape, producing a visual fascination for the sublime landscape that punctuates the narrative.[28]

After an equipment malfunction during the landing on Mars, the other astronauts overcome the technological issues they face to survive and build a home on the planet. The construction of a place capable of sustaining life throughout seasons one and two refers to a location that is tangible. Yet such a feeling of realism is as much related to what can be seen as the understanding of the other qualitative aspects of place: spectacular and awe-inspiring images of the visitation of another planet and a sensual response to the Martian landscape. The exploration of Mars depends on the unprecedented visibility of the planet. The effect of such a geographical extension and the representable enhances the possibility of verisimilitude. Place is therefore concrete and central to the construction of a phenomenal immediacy. The communication between International Mission Control on Earth and Mars acts as a reminder of the ability of television to transport viewers not only around the globe but also to the planets. However, what remains important is not a break from the normal temporal structures but its incorporation of additional modes of historical consciousness and personal history. Beautiful television may provide sublime moments of contemplation of the Martian desert, but any contemplatable mode is complex and not necessarily constructed from a spectacular gaze of the landscape. Rather, the power to transport the audience within the compelling illusion of 'being there' suggests how the gaze is deployed in *Mars*.

High-end television raises the possibility of 'beautiful TV', a term originally associated with Greg M. Smith, whose account of television encouraged the study of its aesthetics in stylistically richer texts.[29] Smith points out that the term 'beauty' is a contentious term rather than 'quality' in the context

---

[28] For a fuller account of the idea of a sublime landscape on television, see Helen Wheatley, *Spectacular Television: Exploring Televisual; Pleasure* (London: I.B. Tauris, 2016), 110–11.

[29] Greg M. Smith, *Beautiful Television: The Art and Argument of Ally McBeal* (Austin: University of Texas Press, 2007).

of making a judgement about a programme. An increased emphasis on the spectacle of landscape cinematography in shows such as *Mars* and *One Strange Rock* suggests how the spectacular can exist as a mode or style within particular high-end programmes. The combining of beauty and pleasure can be extended to the debate about quality in television. Helen Wheatley, commenting on natural history programming in the debate about quality, points to *The Blue Planet* (2001), as an example of the imperatives on broadcasters of the production of beautiful television. Wheatley's focus is on public service broadcasting, especially, the BBC and the situation in the UK. Nevertheless, other shows such as *Frozen Planet* (2011) are examples of the increased importance of the epistemic as a criterion of value. For her, the cinematography in natural history documentaries such as *Frozen Planet* can be argued to be 'beautiful' as a method of producing a gaze in educational programming, which is suitable to high-definition television. Robert Lloyd observed in the *LA Times*:

> The first thing to say about Frozen Planet . . . is that it is gorgeous to behold: lump-in-throat, tear-in-the-eye beautiful. It is the very point of such documentaries to be beautiful, of course, and not merely to honour, record and convey the awesome majesty of the natural world but also to look good on that big, expensive television set you bought yourself for Christmas.[30]

Frozen Planet was broadcast on Discovery, a channel that specializes in documentaries and what the network calls 'human adventure'.[31] The channel was to co-produce shows with the BBC, which, like National Geographic, has sought programmes that popularize educational shows as it draws on an upscale audience.[32] Yet the appeal to an elite audience capable of detecting beauty in its programming has to be understood as a notion of visual codes that define a particular type of gaze within high-end television. In *Mars*, the attempt to produce a cathected spectatorship suggests greater capacities in the image than usually present in more quotidian television drama. Using this logic of value, high-end television drama is more replete as a powerful psychic space.

---

[30] Robert Lloyd, 'Television Review: *Frozen Planet* on the Discovery Channel', *LA Times*, 16 March 2012. Available at: https://www.latimes.com/entertainment/tv/la-xpm-2012-mar-16-la-et-0317-frozen-planet-20120315-story.html
[31] Curtin and Shattuc, *The American Television Industry*, 128.
[32] Curtin and Shattuc, *The American Television Industry*, 129.

Colour grading

In *Mars*, the dramatic use of light and shadow or taut camera movements evokes an on-edge feeling that reflects the dangers facing the astronauts. Other digital effects included replacing visors on the astronaut's helmets to eliminate seeing the reflections of the filming crew. It should be recalled that much of the VFX was made easier by using the ARRI Alexa camera, whose recording format, and its original photography, incorporates much more detail than has been, hitherto, possible in the television image. As a technology of agency that allows the text to be controlled in more detail, HD (2K) and UHD (4K) footage in recent high-end television drama delivers the best result using a HDR. The effect is to reveal subtleties in everything from set design to costumes. According to senior colourist Thor Roos, 'You can see more detail in 4k but HDR takes this to a whole new level. You can see neon lights, spectacular highlights in windows or stained glass. HDR shines in those moments.'[33] For colourists, the development of OLED technology has also meant that a lot of detail is possible that was invisible before. This allows making adjustments to brightness and contrast, as well as colour, and devising aesthetics that overcome older restrictions on viewing technology.

In *Mars*, increased telephilia,[34] due in part to its increased visual capacity in the last decade or so, makes use of structural codes of colourization. These tints (the red surface and pink sky) and lighting enable the spectator develop an interpretative gaze to not only contemplate but analyse its sublime landscapes. In high-end drama, the possibility of the right emotional atmosphere using colour offers an intense and meaningful relationship. This is particularly noticeable in the images on screen in *Mars*, demonstrating again how the show both lures its audience to places of exhibition and constructs an experience of place as sublime. In *Mars*, colour is made to function to indicate the difference between Earth and Mars – and, in this way, between colours associated with life and a waterless desert. In regard to the point about a waterless desert, colour is used to prepare the audience for the goal of discovering water on Mars.

Episode two begins with a view of the Earth in space. We observe and comprehend that it is a blue planet set across the black of space. Next, the colour

---

[33] Anon, 'High Dynamic Range', *Broadcast Tech*, January/February 2016: 44–5.
[34] Anon, 'Telephilia: Has Television Become a More Relevant American Medium Than Art Film?', *IndieWire*, 17 May 2013. Available at: https://www.indiewire.com/2013/05/telephilia-has-television-become-a-more-relevant-american-medium-than-art-film-38350/

palette of shots on Earth, especially inside International Mission Control, is constructed from the usual red-green-blue-colour model during the grading process. Plate 16 is one of the original artistic sketches for the production design in *Mars*.[35] Grading is a visual effect used during post-production to change primary and secondary colouring. As can be seen, dominant hues in Mission Control are blue, as well as the use of secondary blacks so that computer screens and setting appear more 'Earth-like', with its enhanced use of blue. They also duplicate the harsh contrast between blue and black with the earlier shot of the Earth from space.

The scenes of Mars are graded to make it appear less Earth-like. Conversely, this colour grade is used during the flashbacks of Commander Ben as a boy with his father in the desert on Earth. If many of the exterior shots were shot in Morocco in the first series, the grading enhances a sun-bleached effect. However, as we learn watching the show, the idea of a Martian sun-bleach desert as hot is misleading because it is below minus seventy degrees Celsius, making it much colder than any place on Earth. Consequently, the grading by Framestore has been calibrated to inflect this contrast with Earth by producing a sun-bleached desert that is almost hyper-real. This is no Earthly desert but supremely alien and hostile landscape. To achieve such a visual effect required grading that would not use the usual colour model associated by now with Earth but a palette constructed from yellow-cyan-magenta. This inflects scenes such as the astronauts crossing the desert in episode two with a brilliant cool stillness unlike the heat on Earth. Later, at the end of the final episode of series two, one of the astronauts refers again to a heavenly view of the Earth from space and muses on how a 'thin blue-like line atmosphere keeps us alive'. This frightening but awe-inspiring understanding is linked to much of the thematic structure of *Mars*, including the extreme fragility of our own world. Visually, this is strengthened by the keying of turquoise or cyan into the Martian sky so that it appears perpetually over-bright. The visual effect is put to good use by suggesting a delirious feeling which in episode four of season one becomes a heightened sensation of the breakdown of botanist Paul Richardson, played by John Light. In *Darkest Day*, a complex visual system of hues thematically suggests isolation and Richardson's delirium as he comes under strain from living on Mars.[36]

---

[35] MMC Mission Control. Available at: https://www.artstation.com/artwork/vq13E
[36] Original TX, 12 December 2016.

Having the same look throughout in a TV series limits the visual style. But most television drama and colourists maintain the same look for reasons of cost. Nevertheless, colour grading is assuming an importance in high-end drama that, hitherto, has been rare in television, unlike film grading. One problem has been budget plus the fact that television drama often has a fixed transmission date, but with film, there is more flexibility about its release. The use of high contrast and strong colours is an opportunity to give a high-end series a distinct look as an example of beautiful TV. For example, the astronauts incorporate red piping on otherwise grey suits. Other splashes of orange exist when they sit inside the Mars Rover. In *Darkest Days*, a clever use of thematic green enables the viewer to focus on the contrast between Earth and the deadly browns and reds of Mars. When Paul Richardson experiences a psychosis in the mission base on Mars, he wears dark-green pants that match the surrounding shades of green (Plate 17).

A diverse colour palette enables a method of interpreting the script, as well as offering what can be recognized as the technological affordance of a high-quality picture. Colour grading is an economic as much as an artistic marker. It can offer something different from a standard look of television drama: bright, clean and limited by a single visual style. In high-end television, the broader spectrum of colours is likely to become increasingly significant as UHD and HDR assume a growing importance. Colour is changing the look of dramas such as *Mars* more than other technical improvements like higher resolution or frame rate to create new trends in narrative and aesthetics.

Space tourism

Past science fiction on screen has distinguished itself from other genres by its appeal to special effects technologies. Vessels travelling through space and alien landscapes reveal the importance of spectacle to the genre more than many others. If special effects tend to draw attention to an exhibitionistic mode within many sci-fi films at the cinema, they invite admiration for their virtuosity and future technology. Moreover, the codes of visibility on display invite the spectator's gaze. More recently, the appeal to a sustained gaze by the spectator engages particular pleasures about the pristine and sophisticated use of sound and vision not only in the cinema but, to an increasing degree, within high-end television such as *Mars*. Nevertheless, the VFX in *Mars* resists a non-diegetic role. As we have noticed, digital effects have been used to reinforce a sense of materiality in 2033 rather than a simulation of what is technologically impossible.

Consequently, the digital realm of re-creating Mars incorporates a reality not borrowed from older iterations trading on fantastic nostalgia about the Red Planet. If Bradbury was an essentially nostalgic writer, the imaginative milieu in *Mars* is not a ghostly awareness of myths about the Red Planet. Rather the allure of the exotic is about what is happening now technologically and a return to trust in science and its achievements that would have been regarded as naïve in older shows such as *The X-Files*. At the same time, the notion of space as territory in *Mars* is different from a backdrop. The producers of *Mars* selected a specific location on the planet to replicate: the foothills of Olympus Mons, the planet's tallest mountain, where underground lava tubes provide shelter, water and protection from cosmic radiation. If spectacle was avoided earlier by the decision to record the tiny cramped spaces of the ship on which the astronauts travelled on, the first series focuses on how the first Mars settlers construct a bare-bones underground habitat in the tubes. Future missions deliver additional materials, and by series two the colony expands, module by module. Place on Mars not only is a natural location – a landscape – but informs the construction of identity for the future colonists.

Novo Mundo, the first episode, opens with voice-over narration telling the audience, 'We crossed the oceans, we conquered the skies. . . . The heavens beckoned a new generation of innovators and explorers.' The opportunity to explore this terrain is linked to a kinetic experience as the astronauts on first landing travel across the planet to battle harsh Martian conditions to reach base camp. It becomes clear how dusty the road is to the camp and how cold despite being close to the Martian equator. The windblown landscape and rusty surface are the spectacle of a frozen environment, which emphasizes its remoteness from Earth.

The innovation of beauty in the show produces an excess of topographic specificity to get the facts right about its alien environment. In season one, the overarching theme of the Mars exploration is to 'follow the water'. The search begins for an ancient lava tube near frozen water, which can be used to develop a permanent base below Mars's surface. However, the indexicality of the landscape not only is supported by a proliferation of detail but includes a complex relationship that does not depend on its literalness to Mars. A subjective engagement with the planet is required by reproducing the supposed objectivity of the alien landscape constructed from memories of Ben Sawyer, as well as his successor as commander, Hana Seung, as a teenage girl who dreamt of going into space in the series prequel, *Before Mars*.[37] In episode two, 'Grounded', after arriving on Mars, the astronauts are encapsulated on board a transporter, which, with their diverse accents, reinforces an impression of tourists gathered together to gaze upon a foreign country. Textual cues allow viewers to orientate themselves both cognitively and emotionally as places on Mars are initially coded foreign before becoming familiar, and the Earth becomes less of a home to the astronauts.

The second series of *Mars* sees the arrival of greedy corporations looking to extract and exploit the Red Planet's natural resources for commercial gain. The new narrative – which meant more people, more vehicles, more locations – plus a move from shooting on location in Morocco to a studio (and its backlot) in Budapest meant that VFX and use of green screen became more important. There were 1,302 shots that Framestore worked on across 6 episodes, including digital matte paintings of Martian landscapes, new VFX environments, vehicle designs and VFX builds of shuttlecrafts, rovers and a space station, and a Marsquake scene. One of the biggest VFX challenges was to seamlessly match live action-footage shot in the backlot of the Budapest studio (which had been covered with gravel, tons of sand and backed by a vast green screen wall constructed from shipping containers) with sweeping landscape shots taken on location in Morocco.[38] VFX supervisor Robert Harrington explains:

> The series 2 setup was similar-ish to our work on season 1 but the primary cast not leaving Hungary was new and therefore something which required some planning as it meant taking Principal Actor footage shot in what was essentially a supremely-flat, Hungarian car park at a former cold-war missile base – and blending it seamlessly into the ancient fossil-encrusted hills and cliffs outside Erfoud in Morocco where a team, led by Overall VFX Supervisor Russell Dodgson, went to gather environment and lighting plates. A whole lot of driving enabled us to find locations not only topologically good to blend into but also where the 40-degree sun angles the DOP was leveraging in a Budapest summer would cut with sweeping views of the rocky Moroccan landscape in the autumn because, after all, we had the primary cast on one continent, their doubles on another, and it all had to match perfectly.

---

[37] Original TX, 14 November 2016.
[38] Moir, 'Mars Series 2'.

Television space, it has been argued, replaces the physical space we inhabit to produce a complete, contiguous (if virtual) space.[39] However, as we have seen, in *Mars* there are temporal emphases on personal history. Mars is a place that is intimate (the astronauts and their relationships), as well as fantastic. For the spectator, there is the blended sense of familiarity and foreignness, as we go from Earth to Mars. Later, as a place invested in depth and texture, it is possible for Mars to orient the lived experience of the astronauts with the purely spectacular without the suspicion of digital sequences becoming non-diegetic. Temporal signifiers in the beautiful television of *Mars* are a network of 'future memories'.

There is the evolution of a 'tourist gaze' in *Mars*. The use of travel in the show can be compared to the itinerary of a map as ideas of the exotic are chosen for explicit observation, including Mons Olympia and its underground lava tubes. The touristic experience can be understood as a gaze, albeit not necessarily one that halts the narrative in *Mars*. It is possible to say that the 'natural' setting on Mars can be contemplated in its own right for a few moments before shifting back to the narrative. Spectacular television in *Mars* does not rely on a distracted viewer according to the schema set forth by John Ellis about past television,[40] but its visual pleasure depends on a mode of beautiful images in spectacular clarity as an ideal vision. Equally, *Mars* relies on a shared intimacy between the viewer and the astronauts as the landscape becomes an experiential sense of being-there. If high-end television repeats tropes of the spectacular in film, beautiful television is more amorphous in its address. Options to 'just look' exist as Mars becomes a tourist site, but a sense of place is brought to life as a character in its own right as direct connections are made between the physical environment and the various mental states it evokes in the astronauts and viewer.

Conclusion

The theme of realism and the increased trend of new aesthetic techniques are active in *Mars*. Immediacy lies in the ability of the show to return to the viewer what is purportedly taken away with spectacle. The production of spectacle in *Mars* is closely tied up with assertions of authenticity. We have the spectacle of leaving the Earth, landing on Mars and its deserts. The association with Hollywood

---

[39] Karen Lury, *Interpreting Television* (London: Hodder Education, 2005), 147–50.
[40] John Ellis, *Visible Fictions: Cinema, Television, Video* (London: Routledge, 1992).

names such as Ron Howard and Brian Glazer may have raised suspicions that *Mars* would have been organized around the production and consumption of spectacular images. However, as we have seen, television's interest in emotional states through temporal closeness in its creation of a viewing community makes the use of VFX compositing, as well as spectacle, much less important than film. Rather, in *Mars*, VFX and spectacle are normally subordinated to narrative. The blurring of the distinction between fictional and factual segments in the show, to a degree, creates a viewing event on television, which can be discussed later.

Spectacular aesthetics in high-end television drama continue to depend on a different temporal structure that is distinct from it being cinematic. Futurism in *Mars* as a stylistic strategy indicates how the viewer participates in the real world of space exploration by going backwards to archive footage of the Apollo mission before moving to 2033 and beyond. The temporal fluidity capitalizes on tensions in the show between the past, present and future to create a more dynamic appeal of the relationship between Earth and Mars and the spectator and explorer. The spectacle of 'real experience' using a blurring of fictional and factual forms is organized around the rhetoric of ordinary people 'like us' rather than enjoying a special status, although in an exotic place.

Production design from the set to colour grading in *Mars* is constructed around this notion, refusing to emphasize the stardom of space exploration. Nevertheless, a tension exists between this notion and the use of landscape shots of Mars as spectacle allowing two modes: one narrative and the other spectacular, allowing the viewer to better follow the story or contemplate 'beautiful TV'. The development of a complex gaze makes possible the transition from setting to landscape as more attention is given to the Martian deserts and mountain ranges that tantalize in their familiarity to Earth but also in their radical difference. As a function of these modes, style in *Mars* is an example of big-budget, high-end television drama.

Conclusion

Seeing It on TV: Televisuality in the Contemporary US 'High-End' Series has sought to advocate the importance and significance of style to a type of television that has been at the forefront of debates about the medium becoming cinematic. Not only do high-end TV dramas now share finance arrangements with film, as we have seen, they also attract film talents. The demand by Netflix and other networks when commissioning shows has been for directors such as Steven Soderbergh and Martin Scorsese, showrunners like Noah Hawley and actors such as Liv Tyler and Winona Ryder. Similarly, the greater use of DVFX indicates a release of ambition and the possibility of a visual epic not seen historically in scripted TV but more common on film. But the use of film talent or indeed higher budgets and feature cinematography is not the same as proposing that a single, highly differentiated production model exists in US high-end drama. This book is at pains to note that the development of an aesthetic in high-end drama is not the same as claiming a cinematic aesthetic has been transported to television.

Moreover, there is the continuing problem of the high-end series eluding a single categorical definition unlike earlier forms of television drama such as the soap opera, presenting the difficulty of finding a secure analysis. This book demonstrates that one possible taxonomic feature of high-end television is how authorship can be shown to control elements of a programme that builds meaning in a text and seeks interpretative consistency. In turn, this is linked to notions about value in the television series. In many ways, the practice of authorship, including the role of the showrunner, is signified by a professional whose craftsmanship sets aesthetic parameters in a programme. Next to this, prior discourses about a showrunner, director or writer as a mark of quality establish audience expectations. These often determine how various scenes will be shot by turning them into moments of sheer technique. However, despite the importance of a close reading of elements of a programme, this cannot be definitive evidence for a high-end show. Rather, examination of the eight programmes in this book is a demonstration of how a showrunner, director or actor expresses their own personal predilections through complex stylistic structures around, for example, focalization or performance.

In *Seeing It on TV*, a general concept of authorship in the thirteen, nine or fewer episodes of a high-end show begins to establish how visual style becomes a site of particularity because of the control exerted by a showrunner or director. But, crucially, this book has also been careful to understand that they continue to rely on a network, as well as others, that enacts their vision. On the one hand, high-end drama can be categorized as the art of personal expression; its style of tonalities and textures, the expression of a personal vision. On the other, creative tone is less a singular vision but rather the logic of a cluster of independent traits that each show in this book brings together under the broader label of 'original content'. In this way, a general category of authorship within the roles of the showrunner or director is shown in this book to not fully account for how a variable form in high-end drama coalesces within a marketable value.

Instead, stylistic clusters – including cues about temporality and colour grading (*Mars*), remediation and digital aesthetics (*Stranger Things*), or hypersubjectivity in *The Young Pope* – mark the processes of creating value in high-end television. Other examples in this book include the tactics in *The Knick* inspired by indie film practice, with its fast pace of shooting and camera movement, or the remediation of performance in the adaptation of cinema to television that creates fictional worlds in *Fargo*. Similarly, the collision of performance modes in *The Leftovers* suggests a shared and complex authored use of stylistic elements, in order to create a highly affective televisual style. Nevertheless, each of these examples are not simply experiments with style. Within the high-end drama brand name, a programme can be unorthodox in its text and ways of seeing but there are remaining structural requirements conferring the relative legitimacy of a prestige project, and standard factors in play that add to the value of a show.

Televisuality in high-end drama is largely an exchange of competing pressures between the professionalism of the showrunner and team involved in a project, television's heritage as well as newer technologies. Formal strategies in high-end drama, its immanent reading and contested interpretations using sometimes opposing discourses demonstrate that authorship is unstable. At the same time, television's specificity continues to be useful in fixing an understanding of authorship and the professionalism required to work within one medium rather than another. Work by a production designer such as Sophie Becher for *Mars* and the commitment to a tactile realism in space exploration celebrates an intimate experience that is specific to television drama. Digital streaming services in the second decade of the twenty-first century continue to distinguish content in high-end television from affordances in cinema even if, at times, the richer density of the image and ideas about authorship parallel film. Any debate about whether this represents a distinctive modality in television with new cultural values is complex and benefits from a close reading of style. In *Seeing It on TV*, readings map the economic, technological and cultural decisions taken about form, which are used to investigate any claimed uniqueness for a show. Critical work on future Televisuality must continue to demand the breakdown of claims about media convergence, as well as the possibility of the continued specificity of television drama.

Index

accents 91, 94–7, 172
acting styles 96, 141, 148, 151
actors 17, 18, 42, 71–3, 77, 96, 97, 132, 134, 135, 137, 138, 152
The Addams Family 116
aesthetics 26, 27, 113, 114, 121–24, 128, 164, 166, 168, 170, 174
affective styles 28–30
agency, of performer 138
alignment 44, 46, 47–8, 55
allegiance 44, 45, 48, 54–5
allusion 49, 78, 105, 106, 109–10, 115
allusiveness, wealth. *See* wealth of allusiveness
Alpha House 88
'American Quality Drama' (AQD) 14, 42
Amiel, Jack 72
analogue nostalgia 111–15
astronauts 154–9, 162, 164–6, 168, 169, 171–3
authorship 17–22, 25, 34, 35, 110, 111, 152, 175–7
Avatar 2 27

BBC 113, 136, 154, 167
beautiful television (TV) 165–7, 173
The Better Angels 88
Blank, Kevin 26
The Blue Planet 167
Boardwalk Empire 20, 73, 79, 120–5
Bradbury, Ray 165
Brenneman, Amy 135–6
Buck, Michelle 24
Burn After Reading 84
Butler, Jeremy 2

cable channels 14, 44, 59
Cain, James M. 25
Caldwell, John T. 2
camera 17, 18, 26, 41–3, 54, 64, 68–71, 75, 76, 93

camera style 88, 93
carnation 123, 124
Carroll, Noël 109
cast 34, 94–7, 121, 122, 134–7, 140, 141
casting 134–5
Caughie, John 64, 110
character structure 91
cinematic influences 37–40
cinematic performance mode 142, 152
cinematic text adaptation 81–103
Cinemax 59, 73, 78
close-up shots 65
Coen, Joel and Ethan 81, 83–5, 87, 91, 92, 94, 97, 99, 101
Coen brothers 81–4, 87, 91–4, 96, 97, 101
Cold Mountain 34
colour grading 27, 123, 153, 168–70, 174, 176
Comand, Mariapia 38
complexity 12, 23, 44, 55, 57, 117, 131, 132, 146
Complex Serial Drama and Multiplatform Television 2
Complex TV: The Poetics of Contemporary Television Storytelling 2
The Consequences of Love 38
contemporary high-end television drama 14, 33
contemporary television drama 13, 16, 27
contemporary television storytelling 3
Coon, Carrie 137
Cornea, Christine 131
The Crocodile's Dilemma 91, 95
Cronyn, Hume 42
CSI 26
cultural value 73, 103

dead space 53
Deadwood 19

Index

death, anticipation of 43
dialogue 17–19, 95, 97, 100, 109, 117, 142, 144, 150
digital visual effects (DVFX) 26, 103, 108, 119, 159, 175.
    See also VFX
Disneyland 155
distinction 12, 15, 16, 18, 26, 35, 55, 75, 103, 162, 174
The District 135
documentaries 38, 64, 156, 161, 164, 167
Duffer brothers 107, 109, 110, 113–15, 117, 118, 128, 129
Dunleavy, Trisha 2
Dynasty 21

Ebert, Roger 118
Eccleston, Christopher 136–7, 142, 147–52
Ellis, John 173
emotions 15, 29, 30, 42, 87, 126, 141, 142, 144
engagement levels 46–9
episodes 20, 23, 34, 39, 49, 58–60, 68, 74, 75, 85–9, 93, 108, 121, 126, 135, 147
ER 22
Erin Brockovich 75
events 35, 41, 47, 49, 64, 69, 74, 155, 160–2, 164
experts 155, 163
extreme performance modes 140–4

Fargo 11, 24, 81–103
    continuities 91–4
    disruptions of visual style 91–4
    limitations of exhibitionism 94–7
    Noah Hawley 81–9, 91–7
    performance style 94–7
    rupturing style 99–103
    storyworld 89–91
    violent exhibitionism 98–9
Fellini 36, 39
film history 109, 124, 125
first-degree style 18
The Frozen Planet 154, 167
FX 11, 24, 26, 30, 81–3, 103

Garvey, Kevin 137, 140, 147
Genius 154
The Girlfriend Experience 58, 72
Goldberg, Matt 81
Google 105
The Great Beauty 38
guerrilla tactics 69–76
Guilty Remnant (GR) 137, 140–4, 147

Hawley, Noah 81–9, 91–4, 97–9, 101–3
    Fargo 81–9, 91–7
    as scriptwriter 81–7
    as showrunner 87–9
HBO 13, 14, 33–5, 59, 73, 82, 99, 121, 133–5, 154
heritage 115–20
high-end drama 12, 15–17, 19, 20, 26, 28–30, 111, 151, 175–6
    televisuality in 176
high-end television 11–15, 23, 26, 37, 48, 161, 167, 174
    affective styles 28–30
    authorship 17–21, 152
    drama bands 127
    original programming, value 13–17
    reconfiguring televisuality in 9–31
    showrunners 21–5
    technology and image 25–8
    televisual style 17–21
high-end television drama 12, 16, 20, 37, 43, 44, 48, 161, 167, 174
high-end television serial drama 3–5
high-profile television drama 75
Hill Street Blues 15
How We'll Live on Mars 155
hyper-subjectivity 43–6

independent style 57–79
    approaches to realism 76–8
    guerrilla tactics and mobility 69–76
    physicality and intimacy 60–9
In God's Hands 58
intertextuality 110
intimacy 60–9

Jacobs, Jason 63, 79, 123
Jaramillo, Deborah L. 11, 12
John Adams 135

Johnson, Catherine   155
Judging Amy   135

Kermode, Mark   118
The Knick   57–79
Knickerbocker   61, 62, 66, 68, 73–6

La Dolce Vita   39
La Strada   39
The Leftovers   29, 131–52
   production context   133–4
Life on Mars   127
Lloyd, Matthew J.   88, 89, 93
Lloyd, Robert   167
Lombardo, Michael   121
long shot   42, 50, 52, 53, 54, 74
Lord of the Rings   118
Lost   26, 27
Lotz, Amanda   44
L'uomo in più   38

McCabe, Janet   122
Malcolm X   43
Mars   25, 153–74
The Martian   159
Martian Chronicles   165
Martin, Troy Kennedy   18
medium shots   43, 117
Meg Abbott   29, 136, 142–6, 151
Mildred Pearce   25, 33
Miller's Crossing   102
Mittell, Jason   2, 132
mobility   69–76
mode of high-end television   13, 26
Moreno, Julio   50
movie camera   50, 68
MTM: Quality Television   15
The Munsters   116
musical nostalgia   125–8

narrative space, witnessing   49–54
National Geographic Channel   25, 153–55, 161, 163, 167
naturalism   18
Netflix   11, 13, 30, 34, 35, 105, 106, 108, 111, 113, 114, 120, 154
network television   13, 18, 44
   content   13
Newcomb, Horace   14

nostalgia   15, 29, 106, 111, 112, 117, 119, 120, 125, 127, 128
Notes on Film Acting   42

Ocean's Eleven   57
older television drama   14, 87
Olive Kitteridge   33
One Strange Rock   154
original programming   13–17
Our Planet   154

Paper Chase   14
The Passenger   138
passionate realism   33–56
   cinematic influences   37–40
   hyper-subjectivity   43–6
   levels of engagement   46–9
   narrative space, witnessing   49–54
   point of view   40–3
   re-allegiance   54–5
pastiche   84, 106, 110–15, 117, 123
performance   94–7, 131, 132, 137–44, 146, 149–52, 176
performance modes, collision   131–52
   agency, of performer   138
   close reading of   144–7
   extreme performance modes   140–4
   Guilty Remnant   140–4
   pilot episode   138–40
performance styles   94, 97, 138, 144, 147, 148, 152
physicality   60–9
pilot episode   19, 127, 138–40, 142
Planet Earth   154
point of view (POV)   40–3
Poltergeist   107
The Prisoner   24
Private Practice   135
The Public Enemy   124
Purse, Lisa   118

quality   14, 15, 25, 26, 96, 113, 114, 135, 149, 158, 167
Quality Television (TV)   15, 131
Qualley, Margaret   137

Raiders of the Lost Ark   115
realism, approaches   76–8
re-allegiance   54–5

Red camera 73, 108, 113
Red Planet 27, 153, 155, 156, 171, 172
responsibility 151
The Roaring Twenties 124
Rome 121
Roos, Thor 168

Salem's Lot 117
Scarface 124
scene 46, 47, 51, 67, 73, 91, 95, 96, 98, 144, 145, 148–50
Sconce, Jeffrey 50
screen monsters 115–20
screen performance 132, 138, 146
   initiating 134–5
scripted drama 154, 156, 162
second-degree style 18, 36, 41
A Serious Man 84
Sex, Lies and Videotape 57
shot 27, 41, 43, 47, 48, 50, 51, 53, 54, 58, 67, 69, 72, 74, 75, 88, 108, 145, 146, 159
shot-reverse-shot 47, 53
showrunners 21–5, 30, 58, 59, 87, 88, 101, 103, 175, 176
Six Feet Under 135
Smith, Greg M. 2
The Snoop Sisters 126
Soderbergh, Stephen 57–79
The Sopranos 120
Sorrentino, Paolo 33–56
space tourism 170–3
spectacle 12, 25, 26, 63, 65, 66, 153, 157, 160, 161, 167, 170, 171, 173, 174
spectatorship 20, 29, 50–2
Spelling, Aaron 21
Sperb, Jason 112
Spiderman 118
storytelling 3, 5, 21, 26, 27, 34, 36, 43, 45, 57, 74, 100, 101, 108, 132, 145
storyworld 28, 83, 84, 87, 89–91, 94, 96, 109
Stranger Things 105–9

The Talented Mr Ripley 34
television aesthetics 12, 26, 164
television audiences 15, 25, 94

television authorship 20, 81. *See also* authorship
television drama 21–4, 42, 43, 69, 70, 89, 90, 170
television history 15, 129, 155
television image 69, 123, 168
televisionland 128
television performance 132
television production 21, 30, 31, 59
television programmes 12, 25
television realism 57, 64
television seasons 107
television specificity 1–3
television spectatorship 28, 51, 65
television style 17
Television Style 2
television technology 107
televisuality 2, 5–31, 79, 175–7
   in high-end drama 176
   in high-end television 11, 13, 15, 17, 19, 21, 23, 25, 27
   reconfiguring in high-end television 9–31
televisual spectacle 153–74
   beautiful TV 165–7
   colour grading 168–70
   space tourism 170–3
   temporal realism and epistemic 158–65
televisual style 17–21
temporal realism 158–65
texture 27, 112, 113, 119, 173
Thackery 60–3, 65–9, 75, 76
Theroux, Justin 135
tracking shots 70, 71
Traffic 57, 75
True Detective 107
Tyler, Liv 136

US television 3, 9, 14, 15, 23, 88, 107, 116

Vatican 39, 40, 43, 48, 49, 51
VFX 26, 27, 113, 114, 119, 120, 123, 160, 164, 168, 170, 172, 174
Videodrome 107
vintage television cameras 113
Vinyl 120–5

violent exhibitionism   98–9
vocal performance   95, 96, 149
voice   40, 41, 46, 95–7, 140, 149

wealth of allusiveness   105–29
Westworld   82

Winter, Terence   122
witnesses   52, 53, 74

The Young Pope   33–56
Youth   38

www.ingramcontent.com/pod-product-compliance
Lightning Source LLC
Chambersburg PA
CBHW070640300426
44111CB00013B/2193